OAKWOOD RAILWAY WALKS

AYRSHIRE'S FORGOTTEN RAILWAYS

A Walker's Guide

by

Alasdair Wham

THE OAKWOOD PRESS

British Library Cataloguing in Publication Data
A Record for this book is available from the British Library
ISBN 978 0 85361 729 7

Typeset by Oakwood Graphics.
Repro by PKmediaworks, Cranborne, Dorset.
Printed by Berforts Information Press Ltd, Eynsham, Oxford.

Dedicated to the memory of David S. Rutherglen and Ralph Rawlinson who both had a love for exploring disused railways.

Ex- Caledonian Railway '439' class 0-4--4T is on station pilot duties at Kilmarnock on 6th May, 1959. The now demolished Kilmarnock Infirmary is in the background.
Hamish Stevenson Collection

Rear cover, top: Laigh Milton viaduct in 2012. *Author*

Rear cover, bottom: Newmilns viaduct in 2012. *Author*

Published by The Oakwood Press (Usk), P.O. Box 13, Usk, Mon., NP15 1YS.
E-mail: sales@oakwoodpress.co.uk
Website: www.oakwoodpress.co.uk

Contents

Ballochmyle viaduct engineered by Grainger and Miller, 2012. *Author*

Introduction

A surprising amount of railway heritage remains in Ayrshire and hopefully this book will help you to both recognize and appreciate it.

The Scottish Outdoor Access Code (outdooraccess-scotland.com) ensures that people in Scotland have greater access to land than in many other countries. However, anyone accessing land has to act responsibly.

The following points are intended to encourage responsible exploration:

1. Please do not assume that because a journey or place is described in this book that you have permission to follow in my footsteps. Unless a route has been recognized as an official walkway then the fact that I have been able to explore the routes is not meant to imply that a right of way exists or that they are suitable for walking. The description of a route is given to enable you to recognize the railway heritage and learn more about the history of the line and the events that have happened close to the trackbed.
   Please use the grading system which appears in the text:
   - * Interesting to visit, for example, to look at a former station building.
   - ** The route may not be complete, detours may be required, and conditions underfoot, in places, may be difficult. If possible, check out a route beforehand especially in country areas and be prepared for unexpected detours. In preparation for this book I discovered, that on my return to photograph a viaduct, which I had visited only a few weeks earlier, it had now been fenced off. Conditions can change at any time.
   - *** A recognised walkway.
2. If you do intend to walk any part of a route, where possible, seek permission from the landowner who will probably be pleased to let you walk the trackbed. Being a responsible explorer will promote goodwill and allow others to follow in your footsteps. Seek permission where possible and respect the Scottish Outdoor Access Code. You should never cross fields of crops, although you may walk along the margin of a field where no crops are growing. You should never enter a field where you would disturb cattle or sheep. Access will always depend on courtesy and mutual trust.
3. Many former station buildings are now private residences and while owners are usually pleased to talk about the history of their properties, there is no right of access. No-one wants a walker in their back garden.
4. Always keep away from dangerous structures. Most of the viaducts, bridges and tunnels have not been maintained for over 30 years, some a lot longer. Do not cross fences or barriers erected for your safety. Do not cross railway tracks or enter railway property.
5. All distances given are approximate. A missing bridge can result in a lengthy detour. Use an up-to-date map. I have found the Ordnance Survey Explorer series to be the most useful.
   The Ordnance Survey Explorer Maps I have used are:
   - 326 *Ayr and Troon*
   - 327 *Cumnock and Dalmellington*
   - 328 *Sanquhar and New Cumnock*
   - 333 *Kilmarnock and Troon*
   - 334 *East Kilbride, Galston and Darvel*
   - 341 *Greenock, Largs and Millport*
6. Be aware of the weather. In Scotland it can change very quickly. Be equipped and, in the more remote sections, check the bus or train times carefully or arrange for someone to pick you up.

Chapter One

A View of Ayrshire

Robert Burns, Ayrshire's most famous son, never mentioned the Isle of Arran in any of his poems. The beautiful sunsets, seen from the Ayrshire coast, as the sun dips behind the jagged peaks of Arran's mountains, in a blaze of red, are unforgettable. Those who live in Ayr, as I do, are surprised that the poet never drew inspiration from it and neglected to mention the island in any of his poems. It is like a resident of Edinburgh writing about the city but never mentioning the Castle. Was our National Bard short-sighted?

Arran is situated in the Firth of Clyde leaning closer to the Kintyre peninsula than to the Ayrshire coast and as far away from the Ayrshire coast as England is from France. The island offers an uninterrupted and unique view of Ayrshire's coast especially from its many hilltops. Ayrshire, as seen from Arran, is surrounded by a rim of hills and high moorland to the north, east and south, with a large flattish plain in the centre drained by several rivers, mostly flowing into the Firth of Clyde. The counties of Renfrewshire, to the north and Lanarkshire to the east border Ayrshire with valleys acting as corridors between the counties. To the north the River Garnock has created the Garnock Valley by cutting through the boulder clay, left by glaciation, as it snakes its way towards Irvine Bay.

The River Irvine also meanders towards Irvine Bay but from the east along the Irvine Valley passing through Kilmarnock en route. The two rivers converge, at Irvine harbour, just prior to entering the Firth of Clyde. The distinctive volcanic core of Loudoun Hill, visible from Arran, where Robert Bruce defeated an English force, indicates the direction taken by the River Irvine from the east. To the south the hills of Dumfriesshire and Galloway form a barrier between Ayrshire and its southern neighbour pierced only by the Nith Valley, through which the River Nith flows turning south, towards the Solway Firth and the Doon Valley, through which the River Doon flows north to reach the Clyde coast. Ayrshire is a fascinating county, with a rich history, beautiful scenery and a mild and damp climate. In 1996 Ayrshire was divided into three smaller local authorities as part of local government reorganization. These are North, East and South Ayrshire.

From Arran there is a clear view of Ayrshire's western seaboard. Ardrossan, the ferry terminal for Arran, and slightly south-east Saltcoats and Stevenston, known collectively as the 'three towns', set around a sheltered bay, are visible. Next the sand dunes of the Ardeer peninsula, bounded on the west by the north end of Irvine Bay and on the east by the River Garnock, separate Stevenston from Irvine, the next town down the coast. One town visible only from the island's highest peaks is Largs - the ferry port for the island of Cumbrae. Largs is to the north of Ardrossan, round the coast, on the mainland opposite the Island of Cumbrae. This part of Ayrshire, including the Garnock Valley and Arran is now known as North Ayrshire, with Irvine as its administrative centre, and stretches to the south of Irvine where South Ayrshire begins. A large paper

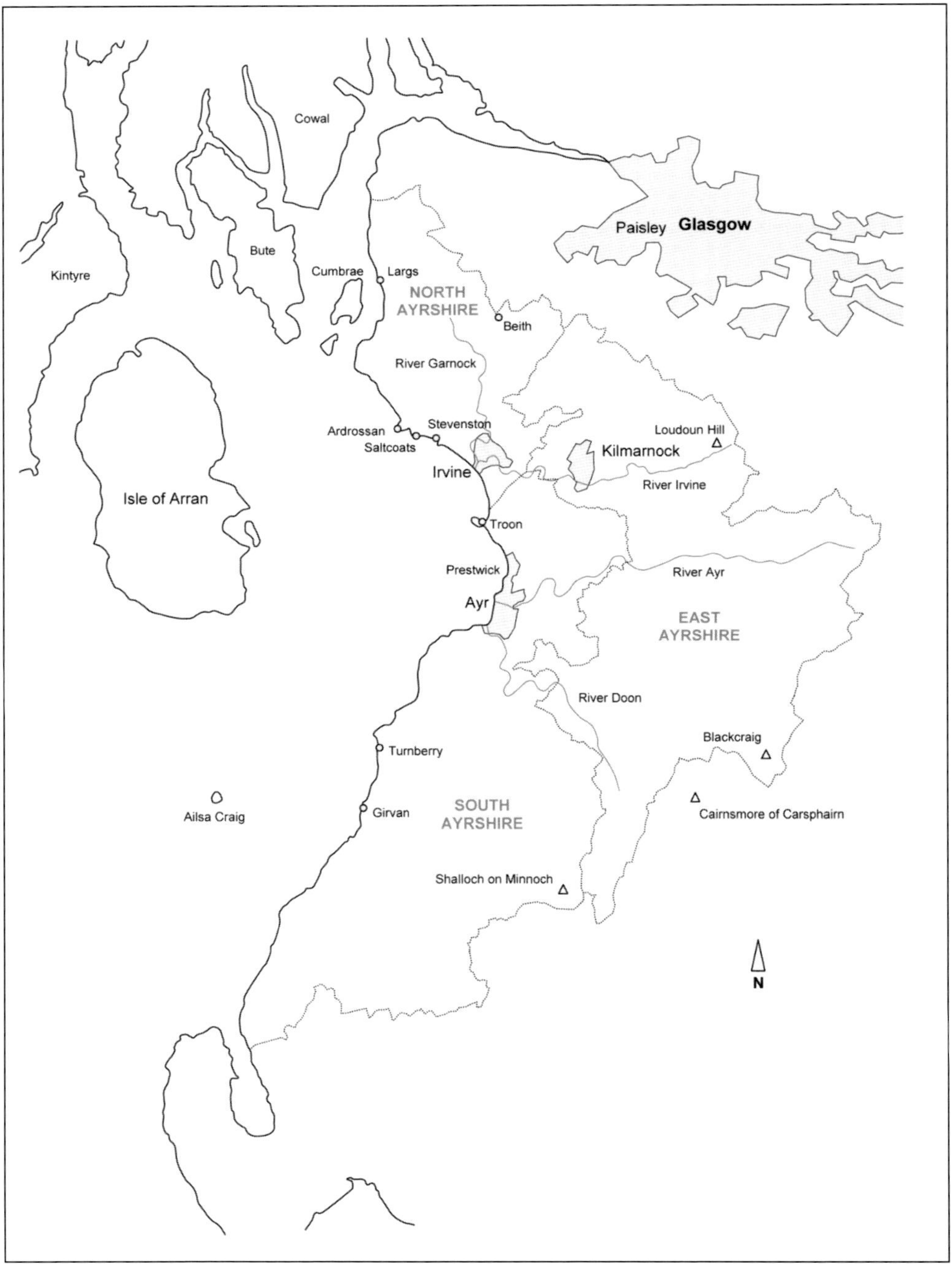

Cowal
Paisley
Glasgow
Bute
Kintyre
Cumbrae
Largs
NORTH AYRSHIRE
Beith
River Garnock
Ardrossan
Stevenston
Saltcoats
Loudoun Hill
Kilmarnock
Irvine
Isle of Arran
River Irvine
Troon
Prestwick
River Ayr
Ayr
EAST AYRSHIRE
River Doon
Blackcraig
Turnberry
Ailsa Craig
Girvan
SOUTH AYRSHIRE
Cairnsmore of Carsphairn
Shalloch on Minnoch
N

mill visible from Arran is situated on the boundary between North and South Ayrshire.

Troon jutting out into the Firth of Clyde, on an exposed short promontory of land, like a cocked pinkie, separates Irvine Bay from Ayr Bay to the south. From March to October a ferry service operates from Troon to Northern Ireland. Behind Troon is Dundonald Hill, a well known landmark for pilots with its radar transmitter used as a beacon by flights across the North Atlantic. To the south of Dundonald Hill is Glasgow Prestwick Airport, with its development favoured due to the fog-free climate on this part of the coastline. The international airport, largest in size, although ranked only fourth in Scotland for the number of passengers, is also important for air freight and is used for military refuelling. It is also famous for a brief stopover by Elvis Presley in 1960. Surely it is a malicious rumour that the great man might have been seen in London two years before.

The resort towns of Prestwick, to the north and Ayr at the mouth of the River Ayr stretch along Ayr Bay. The River Ayr rises on the eastern boundary between Ayrshire (East Ayrshire) and South Lanarkshire, near the mining village of Glenbuck, now destroyed by opencast workings and in its nearly 40 mile length traverses the whole county. In its middle section, near Ballochmyle the soft red sandstone has been gouged out by the river to form a deep gorge. Ayr is the administrative centre for South Ayrshire and the heart of 'Burns Country' with the poet born at Alloway, now a suburb of Ayr.

To the south of Ayr, the River Doon reaches the coast close to where Greenan Castle, perched on a cliff top, can be spotted by eagle-eyed observers on Arran.

Greenan Castle in 2011. A short distance from the castle was the Prisoner of War camp from which 97 Italians escaped in 1944. *Author*

Village of Dunure from the sea with the trackbed of the Maidens & Dunure Railway to the rear of the houses, 2011. *Author*

Culzean Castle in 2011. It was designed by the Scottish architect Robert Adam for the Earl of Cassillis. *Author*

South-west the sheer rock faces of the Heads of Ayr, the remnant of a volcanic core, dominate the low Carrick coastland. The coast is overlooked by the Carrick Hills with yet more transmitter masts. In the distance are the Galloway Hills with the prominent peaks of Blackcraig, Cairnsmore of Carsphairn and Shalloch on Minnoch visible on a clear day.

Along the Carrick coastline the small fishing village of Dunure is reached, then the majestic Culzean Castle perched on more cliff tops, Maidens another fishing village, the lighthouse at Turnberry, a backdrop to many a golfing drama, and eventually round to Girvan. The Water of Girvan reaches the sea through the small harbour at Girvan. Out to sea from Girvan, but prominent from almost anywhere on the Carrick coastline, is the small humped island of Ailsa Craig, another volcanic core, a landmark on the crossing to Ireland, often referred to as Paddy's Milestone. The Ayrshire coastline continues south to Loch Ryan. The coastline offered another route between Ayrshire and Galloway avoiding the hills further inland.

East Ayrshire, the third of the three councils created from Ayrshire when Strathclyde Regional Council was disbanded, stretches from near Stewarton in the north, east to both Darvel and Muirkirk and includes the Doon Valley to the south. Kilmarnock, inland from Irvine is where the administrative headquarters is located. Kilmarnock and Ayr with populations around 50,000 are the two largest towns in Ayrshire.

The hills surrounding Ayrshire are composed mainly of moorland, with the natural goodness of the soil having been long washed down to the fertile flat land which is drained by many rivers. Ayrshire is well known for its agriculture, a testimony to generations of farmers who have worked the land. The warm and wet climate in Ayrshire is ideal for the growth of grass from which the many dairy herds benefit. More of the land near the coast where the soils are drier and rainfall lower is given over to crops, including the famous Girvan tatties especially on the raised beaches of the Carrick coastline. Sheep become more prevalent towards the higher moorland but are often brought down to lowland farms after the summer grazing is over.

If farming traditions have helped shape the county then so also has the coal mining industry. Etched in many small communities is the memory of hardship as deep pits harvested the bounty left by carboniferous forests which once covered much of central Scotland. Early demand for coal came from farmers requiring coal to burn lime to improve the soil and near the coast, at Saltcoats and Ayr, for use in salt production. Much of the coal was exported to Northern Ireland which led to the development of Troon, Ardrossan and Ayr harbours. Today Northern Ireland's coal burning power stations remain a major market for Ayrshire's coal.

Coal extraction in north Ayrshire spread to the Dalry and Kilmarnock areas but by 1947, at the time of nationalization, this area was in decline. After World War II, with the development funds provided by nationalization, the Central Ayrshire Coalfield dominated coal production with all but 12 of Ayrshire's deep coal pits. This coalfield, stretched across the county from near Ayr to Muirkirk in the east and as far south as New Cumnock and Dalmellington. There was also a small coalfield in the south-west of the county centred on Dailly, between Maybole and Girvan. Deep mining has now ended and many communities are still recovering from the loss of employment. Today only opencast pits scar the land.

However, it was the existence of ironstone deposits along with the coal which transformed Ayrshire's industry and led to the county becoming a major producer of iron. Over 120 years ago there were over 40 furnaces operating with one of the earliest at Muirkirk. Ironworks at Waterside, near Dalmellington, Lugar, Kilwinning and Stevenston survived until the 1920s, latterly using imported ores. In the Garnock Valley the Glengarnock steelworks continued until 1985.

With a ready supply of iron many other industries developed, such as the Caledonian Foundry of Andrew Barclay, Sons & Co. Ltd factory in Kilmarnock, famous for building locomotives, but now Wabtec Rail Scotland overhauls railway stock in the town. Other companies produced waterworks equipment, ball bearings, parts for cars, trucks, brick, tiles and sanitary ware. Carpet manufacture, manufacturing of shoes, manufacturing of combine-harvesters and, of course, until recently Johnnie Walker whisky also helped to establish Kilmarnock as the major industrial centre for Ayrshire. Sadly, most industries have now closed.

Ayrshire was also once famous for the production of textiles, clothing and carpets. Starting as a cottage industry, often as a means of farming folks supplementing their income, during the winter the demand rose for wool and linen. With supplies of wool and flax not keeping up with demand cotton was imported, although the American Civil War disrupted the supply. Catrine was famed for its cottonworks as was the Irvine Valley for lace and Stewarton became known as the 'Bonnet Town' for its manufacture of bonnets and regimental headgear. Textile production was also important in the Garnock Valley.

A chemical industry developed among the sand dunes to the south of Stevenston, at Ardeer, where Alfred Nobel, looking for an isolated site to experiment with explosives, started the manufacture of dynamite. In time ICI operated the site which developed into a large complex producing many chemicals but the site has declined to a shadow of its former grandeur.

Road improvements in the later 18th century enabled transportation of materials by labourers hauling the raw materials to and from towns and ports by cart. People had to travel on horseback or by horse-drawn carriage or simply walk the rutted roads. There were only two short canals in Ayrshire at Muirkirk and Saltcoats. Waggonways, where loads were hauled by horses along plateways, were an improvement but with the arrival of the railway era in the mid-19th century they were overtaken by the more efficient iron roads with their steam driven engines which did so much to connect Ayrshire's industries. So in the mid-19th century, blessed with rich coal deposits, fertile fields and with traditional industries like textile and weaving, Ayrshire's industry was ready to take advantage of the railway era and flourish.

For many years Ayrshire had one further advantage. With the upper reaches of the River Clyde not navigable, for larger ships, until the 19th century, the ports on the Ayrshire Coast of Ardrossan, Saltcoats, Irvine and Ayr were vital for the export of coal and other commodities and for importing goods. Coal from the Lanarkshire coalfield also had to use Ayrshire's railways to reach the ports. Competition for the right to carry the coals became intense between railway companies.

The railways also allowed Ayrshire's people to travel to Glasgow to the north and Dumfries, with access to England to the south. In time a busy tourist trade developed with many 'day trippers' visiting the coast for a day out or for their annual holidays. Steamer trade on the Clyde carried many passengers from Ayrshire's ports to the islands, Arran included, or simply for a sail 'doon the watter'.

Golf also attracts many to Ayrshire which boasts many fine courses, two of which Royal Troon and Turnberry are on the British Open Golf Championship circuit. Indeed the first 'Open Championship' was held at Prestwick Golf Course in 1860. The Ayr coast is a golfers' paradise unequalled anywhere else in the world and the railway played its part in promoting golf courses, particularly at Turnberry and Troon. Famous courses line both sides of the railway from Irvine south to Ayr with the added attraction, on good days, of views of the mountains of Arran and Ailsa Craig.

It may be puzzling why Burns never mentioned Arran in his poems but we know why he never wrote about the railways as he died in 1796 before the railway era began. However, he would have been aware of some of the early waggonways which were close to the River Ayr. Both Robert Burns and the railways have produced a lasting legacy for Ayrshire and while their contributions were very different each proved vital, in its own way, to the development of Ayrshire life. Burns' poems and their acute observations say much about human nature but the railways also have a lot to say about man's ability to harness inventions for his own benefit. Robert Burns, I'm sure, would have spoken kindly about the travails of the railwayman but I suspect less kindly of their bosses and the pit owners.

Turnberry Hotel in 2011. It was designed by the famous railway architect James Miller.
Author

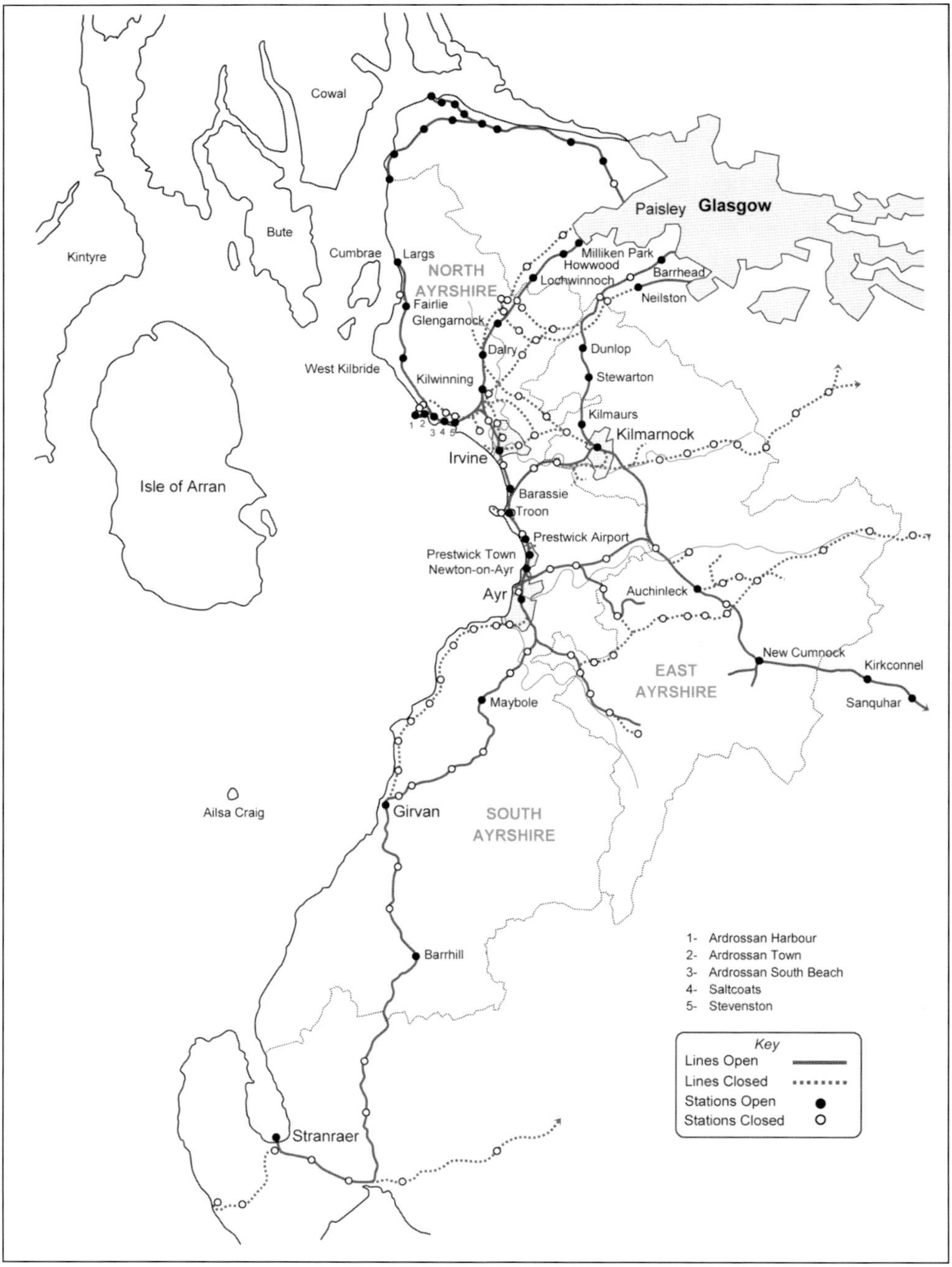
Cowal
Paisley
Glasgow
Bute
Kintyre
Cumbrae
Largs
NORTH AYRSHIRE
Milliken Park
Howwood
Lochwinnoch
Barrhead
Neilston
Fairlie
Glengarnock
Dalry
Dunlop
West Kilbride
Kilwinning
Stewarton
Kilmaurs
1 2 3 4 5
Kilmarnock
Irvine
Isle of Arran
Barassie
Troon
Prestwick Airport
Prestwick Town
Newton-on-Ayr
Ayr
Auchinleck
New Cumnock
Kirkconnel
EAST AYRSHIRE
Sanquhar
Maybole
Ailsa Craig
Girvan
SOUTH AYRSHIRE
Barrhill
1- Ardrossan Harbour
2- Ardrossan Town
3- Ardrossan South Beach
4- Saltcoats
5- Stevenston
Key
Lines Open
Lines Closed
Stations Open
Stations Closed
Stranraer

Chapter Two

Ayrshire's Railway Network

The Kilmarnock & Troon Railway (K&TR) was the first railway in Scotland authorized by an Act of Parliament (27th May, 1808) but also holds several other records. After four years of construction the Duke of Portland's Kilmarnock and Troon Railway was opened on 6th July, 1812, over 200 years ago. At just over nine miles in length, the K&TR ran between Troon harbour and Kilmarnock and was constructed using short cast-iron rails or plateways. For many years horses provided traction either to transport coal or other goods but even before the railway was officially opened passengers were being carried in what was Scotland's first railway passenger service and one of the first in the world. The railway was enthusiastically embraced by the business folk of Kilmarnock and in the town of Troon, which can trace much of its prosperity to the growth of this and later railways.

It was an experiment on the line by the famous engineer, George Stephenson, around 1816, with a steam engine known as *The Duke*, witnessed by a crowd of thousands which heralded the early dawn of a new age. Ultimately the experiment was unsuccessful with *The Duke* being too heavy for the cast-iron rails and it was 1825 before the first steam passenger train ran on the Stockton & Darlington Railway. However, Ayrshire played an important, if oft neglected, role in the evolution of the steam engine.

The oldest surviving multi-span bridge in Scotland built to carry a railway over a river and indeed one of the oldest such in the world was also part of the original K&T route. The stone four-arch Laigh Milton viaduct crosses the River Irvine near Gatehead and was in use until 1846, when the K&TR was converted to locomotive working and a new viaduct opened slightly to the south. The viaduct has recently been renovated as befits its historic importance.

The Kilmarnock & Troon Railway displayed the features that were to be typical of so many Ayrshire lines, as it collected coal from coal pits, transported the coal to a harbour, carried passengers and was a catalyst for the development of the local economy.

In 1831 the Ardrossan & Johnstone Railway, following the route originally planned as a canal, from the harbour at Ardrossan, opened as far as Kilwinning. It was an attempt to link up with another section of canal already constructed south from Paisley and which had been opened as far as Johnstone (Renfrewshire) by the Johnstone Canal Co. By 1840 the railway had separated from the canal company and became known as the Ardrossan Railway.

In 1837 the Glasgow, Paisley, Kilmarnock & Ayr Railway (GPK&AR) Act was passed, promoted by Glasgow businessmen, enabling a railway to be constructed between Glasgow and Ayr, with links at Dalry to Kilmarnock and at Kilwinning with the Ardrossan Railway. The 40 mile route was built in stages from Ayr (Newton terminus) towards Glasgow, tackling the easier and flatter coastal section first. The first engine called *Mercury* and its tender had to be brought from Glasgow, drawn by horses. Prestwick and Irvine stations were opened on 5th August, 1839 and Kilwinning was reached on 23rd March the following year. The route chosen was through the Garnock Valley reaching Beith, close to the county boundary with Renfrewshire, in the same year on 21st July. On the same date the line from the Glasgow end had opened as far south as Howwood (originally spelt with one 'w') in Renfrewshire. The following month on 12th August, 1840 the route was opened throughout. The railway had an immediate impact on Ayrshire's economy with coal exports increasing and ironworks being established at Dalry and Glengarnock. The coastal resorts grew in size and holidaymakers began to make the journey to enjoy the beaches and fresh air. With a new harbour at Ardrossan a steamer service was inaugurated between Ayrshire and Liverpool. The railway company trumpeted this as the introduction of a '24 hour service'* between Glasgow and London, using train, boat and then train from Liverpool. The service was unsuccessful and lasted less than a year.

The townsfolk of Kilmarnock had been disappointed at being bypassed by the initial railway route taken by the GPK&AR, despite proposing an alternative and more direct route which was, however, let down by more demanding gradients. It was to be another 40 years before a direct route between Glasgow and Kilmarnock was achieved. In the meantime the townsfolk of Kilmarnock swallowed their pride and accepted branch line status when the branch from the main line starting at Dalry was completed (4th April, 1843). The GPK&AR also obtained a long lease for the Kilmarnock & Troon Railway and upgraded it from a waggonway, which reopened using locomotives on 1st March, 1847, the same day as the Irvine harbour branch opened. The lease on the K&TR was eventually bought out by the Glasgow & South Western Railway (G&SWR) in 1899.

As railway development expanded in Ayrshire a branch from Crosshouse, near Kilmarnock on the Kilmarnock to Dalry branch, at Busby Junction, to Irvine was opened (22nd May, 1848). The same year the railway network spread east with branches from Kilmarnock to Auchinleck, Auchinleck to Muirkirk, with a branch to Lugar ironworks (*see map page 74*) and Hurlford to Galston (Irvine Valley) being opened (9th August) (*see map page 110*). The rail link to Muirkirk linked up with the ironworks in the village and surrounding coalmines. A branch from the Kilmarnock & Troon Railway, known as the Fairlie branch, served coal mines south of Kilmarnock and opened on 26th February, 1849 (*see map page 110*). On 20th May, 1850 the railway was extended further eastwards along the Irvine Valley from Galston to Newmilns encouraged by the revenue generated by the cotton industry and yet more coal traffic from the pits in the area. The economic benefits of the burgeoning railway network were beginning to be felt all over Ayrshire.

With branches connecting communities and industries, a gap in the market was becoming more apparent – a link with England. To further this end the GPK&AR came to an agreement with the Glasgow, Dumfries & Carlisle Railway (GD&CR) in 1845, but the latter's Bill was rejected that year being considered directly competitive to a Caledonian Railway (CR) Bill for a railway by Beattock and Annandale which was passed by Parliament. The two companies' intention was to extend their lines along the Nith Valley, the GPK&AR from the north, and join up near Cumnock. A further Bill the next

* The journey actually took 26½ hours.

year was passed, by which time the GD&CR had been dissolved and reformed and agreement reached with the CR to reach Carlisle with the last stretch over the 'Caley' line. After further Parliamentary amendments the GD&CR was again dissolved and their shareholders became shareholders in the GPK&AR. The latter's name was changed to the Glasgow & South Western Railway on the day that the line opened throughout.

The link to the south was opened on 28th October, 1850 and on that day the Glasgow & South Western Railway was created, which became the major railway company in Ayrshire complete with access to the outside world and with a determination to defend its hinterland. The G&SWR played an important role in Ayrshire's railway history until the reorganization of the railway network in 1923, when it became part of the London, Midland & Scottish Railway (LMS). The newly formed company owned just over 171 miles of track, not all in Ayrshire. When it was merged to form the LMS it owned just over 493 miles of track from Greenock and Glasgow in the north and south to Gretna. It also owned part of the Port Road, the railway from Dumfries to Stranraer, with a branch to Kirkcudbright and a westerly coastal route south from Girvan to join with the Port Road at Challoch Junction.

The GPK&AR south of Kilmarnock required four major viaducts, Kilmarnock Water, Hurlford, Ballochmyle and the Lugar or Templand viaduct along with the 680 yard Mossgiel tunnel. The viaducts were designed by the famous railway engineers Grainger and Miller who had a major influence on the development of railways in Scotland. There was a local connection as John Miller was born in Ayr in 1805. The 23-arch Kilmarnock Water viaduct still dominates the town centre on the southerly approach to Kilmarnock station, crossing both streets and the Kilmarnock Water. The most iconic railway structure on this line, however, is the Ballochmyle viaduct crossing the deep red sandstone gorge created by the River Ayr. Innovative in design when constructed, the long semi-circular central arch of 181 ft, flanked by six smaller arches, was the largest stone arch in the world at the time. The viaduct used mainly local red sandstone but hard stone from Dundee was used to form the arch ring. From rail to river is a height of 163 ft. The viaduct also had a fleeting appearance in the film *Mission Impossible* when it appears in the train and helicopter sequence as the train is meant to be entering the Channel Tunnel with Tom Cruise clinging to it. The Lugar or Templand viaduct, near Cumnock, was another notable viaduct with 14 semi-circular arches and towering 145 ft above the Lugar Water. This was not an easy route to construct and in addition to the ground works by the GPK&AR, the GD&CR had to bore the 1,410 yards-long Drumlanrig tunnel and construct several viaducts.

By 1854 the G&SWR had absorbed the Ardrossan Railway and its largely coalmining branches at Doura, Fergushill and the extension to Perceton, north of Irvine. These lines helped to supply coal to the Eglinton ironworks at Kilwinning which was operating by 1845.

The 1850s saw further expansion with a railway extending south and climbing through the Doon Valley to reach Dalmellington with the opening of the Ayr & Dalmellington Railway (A&DR) (*see map page 74*). The railway opened for goods on 15th May, 1856 and for passengers on 7th August, 1856.

Ballochmyle viaduct engineered by Grainger and Miller, 2012. *Author*

Lugar viaduct or Templand viaduct north of former Cumnock station site engineered by Grainger and Miller, 2011. *Author*

The connection to the Dalmellington ironworks at Dunaskin allowed the expansion of this industry in the remote valley. The constant demand for coal and ironstone led to a network of mineral lines in the hills surrounding the works and eventually from further afield. Passengers using the service on the first day could use the temporary passenger station at Ayr Townhead on the south side of the river close to the present site of Ayr station with the railway having been extended over the River Ayr to the new station. Ayr North Side continued in use until 1st July, 1857, after that date Ayr North Side station (Newton terminus) was used only as a goods station (*see map page 28*). On the same day Ayr Townhead was made permanent and became known simply as Ayr. The G&SWR took over the running of the A&DR on 1st August, 1858.

In 1856 the Ayr & Maybole Railway which shared the same trackbed as the A&DR as far as Maybole Junction (later renamed Dalrymple Junction), south of Ayr, began operating to Maybole. In 1860 the railway was extended south-west from Maybole (Maybole & Girvan Railway), along the valley through which runs the Water of Girvan, to Girvan, stopping on the north side of the river with a goods line crossing the river to reach the harbour. The railway enabled holidaymakers to enjoy the town's harbour and beach, including sea trips to Ailsa Craig. Fish landed at the harbour could also reach the market in Glasgow more quickly.

The railway network became ever more complex, with the addition of a cross-country line, on 1st September, 1870, from Ayr to Mauchline connecting to the line south of Kilmarnock which involved the construction of the nine-arch Failford viaduct (*page 74*). In turn, in 1872, this led to a further route called the Ayr & Cumnock Railway (A&CR), which branched from the Ayr to Mauchline line at Annbank and looped south, crossing the Enterkine viaduct, which required 14 stone piers to cross over the River Ayr, before passing through Cumnock and reaching the railway to Muirkirk on the moor at Cronberry. The same year or beginning of 1873, another cross-country route linking the Ayr & Dalmellington Railway with the A&CR was opened, which ran from Holehouse Junction on the A&DR to Belston Junction on the A&CR. This line was often referred to as the Rankinston branch. Delivery of coal to furnaces and ports from pits along the routes was the main purpose of the lines but there was a limited passenger service when the line was upgraded from a mineral line during 1883.

The route through Kilmarnock to the south, by Dalry, was a long haul and pressure built again for a more direct line. On 26th June, 1873 the Glasgow, Barrhead & Kilmarnock Joint line was opened to Kilmarnock and the town truly became a railway centre with lines reaching it from all directions. The line was operated jointly between the G&SWR and the CR and was a sensible compromise, for once, between the two companies.

In the same year (1st January, 1873) the Caledonian Railway extended the line which terminated at Muirkirk east to Douglas in Lanarkshire for goods and the following year (1st June, 1874) for passengers. Slowly the corridors linking Ayrshire to its neighbouring counties were acquiring railways.

In an era of rapid railway development it was logical to want to extend the railway south of Girvan, requiring a new viaduct over the Water of Girvan, to link with the Port Road. This ran from Dumfries to the ferry port of Stranraer in

Kilmarnock station in 2012. *Author*

Ayr station in 2012. *Author*

the sheltered waters of Loch Ryan, to provide competition for the Irish trade. The terminus of the Port Road was originally intended as Portpatrick but the harbour was too exposed in rough weather and not capable of expansion and instead Stranraer became the ferry port for crossings to Ireland. The Girvan & Portpatrick Junction Railway (G&PJR) was opened on 5th October, 1877 and joined the Port Road at Challoch Junction, a distance of just under 31 miles over remote moorland with testing gradients and almost no local population to support the railway. Many tunnels and bridges had to be constructed, including the 543 yards-long Pinmore tunnel and the 11-arch Kinclair viaduct within the first six miles. This roller coaster railway peaked at Chirmorie Summit 690 ft above sea level before leaving Ayrshire and entering Galloway. The incentive was to service the short sea crossing to Ireland but while the sea crossing from Stranraer was short the railway journey from Glasgow was long and the longer sailing from the Clyde remained more popular. Revenues were meagre and eventually a legal dispute, caused by arrears of payments due, stopped the G&PJR using the rails between Challoch Junction and Stranraer in 1882; but this was settled by August 1883 and the service resumed.

In 1878 the expansion of the railway along the coast north of Ardrossan began with a branch from Ardrossan to West Kilbride opening on 1st May continuing to Fairlie two years later (1st June, 1880), with a short extension to Fairlie Pier station and eventually opening to Largs on 1st June, 1885. Largs had finally been reached from the south, at the end of a long loop from Kilwinning after the G&SWR and the CR had proposed different routes to reach the seaside resort. Before the Largs branch was completed there were plans to reach Largs by railway from Wemyss Bay to the north (CR) and later across the moor from the Elderslie to Greenock route, north of Kilmacolm. Neither plan was successful.

Ayr's new station, slightly to the south of the existing station was officially opened on 12th January, 1886 followed on the 1st June by the landmark red sandstone Ayr Station Hotel, looking like a French chateau, which still dominates the top end of Burns Statue Square in the centre of the town.

The late-1880s saw a determined attempt by the Caledonian Railway to intrude into Ayrshire. Keen to carry coal on its own lines to the ports in Ayrshire and not be beholden to any other party, it obtained authorization to build a 6¼ mile link from the jointly run branch to Beith south to Kilwinning (Barrmill & Kilwinning Railway). With the encouragement of the Earl of Eglinton, always eager to encourage the further development of Ardrossan harbour, the project was extended. From Kilwinning another line was built to Ardrossan, where eventually new harbour facilities were constructed. The Lanarkshire & Ayrshire Railway (L&AR), as the railway became known, opened on 4th September, 1888, and a branch to the Nobel's explosives factory at Ardeer (3rd November, 1888) and a link to the G&SWR at Ardrossan harbour (30th November, 1888) quickly followed. The following year a 4¼ mile branch west to Kilbirnie (2nd December, 1889), from Giffen station on the Barrmill & Kilwinning Railway was operating and by 1890 the L&AR was operating out of its own pier at Ardrossan - Montgomerie Pier (30th May, 1890). A branch south to Irvine was also opened (2nd June, 1890). For the first time the CR had its own access to Ardrossan and its route was almost three miles shorter. The L&AR

Troon station looking towards Glasgow on 4th November, 1958. The original design was by James Miller. *Hamish Stevenson Collection*

A view from almost the same spot in 2012. *Author*

was an initial success as local industry welcomed the competition offered by the Caledonian-backed railway and a breaking of the stranglehold held by the G&SWR. Traders from Ayr and even further south in the county pleaded with the Caley to extend its railway south to Ayr.

So strong was the determination of the CR not to share revenue with the G&SWR that it built another line into Glasgow from Giffen (south of Barrmill) in 1903 so that it would not have to share revenue with the G&SWR on the Glasgow, Barrhead & Kilmarnock Joint Line. In Ayrshire this meant that even the Beith branch, which the CR jointly owned anyway, was partly duplicated with a track being built to the south of the Beith branch from Lugton as far as Giffen Junction. This completed the construction of the parallel line and underlined the determination of the CR to provide its own line into Ayrshire. The CR could now carry its own coals to Ardrossan.

With the upper reaches of the Clyde becoming navigable the route was built too late and by 1907 coal traffic was been diverted to the newly-opened Rothesay Dock, at Yoker, closer to the coalfields of Lanarkshire. The fortunes of the L&AR soon declined despite valiant efforts to replace coal traffic, including transporting 'offal', which wasn't always appreciated by locals as the contents of open wagons decayed in sidings over weekends.

In the 1890s the rate of branch line development slowed for the G&SWR. The Monkton & Annbank Railway (3rd March, 1892) provided another useful coal crosslink between Annbank, on the Mauchline branch and Monkton Junction, north of Prestwick station on the Ayr to Glasgow line (*page 74*). The same year a new station was opened in Troon (2nd May, 1892) and the original route became known as the Troon Avoiding Line since it bypassed the new station. The original station, opened in 1840, became the goods station and was known as Troon (Old). The new station was more centrally situated for passengers. A short loop was added to allow access to Troon harbour from the south and making a connection to the K&TR line. Another railway bridge over the River Ayr was added in 1899, when a short extension over the river to reach the South Quay was completed. The branch passed through the original Ayr Passenger (North) station building.

The railway in Irvine Valley which stopped at Newmilns was again extended further east, this time to Darvel (1st June, 1896) meaning that all the small towns in the Irvine Valley were linked by rail, giving easy access to Kilmarnock and beyond (*page 110*).

Ownership of Troon harbour was transferred from the Duke of Portland and vested in the G&SWR in 1901. Also at the start of the 20th century more new lines were added as the network became ever more complex. In 1902 the Gatehead & Hurlford (G&H) line, providing a route to the south of Kilmarnock and reducing the need for traffic to pass through the town, opened for goods and minerals on 14th July (*page 110*). This was extended in 1904 with the construction of the Riccarton Loop from Kay Park Junction, just over a mile south of Kilmarnock station, south to Bellfield Junction on the G&H line. It never had a regular passenger service but was useful to relieve pressure on Kilmarnock and allow trains to avoid delays. Part of the Riccarton Loop remains used to service an oil depot.

On 1st September, 1903 the Catrine branch from Brackenhill Junction, south of Kilmarnock, near Mauchline was opened allowing rail access to the cotton mills (*page 74*). In 1905 the line east of Darvel was extended to Strathaven in Lanarkshire and worked jointly by the G&SWR and the Caledonian Railway which involved building the 13-arch brick Loudounhill viaduct in the lee of Loudoun Hill (*page 110*).

On 1st June, 1905 to relieve pressure on the railway between Dalry and Glengarnock a loop line was built, the Dalry & North Johnstone line (Lochwinnoch Loop), from Brownhill Junction north to Cart Junction in Renfrewshire enabling trains to bypass this busy section.

The final railway opened (1st May, 1906) in Ayrshire was the Maidens & Dunure Light Railway (M&DLR), which took advantage of the less demanding engineering specifications for light railways but with a speed restriction of 25 mph. This slow meandering route was a most picturesque journey along the Carrick coastline, linking Ayr (Alloway Junction) and Girvan and was intended to deliver passengers to the grand Turnberry Hotel, built as a railway hotel, complete with its famous golf links (*page 26*). The railway track ran behind the hotel ensuring that the view from sea-facing bedrooms was not spoiled. The route inevitably became known as the 'Golfers' Railway'.

There is one final railway which was built early in the 20th century but does not have an opening date. This strange state of affairs was due to inter-company rivalry. The Mid-Lanark, Spireslack & Muirkirk Railway was authorized by an 1896 Act of Parliament, along with several other lines in Lanarkshire, but was never opened. It left the Muirkirk to Lanark branch just east of Muirkirk station and climbed into the hills behind Glenbuck, requiring three viaducts in fewer than three miles (*page 74*). The Spireslack extension was a symbol of the intense rivalry between companies jockeying for position and wishing to give no advantage to another company and its story is told in Chapter Four.

The G&SWR was still seeking to expand its influence and control at the end of World War I and in 1919 Ayr harbour, run by the town council and appointed trustees, had its ownership transferred to the railway company.

Loudounhill viaduct on 30th August, 1961 with Loudoun Hill in the background.
Roy Hamilton/Hamish Stevenson Collection

In Ayrshire the railways were a force for good, linking communities, empowering industries, by providing a system which allowed goods and commodities to be transported more easily and increasing the scope for visitors to discover Ayrshire's scenic attractions, beaches and golf courses. The G&SWR was also good for Ayrshire but doggedly protected its own interests. Competition from the Caledonian Railway was late and while welcomed by many, was undermined by the decline in importance of Ayrshire's ports at the end of the 19th century. Competition and introspective rivalry had, however, built a system with a wasteful duplication of routes, acceptable when the railways were the only means of transport. The 20th century was to change everything. The railways now faced strong competition from road transport and an improving road network. Trucks and buses could use any road and did not require high maintenance iron tracks. It was inevitable that the railway network would face challenges and change.

Decline of the Network

The expansion of the railway network in Ayrshire stopped in the early years of the 20th century. Some of the last lines to be built were never economically viable and so it proved that within a quarter of a century the economic conditions and the inexorable rise of the internal combustion engine had created conditions that started a cull of the county's railway infrastructure

In railway chronologies of Ayrshire there is a gap between 1906 and 1930. Wartime restrictions meant the temporary closure of some stations as an economy measure but otherwise the railway network was unchanged. The Grouping of the railways in 1923 brought pressure for rationalization and in Ayrshire, the London, Midland & Scottish Railway took over responsibility and began to look for savings. By the 1930s some routes were struggling.

The earliest victim was the branch of the Lanarkshire & Ayrshire Railway, from Kilwinning to Irvine which closed to passengers on 28th July, 1930 and by the end of December 1939 the route was closed completely. Another short branch from the L&AR, the branch to Kilbirnie, between Giffen and Glengarnock, was another early closure on 1st December, 1930.

The wisdom of constructing the Golfers' Railway must be questioned as the route from Alloway Junction to Turnberry, a significant swathe of the line, 14 of its 19½ mile length, was closed to passengers on the 1st December, 1930. A goods service struggled on until the 1950s. An attempt, in 1932, to revive the route, by providing a twice-daily through route to Kilmarnock, linking with the Glasgow (St Enoch) to London (St Pancras) service lasted only a year. The remaining section from Girvan to Turnberry closed to passengers in 1942 and meant that hotel guests could no longer arrive by train, a consequence that has not hampered the attraction of the hotel. A short section of the railway was reopened from Alloway Junction to take passengers to Butlin's Holiday Park, beside the Heads of Ayr, in 1947 but this was closed in 1968.

The 1940s saw two lines close. Another of the lines constructed in the 20th century, the short Catrine branch, was next to go on 3rd May, 1943 for passengers and the short coal route from Monkton Junction to Annbank was abandoned on 15th November, 1949.

Between the wars Troon harbour experienced a sharp decline in business with the closure of many of Ayrshire's blast furnaces, problems with flooding in local coal pits and iron ore and limestone imports being diverted to Glasgow's ports and off Ayrshire's railways. Ayr harbour retained more business but still experienced a decline.

The 1950s saw the closure of the Holehouse Junction to Belston Junction route to passengers (3rd April, 1950) and the total closure of the section from Holehouse Junction to Littlemill Colliery, near Rankinston on the same day. Auchinleck to Cronberry followed three months later (3rd July, 1950) and the Ayrshire & Cumnock Railway route, which joined the Auchinleck to Cronberry section at Cronberry, closed to passengers just over a year later (10th September, 1951). The Littlemill to Belston Junction line lasted until 1st January, 1975 shortly after the Littlemill Colliery closed. The mainstay of these lines was the collection of coal from the pits and while attempts had been made to develop passenger traffic it had never been successful. The A&CR was also closed for freight east of Belston Junction but the section between Annbank to Drongan, where a mineral line had been built to the Killoch Colliery, opened in 1960 as one of the National Coal Board's 'super pits', survived. This line now serves the Killoch Washery and coal disposal point, at the site of the closed pit, and is still in use.

The 1960s saw the Beeching cuts take effect. The Beith branch closed to passengers (5th November, 1962) and to goods (5th October, 1964). April 1964 saw passenger services on the Ayr to Dalmellington, Crosshouse to Irvine, and Hurlford to Darvel lines withdrawn, the latter two originating at Kilmarnock. The 11th October, 1965 saw the complete closure of the Crosshouse to Irvine branch.

The Port Road was closed east of Challoch Junction (14th June, 1965), breaking the direct 73 mile route between Dumfries and Stranraer. Rail services to Stranraer were diverted north along the Nith Valley route, cross-country by Kilmarnock and Troon and then south by Girvan, almost doubling the length of a journey by rail between Dumfries and Stranraer. Even after the Kilmarnock to Troon Railway 'closed' in 1969 (3rd May), the midnight 'Paddy', as the boat train to Stranraer was called, still used the line.

The 1st January, 1968 saw passenger services withdrawn between Castlehill and Parkhouse junctions and from 6th May, 1968 formally between Montgomerie Pier and Stevenston No. 1 as the duplication of lines around the three seaside towns was tackled. The year 1967 saw a decline in the lines around Troon, with the harbour branches all being closed by December 1973. A short stub remains of the Troon Avoiding Line, used when Glasgow to Ayr was being electrified, but the rest of the Barassie Junction to Lochgreen Junction was closed by the end of November 1982.

The 1970s saw further pruning with Mauchline to Ayr (May 1975) and Byrehill Junction to Dubbs Junction, near Kilwinning (13th June, 1977) closing to passengers. Freight traffic ceased on the Ayr to Mauchline line in 1985 but restarted in 1988.

Ayrshire's Railways Today

The railways, which had once provided a vital link for isolated communities and a means of exploring the outside world denied to people previously, almost succumbed to the internal combustion engine, especially with the demise of the coalmining industry. The railway network in Ayrshire was drastically pruned and some felt left to wither and die. However, the mood is changing yet again and in this environmentally conscious age the railway system has once again become important, being more environmentally friendly and having a lower 'carbon footprint'.

The backbone of the old Glasgow & South Western Railway network in Ayrshire survives but most of the branches have been hacked off. What remains is generally well used.

The Glasgow to Ayr line, electrified in 1986, with its branches at Kilwinning to Ardrossan Harbour and Largs, provides a reliable and regular service for commuters between coast and city with pressure mounting for more frequent services. South of Ayr the route to Stranraer continues to provide a service but questions arise about its long term future, especially after the ferry service to Ireland was moved from Stranraer town further up Loch Ryan to a new ferry terminal at Cairnryan and passengers are being bussed from there direct to Ayr station.

The Glasgow, Barrhead & Kilmarnock line, having been singled in 1966 and with all intermediate stations between Barrhead and Kilmarnock closed, has now being upgraded, with a doubling of the track from Lugton to Stewarton. Intermediate stations at Dunlop, Stewarton and Kilmaurs already reopened have been upgraded. South of Kilmarnock the Nith Valley route is also busy and requiring upgrading and stations have been reopened at Auchinleck, New Cumnock and Sanquhar.

The Troon & Kilmarnock Railway, now known as 'The Burns Line', was reopened on 30th September, 1996 with the advertising slogan 'The best line since *Auld Lang Syne*', and provides a regular service between Kilmarnock, Ayr and Girvan. I wonder how many passengers appreciate the historical significance of the route.

Coal traffic continues with some still exported to Ireland. The cross-county Ayr to Mauchline line is open for freight traffic, with the branch to Killoch Washery and coal disposal point still in use. Part of the Dalmellington Railway operates beyond Dunaskin to the Chalmerston opencast coal terminal, near Dalmellington. Coal is still delivered from these sites to the harbour at Ayr for export to Northern Ireland. Coal loading points near New Cumnock have generated business for the railways, although some plans to link opencast pits to the rail network have failed to materialize, such as the link between Auchinleck and Powharnal opencast coal pit, near Cronberry.

Modern industry has shown some willingness to use the railways with a siding built to connect what is now the DSM chemical factory (formerly Roche) at Dalry, which is involved in the production of vitamin C amongst other products. A short branch to serve the Caledonian Paper Mill at Irvine was built to receive consignments of china clay.

The railways in Ayrshire do not only have a history and a rich heritage but a future. Exploring the heritage reveals a lot about Ayrshire's industrial and social history.

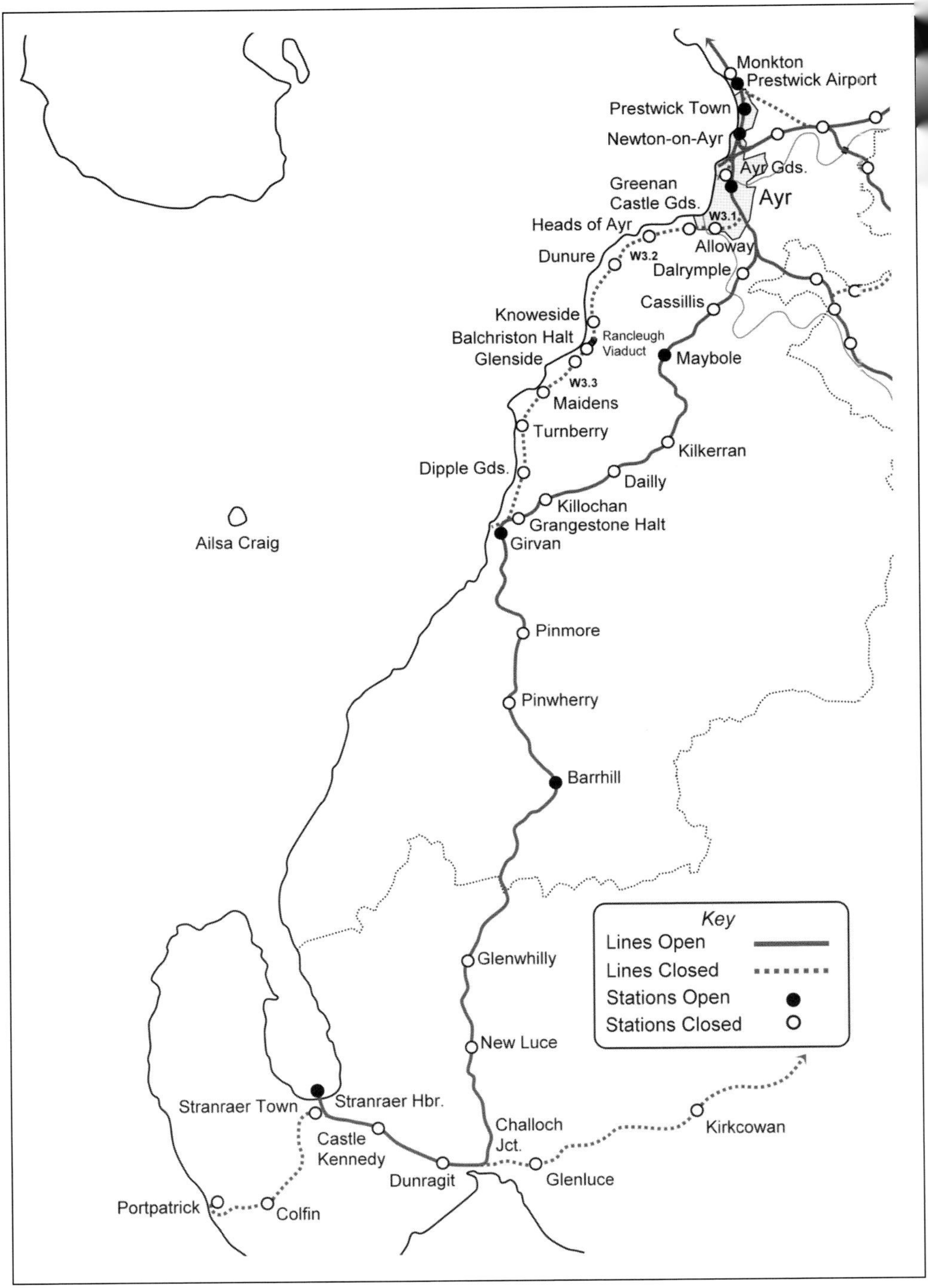
Monkton
Prestwick Airport
Prestwick Town
Newton-on-Ayr
Ayr Gds.
Greenan
Castle Gds.
Ayr
W3.1
Heads of Ayr
Alloway
Dunure
W3.2
Dalrymple
Cassillis
Knoweside
Rancleugh
Viaduct
Balchriston Halt
Glenside
Maybole
W3.3
Maidens
Turnberry
Kilkerran
Dipple Gds.
Dailly
Killochan
Grangestone Halt
Ailsa Craig
Girvan
Pinmore
Pinwherry
Barrhill
Key
Lines Open
Lines Closed
Stations Open
Stations Closed
Glenwhilly
New Luce
Stranraer Town
Stranraer Hbr.
Castle
Kennedy
Challoch
Jct.
Kirkcowan
Dunragit
Glenluce
Portpatrick
Colfin

Chapter Three

Railways to the South of Ayr

Ayrshire was not always an easy county to get around and in the 18th century the roads there were considered amongst the worst in the country and for a large part of the year almost impassable. Two Acts of Parliament in 1767 and 1774, the Ayr Road Acts, allowed for trustees to set tolls and raise capital for the building and maintenance of 63 roads within the county, with a combined length of 550 miles and a network of roads slowly developed. There were interesting exemptions to the tolls. No tolls were paid by those going to worship or carrying stones for repairing the roads or for coal going for export.

Horses provided most of the pulling power and before the railways if goods had to be transported you had the choice to carry them yourself or employ a carter. With roads in poor condition and often no more than rough tracks, no journey was easy.

In the late 18th century the movement of coal from the many small pits, often to the coast for export principally to Ireland, was becoming increasingly important. By this time coal was no longer just a domestic fuel but used to fire saltpans and limekilns and for stationary steam engines. These were the work horses for the textile industry and also used to pump water from mines shafts as the search for coal took miners ever deeper underground. However, heavy loads of coals were slow and difficult to move over uneven terrain and by the end of the 18th century the development of waggonways made it easier to transport coal from pits, or stones from quarries to the towns and harbours where there was the greatest demand. Waggonways used iron or wooden rails to guide the wheels of wagons often with cobbled stones between the rails to provide grip for the horses pulling the heavy loads. Around Ayr there were several waggonways. On the north side of the River Ayr in the Parish of Newton upon Ayr around 1765 several coal pits had been sunk. The coal pits were linked to the harbour by waggonways. Initially the waggonways stretched only a few hundred yards but as coal pits were worked out distances increased. By 1784 a waggonway was operating between Auchincruive Estate, the home of the Oswald family, and the coast at Newton, a distance of about four miles.

The Ayr waggonways seem to have been edge rails, not plate ways. Horses could pull a load of about eight tons of coal; carried in six wagons at a speed of three mph with each horse delivering an average of 70 tons of coal a day To speed up transit passing places were needed to allow wagons to pass each other. The genesis of a railway system was emerging.

The waggonways around Newton were still in use when the construction of the Glasgow, Paisley, Kilmarnock & Ayr Railway began in Ayr around 1838. The terminus of the GPK&AR was north of the river, in the Newton-on-Ayr area and ended only yards from the River Ayr. An amendment to the Act authorizing the railway was necessary forbidding the railway interfering with the operation of the waggonways in the area.

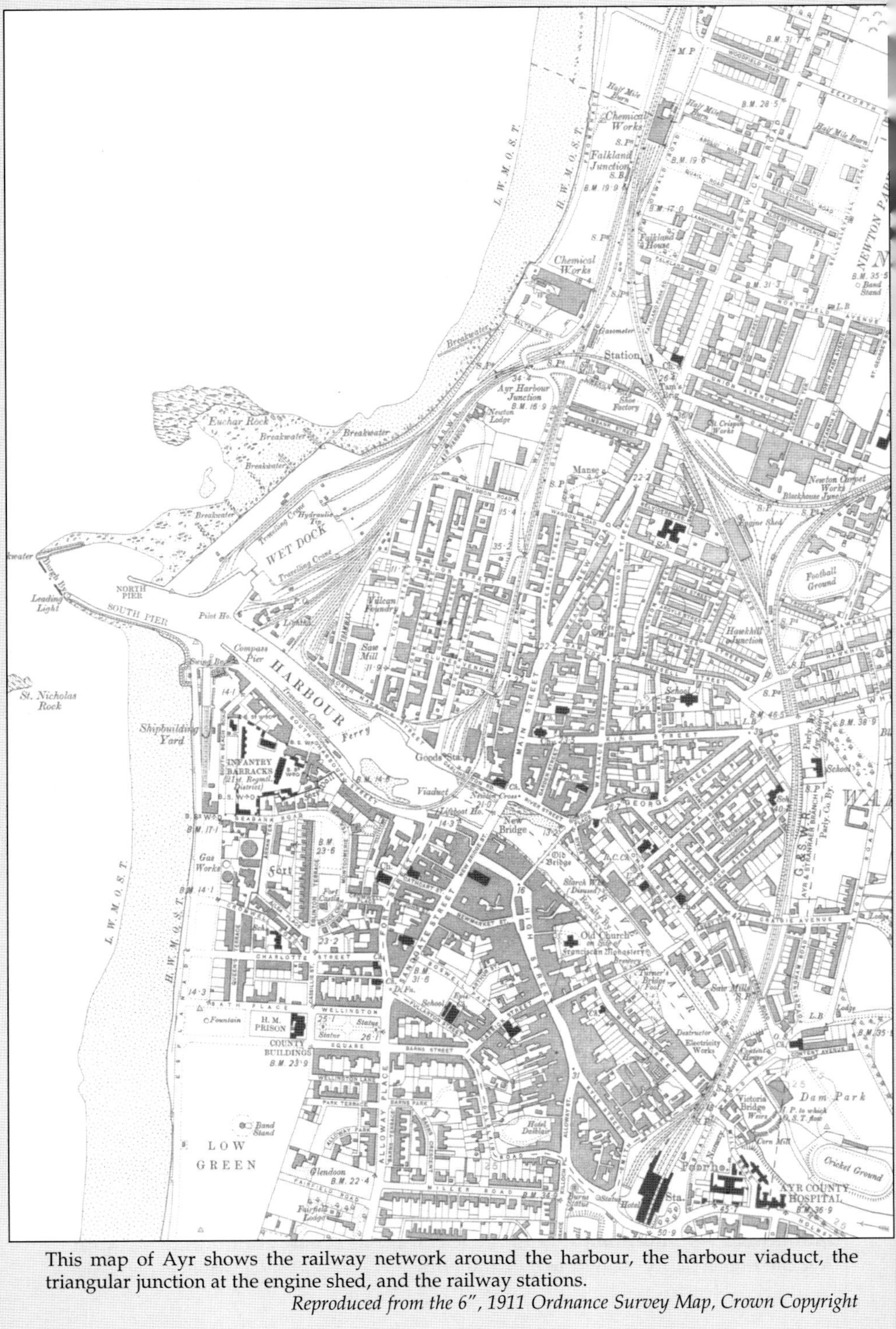

This map of Ayr shows the railway network around the harbour, the harbour viaduct, the triangular junction at the engine shed, and the railway stations.

Reproduced from the 6", 1911 Ordnance Survey Map, Crown Copyright

By 1853 the Glasgow & South Western Railway, the successor to the GPK&AR had plans to carry the railway over the River Ayr southwards. However, arrangements still had to be agreed with the owners of the waggonways to permit the extension without interfering with their operation. An extensive system of waggonways now existed around Ayr and reached as far as Annbank, five miles to the east, beyond the River Ayr. Remnants of the waggonways still exist today, particularly around the Auchincruive Estate and are explored further in Chapter Four.

The railway terminus north of the river was certainly convenient for the harbour but less so for those wanting to visit Robert Burns' birthplace in Alloway or spend a day on Ayr beach, both to the south of the river. However, if tourism was still in its infancy, the Dalmellington Iron Company's (DICo.) works at Dunaskin in the Doon Valley, to the south of Ayr, were already in production having been built in the 1840s. The company was owned by the Houldsworth family who had developed their expertise in the cotton industry, but foreseeing a slump in the cotton trade had switched to iron production. The DICo. wanted the railway to be extended south over the river as soon as possible to help develop their business. All the materials originally required to build the furnaces had been carted from Ayr by road to Dunaskin, a distance of around 13 miles with some steep ascents. It took 24 pairs of horses just to carry the great beam for the engine house up to Dunaskin. After the ironworks opened lines of carts were required to take the limestone up and bring the pig iron down. A common sight in Ayr High Street was rows of carts left while thirsty carters enjoyed refreshment in the local taverns and the horses were rested. While this arrangement meant that pig iron could reach Ayr, the Houldsworths wanted to take their product directly to the expanding markets around Glasgow. A railway to the works would be far more efficient and was vital for their business plan.

Ayr Old terminus (Ayr Goods) in the early 1970s. *Hamish Stevenson Collection*

Further extension of the railway system south of the river was also envisaged to build a route to Portpatrick with the potential of traffic from the Galloway port to Ireland. Two companies were bidding to reach Galloway. The Glasgow & Belfast Union Railway (G&BUR) produced a Prospectus with a coastal route, firstly inland to Maybole and then to Girvan and the south while the Ayrshire & Galloway Railway (A&GR) wanted a direct route south to Dalmellington and then through the Galloway Hills to Balcary Bay on the Solway coast. No one could accuse railway promoters of lacking ambition, even if the A&GR's knowledge of the obstacles presented by geography was less than impressive.

It was only around 50 years earlier that a road, as a result of the Ayr Road Act, had been built through the Doon Valley to reach Dalmellington and, like the road today, it avoided the route taken by the River Doon until it reached Patna. The first road to Dalmellington had almost avoided the valley altogether preferring to cross the hills to the east of the valley which was considered safer for travellers. Around the Dalmellington ironworks at Dunaskin coal from local mines struggled to reach the furnaces, such was the state of the roads. A railway was a necessity to develop the ironworks and to supply them with coal and other raw materials and to take away the pig iron. A railway network linking local mines to the main line and the ironworks would be even better.

The Glasgow & Belfast Union Railway obtained an Act of Parliament in 1846 but did not proceed. A branch from the main G&BUR route would have taken the railway to Smithston Farm, a distance of nine miles from Ayr but still four miles short of Dunaskin. From there the Ayrshire & Galloway Railway would have continued to the ironworks and south to Dalmellington and then onwards to Galloway. Despite backing from the Glasgow, Paisley, Kilmarnock & Ayr Railway and the Houldsworths, for the section to Dalmellington to be completed, the A&GR had insufficient funds and the business confidence to start construction from Smithston Farm.

To the Houldsworths this was frustrating and even the proposed railway from the ironworks south to the pits at Sillyhole, near Dalmellington was not proceeding quickly enough due to difficulties in stabilizing the surface of the marshy ground that the railway had to cross at Sillyhole. It took until 1849 for this section to be completed by the A&GR with the Dalmellington Iron Company working it. Horses, at this time, were still providing the pulling power.

If the A&GR's plans had not progressed sufficiently then the G&BUR's progress was worse. By 1852 no track had been made on its projected main line, south from Ayr, or on the branch to Smithston Farm. In 1850 the Glasgow & South Western Railway was created absorbing among others the GPK&AR. Directors of the G&SWR met with the Houldsworths and an agreement was reached. The result was that the A&GR was wound up with the Dalmellington Iron Company giving several guarantees, including a minimum return for the new company operating the lines and a promise to build no rival lines. A new Bill was passed through Parliament on 4th August, 1853 and the Ayr & Dalmellington Railway was formed. Work began to construct the railway from a new junction (Falkland Junction), north of the terminus in Ayr, across the River Ayr to reach the ironworks. This was not an easy route to construct requiring several new bridges in Ayr, sections of high embankments, deep cuttings and one major viaduct, near Dalrymple on the often steep climb to the Doon Valley. With the section between Sillyhole and the ironworks already finished it required only a short further section from Sillyhole to Dalmellington to be constructed and the route from Ayr to Dalmellington was finally completed. Trains started transporting the pig iron down to Ayr on 15th May, 1856 and a passenger service started from Dalmellington to Ayr on 7th August the same year. On 19th August a new temporary station was opened on the south side of the River Ayr at Ayr Townhead, sometimes referred to as Ayr South Side, with passenger trains still continuing to use the original terminus, then called Ayr North Side. Within a year (1st July, 1857) the station at Ayr Townhead, thereafter simply known as Ayr, became permanent and Ayr North Side ceased to deal with passengers and dealt solely with goods.

The new development created disruption in Ayr with several new bridges required from what became Falkland Junction, where the new line deviated from the existing track half-a-mile north of Ayr North Side. The main road was now forced to cross over the line by a new bridge known locally as Tam's Brig, probably named after a local farmer Tam McCreath. Within 30 years, 1886, a third station was required in Ayr, close to the Townhead site but 900 yards further south. A railway hotel, known simply as the Station Hotel, built of local red sandstone, formed part of the new station. The railway station and hotel was now an important landmark in Ayr dominating the top of the town. The third station was more convenient for the town and Ayr beach now being developed for holiday makers.

Ironworks have an insatiable demand for coal and the hillside at Dunaskin and the plateau above were the site of many coal and ironstone pits, some worked by incline. By the early 1860s the mines at Sillyhole had reached the end of their productive life, being prone to flooding, and new pits were developed to the east of Dalmellington towards Cumnock. At the same time DICo. were developing ironstone pits at Carbieston near Coylton connected to the A&DR railway by a mineral line. By the mid-1870s this line was extended to Coylton and further pits were opened. In 1873 a branch from the A&DR was opened from Holehouse Junction to Belston Junction where it joined up with the newly opened Ayrshire and Cumnock Railway. Known as the Rankinston branch it provided a useful cross-country link. DICo. was facing competition for the coal reserves firstly from the Summerlee Iron Company who withdrew when their pits, near Smithston Farm, were worked out by the early 1870s, and then from Merry and Cunninghame who operated the Glengarnock ironworks in north Ayrshire at Glengarnock. Merry and Cunninghame extracted coal from pits near Rankinston on the northern slopes of the plateau and the Rankinston branch allowed them to transport coal north.

When constructed the Ayr & Dalmellington Railway route was single track but work had also begun on doubling the trackbed for four miles south of Ayr and by 13th October the same year (1856) a new route was completed to Maybole. The Ayr & Maybole Railway shared the first 4½ miles with the Ayr & Dalmellington Railway but at Dalrymple Junction it went its own way to reach Maybole, a further distance of almost six miles. Just over three years later the railway had reached Girvan journeying beside the Water of Girvan for most of the route. A small coalfield provided some useful local business for the railway and some coal was exported to Ireland from Girvan harbour. When the railway was extended beyond Maybole the original terminus station was closed and became the goods station for the new Maybole station on the through route.

The continuation of the railway south to Galloway, from Girvan, the dream of many railway promoters, was eventually achieved when the 30 mile gap between Girvan and the Portpatrick Railway was completed by the Girvan & Portpatrick Junction Railway. At last the journey by rail from Glasgow could compete in the time taken with the sailing from Ardrossan to Belfast. The previous long railway route via Kilmarnock and Dumfries and then west to Portpatrick was considerably shortened by the new route. The route, difficult to build and to operate with challenging gradients had only one purpose in mind – Ireland. While intermediate stations were opened there was little local passenger traffic. Today the line is under threat as already explained.

The railway development south of Ayr was not complete, however, and in 1906 the Maidens & Dunure Light Railway was opened between Alloway Junction and Girvan Junction. The line sought to attract golfers to the grand new railway hotel at Turnberry, built by the G&SWR, and took an attractive coastal route. While the hotel has gone on to be one of the world's top hotels its railway connection has long since been lost. The railway also provided a connection to the heart of the Burns' Country at Alloway, but in this it had been beaten by a tram service from Ayr which was already operating.

Maybole Goods, the site of the original station. *Hamish Stevenson Collection*

Exploring the Railway Heritage

Places of railway interest and disused branches are described in sequence starting north of the River Ayr at the site of the original terminus of the GPK&AR and proceeding south.

The exploration of the railways to the south of Ayr begins at the site of the original terminus of the GPK&AR which is found on North Harbour Street beside the New Bridge (map reference 338222) across the River Ayr. From the road bridge the first evidence of a earlier railway can be seen - the piers of a former railway bridge over the river. The piers curve towards the river mouth, to the quay side on the south side of the harbour where the fishing fleet was once based. (*) Fish landed at the fish market on the south quay were transported to Glasgow markets across the railway bridge. The bridge which was constructed in 1899 was a five-span girder bridge (337223) built on masonry piers. It was used less frequently as goods traffic concentrated on the north side of the river and it closed by the early 1960s. Thereafter it was used only as an unofficial shortcut, by daring or inebriated townsfolk, before the metal girder structure was removed in 1978. In March 1949 the *Cornish Coast* a ship being refitted in the shipyard, broke loose from her moorings and crashed against the bridge dislodging part of the girder structure from the piers and dislodging one of the piers. The piers bear testimony to the damage and one has been repaired with brick.

New red brick flats on North Harbour Street, next to a former church, have been built on the site of the station buildings (337223) but the piers of the old railway bridge indicate the station's location. A two-storey sandstone building, the station was altered to allow trains to pass through it and across the bridge. Behind the new houses is a fan-shaped area where the sidings were located. This area is now a car park. Some of the original boundary walls are still extant. The railway also extended from the station along the north quay. Short sections of the trackbed from the site of Ayr North Side station can be traced back to the junction, particularly behind Newton House, on Green Street Lane and close to the prominent gasometer beside Limekiln Road (339231) where a road bridge crosses the trackbed. The junction site was just to the north of Limekiln Road. En route you cross Waggon Road which follows the line of a former waggonway.

In a section of the town which has always been industrialized railway sidings still serve the harbour and Falkland Yard. The Port of Ayr remains busy today with coal being shipped across to Northern Ireland in a continuation of a process which has gone on for several hundred years. Fertiliser, scrap metal, rock salt and timber also pass through the harbour. The former Scottish Agricultural Industries building remains between the railway and the coast. The south quay now only enjoys seasonal visits from PS *Waverley*, the last seagoing paddle steamer in the world.

Beside Newton-on-Ayr station (341232) is Tam's Brig which carries the main road over the railway and to the east of it is the recently closed Ayr traction maintenance depot and the start of the now freight-only Mauchline branch. Somerset Park, the home of Ayr United Football Club, is located beside the former depot and the start of the Mauchline branch. Records show there was also a

Ex-LMS Compound 4-4-0 No. 1171 and a Hughes-Fowler 'Crab' 2-6-0 depart Ayr station with a Glasgow-Stranraer boat train. *Hamish Stevenson Collection*

Remnants of the railway bridge to South Harbour Ayr in 2012. *Author*

Ayr Harbour branch on 16th April, 1965. The line to Ayr Goods is in the foreground, Falkland Yard in the distance, and the line from Newton Junction runs left to right.
Hamish Stevenson Collection

Newton-on-Ayr station on 19th June, 1954, looking towards Prestwick. The line to left is the Ayr harbour branch.
Hamish Stevenson Collection

Ex-LMS '2P' class 4-4-0 No. 40638 passes Ayr shed on 2nd July, 1949, with Newton-on-Ayr station in the distance. *Hamish Stevenson Collection*

McIntosh '3F' class 0-6-0 No. 57580 and Pickersgill '3F' No. 57658 outside Ayr shed on 17th May, 1958. *Hamish Stevenson Collection*

Newtonhead station which opened in 1864 but closed by 1868. The *Ayr Advertiser* of 1864 described it as the 'Newtonhead Ticket-Box' and went on to say that the 7.23 am and 5.00 pm trains from Ayr, and the 7.15 am and 4.30 pm trains from Glasgow were now to stop at Newtonhead. The paper was surprised that no tickets were to be issued for any station south of Kilmarnock, nor for any station on the Maybole or Dalmellington lines. If you wanted tickets for those destinations you had to go to Townhead station. While the exact location of the Newtonhead Ticket-Box is not known, it must have been on the main line.

From the Ayr depot the line crosses the river by a four-span masonry structure, completed in 1856 but rebuilt around 1878, to reach Ayr station. Ayr station (340214) is a two-platform through station with two north-facing bay platforms. Sidings to the west have been removed and the land is now occupied by a car park and housing.

South of Ayr station the line once passed through open countryside which has gradually been built upon. Narrow single-arch rail bridges are a 'pinch point' for the volume of road traffic not envisaged when the line was built when the trackbed was surrounded by fields. Just north of Belmont level crossing was a wooden halt built for horse race fans to use when the racecourse was located to the south of the town. No evidence of it remains.

Alloway Junction, 1¼ miles south of Ayr station, is where the Maidens & Dunure Light Railway left the main line. The junction is located next to the Ayr bypass and is inaccessible.

Maidens & Dunure Light Railway

Why call the Maidens & Dunure Light Railway after two small fishing villages when the railway didn't pass through either of them? Why not call the railway the Alloway & Turnberry Light Railway? More people would surely understand the link with Robert Burns' birthplace and the Turnberry Hotel, after all was the *raison d'être* for the line, a new links golf course good enough to attract golfers from all over the world. Maybe indeed the nickname for the line: the 'Golfers' Line', made most sense. Whatever the reasoning behind the name, the construction of the line was a bold, and eventually unsuccessful, railway project, but one that left memories, now very distant, of a wonderfully scenic route along the Carrick coastline.

Light railways had a speed limit of 25 mph and in return for the speed limit the restrictions on gradients and curves were less demanding. This does not imply, however that the engineering of the route was simple and the M&DLR had one tunnel, a covered cutting, 65 bridges and three significant viaducts in 19½ miles. It was an expensive line to build and consequently difficult to make a return on the financial outlay. Too few passing loops hampered the service with trains having to wait while another train cleared the next section. An average journey time of an hour was also quite slow and an express train faced a final slow section to reach Turnberry. Forget the view, let's get on with the golf could have been a response from impatient golfers. Journeys at speeds of 60 mph on the Ayr to Girvan via Maybole section provided a quicker journey.

Passenger numbers were disappointing and given the remote location of some of the stations, this was not surprising. Even Alloway station did not attract large numbers of Burns' devotees and faced competition from a tramway system which reached Alloway, from the town of Ayr, four years before the M&DLR opened. The trams ran for 30 years but increasing maintenance costs and replacement of rolling stock resulted in the system running at a loss and they closed in 1931, one year after Alloway station was mothballed. The lure of Robert Burns was not strong enough to make a profit.

Alloway Junction to Maybole Road

The short section between Alloway Junction site and Maybole Road (A79) is now overgrown, the slopes of the steep embankment swathed in trees.

WALK 3.1 MAYBOLE ROAD TO GREENAN CASTLE SIDINGS

Distance: 2.25 miles (***) one way.
Start: Maybole Road (A79) (349187), close to the A77 bypass. Parking nearby. Start of walk clearly signposted as part of a local cycle path.
Finish: Greenan Castle sidings beside A719, limited off-road parking.
Terrain: mostly tarmac but section beside Greenan Castle can be muddy underfoot.
Facilities: Alloway village, Robert Burns Birthplace Museum, no public toilets.
Further options: Having reached the site of Greenan Castle sidings the walker can retrace steps or follow the blue National Cycle Network (NCN) Route 7 signs, pass Greenan Castle to reach the shore. From the shore walk along the promenade to reach Ayr following NCN Route 7.

On both sides of the trackbed houses now encroach, with back gardens overlooking the former railway, as housing has been built between Alloway village and the Ayr to Stranraer Road (A77). Between Maybole Road and Alloway station the trackbed loses height, and quickly enters an almost continuous cutting. At Doonholm Road the railway passed, at an angle, under a metal plate girder bridge and turned towards the site of Alloway station. Doonholm literally means the meadow by the Doon, which is appropriate as the River Doon is now only a short distance away. Several of the bridges and the entrance to Alloway tunnel have now been narrowed by infilling with concrete around a circular corrugated metal sheet which has strengthened the bridges and the entrance to the tunnel.

The walk continues beside a section of road only recently opened. This short link section was built, as part of an agreement, to allow road traffic an alternative route to reach Turnberry, enabling the British Open Golf Championship and other competitions to continue to be staged at Turnberry golf course. The new road, an extension of Murdoch's Lone, previously a cul-de-sac, has been constructed between a new roundabout on Doonholm Road and Murdoch's Lone. When the railway was opened Murdoch's Lone had not been constructed, indeed the road was partly built over the former goods yard at the station. The former railway runs parallel to the road in a shallow cutting. There are two new overbridges on this section of trackbed, built over the station site, one leading to a housing estate and the next one, a wooden structure, allowing visitors to the new Robert Burns Birthplace Museum easy access between the museum, located on the south side of Murdoch's Lone with Burns Cottage, a short distance to the north on the other side of the railway. The Robert Burns Birthplace Museum, operated by the National Trust for Scotland, has been a major development, replacing the Burns National Heritage Museum, on the same site, and is proving to be a popular tourist attraction, paying homage to Scotland's national poet and well worth a visit. Murdoch's Lone was named after John Murdoch, a tutor of the young Robert Burns for a short time in both English grammar and French.

On the approach to the station and before the first of the overbridges the cycle path deviates slightly from the former railway trackbed. Sadly, there is nothing of the old station remaining. The site has been cleared. Alloway station was sited in the cutting and consisted of an island platform (333182). The chalet style station building, with overhanging canopies to both sides and a long 550 ft platform with regularly-spaced flower beds made for an attractive scene, which, when built, was in the middle of the countryside. There was a signal box and a wooden footbridge which provided access to the platform and provided a good vantage point for those photographing the station. The station master's house still exists, now separated from the station site by the road. At a higher level extending across what is now the road and occupying most of the space between the station and Alloway Parish Church was the goods yard. The Maidens & Dunure Light Railway built a large wooden shed with a curved roof, which met with the disapproval of locals who felt that it was not appropriate to have such a building so close to the Burns Monument. The monument built in a Grecian style and copied from the monument of Lysicrates at Athens was set in a nearby flower garden and was completed by 1823. The shed was soon removed.

The footbridge was the scene of a most unfortunate incident, in June 1948, when an excursion train carrying over 700 people on a Sunday School excursion from Troon Old Parish Church, to picnic at Burns Cottage, arrived at the station which had been rarely used since its closure in 1930. As the excited crowds spilled from the train they crossed the footbridge which had become rotted and gave way under the pressure of so many bodies. One elderly lady died of her injuries and several others were also hurt.

Beyond the station was Alloway tunnel, the only tunnel on the line. Double width and 140 yards long it passed under the B7024 and curved south-west towards the River Doon, narrowly avoiding the ruined Alloway Kirk and graveyard. This was the scene in Burns' famous poem *Tam O'Shanter* where Tam encounters the witches' coven. Burns' father, William Burnes, is buried in the graveyard. Today the entrance at the station end has been reduced in size to from a circular entrance extending a short distance into the tunnel under the road; otherwise the tunnel is square shaped. The tunnel is permanently lit and

Alloway station site with the entrance to the tunnel in the distance, 2012. *Author*

its construction can be clearly seen consisting of vertical concrete walls with girders laid between them. Between the girders are concrete arches.

As the trackbed emerges from the tunnel mouth, it initially retains the high concrete walls but they quickly step down in height as the railway approaches the crossing of the River Doon. Part of the wooden signalling support is still attached to the concrete wall by the tunnel entrance. The square cut of the tunnel is apparent from this end. Also located here is Mungo's Well, named after St Mungo, the local patron saint, which ran dry for a short time when the tunnel was being constructed and looks to be in the same state again today. The well also features in *Tam O'Shanter*, as Tam tries to escape the witches and passes Mungo's Well where it's said that 'Mungo's mither hanged hirsel'.

The eastern edge of Cambusdoon Estate lay to the right of the railway at this point, where it emerges from the tunnel, and was bought and developed by James Baird, whose name features frequently in Ayrshire's railway and industrial history. Baird, along with his brothers, established William Baird & Company which built up a vast portfolio of iron furnaces and coal mining interests in the county and throughout central Scotland and Cumbria. The Baird brothers employed 25,000 people by the mid-1860s and ranked amongst the biggest iron producers in the world at that time. He built a grand neo-baronial mansion in the estate and also paid for the gothic style Alloway Parish Church. Baird also helped to develop the Ayr docks but was not as generous to his employees, many who lived in sub-standard accommodation. His mansion was used for a while as a school, after his death, but in 1970 it burnt down with only an archway remaining today. In 1931 William Baird & Co. bought the Dalmellington ironworks and formed Bairds & Dalmellington Ltd.

Alloway tunnel now open as a cycle path, looking towards the Doon viaduct in 2011.
Author

A short distance from the tunnel the railway then crossed the River Doon, at a height of 28 ft, by a four-arched viaduct (321180). The two main central arches are larger, with a smaller outer span arch at each side. The bridge is a brick and stone clad concrete bridge, complete with mock castellated parapets. A metal fence has been added along the parapets for safety reasons since the viaduct was reopened as part of the cycle route. While the tunnel was built for two lines, the viaduct could only carry one. When the extension of Murdoch's Lone was being planned, one proposal was to use the tunnel for the road. This was rejected because of the cost of widening the viaduct.

Looking up river from the viaduct, the red sandstone single-arch road bridge, built in 1816, can be seen and through its arch the famous 15th century Brig O'Doon, where in the poem *Tam O'Shanter*, Tam narrowly escaped capture by the angry witches by crossing the River Doon, which stopped the witches chasing him as they couldn't cross running water. His mare, however, lost her tail as it was grabbed by one of the witches as he reached the bridge.

Downstream the River Doon flows towards the sea at Doonfoot. The redevelopment of the tunnel and viaduct allows many to enjoy this alternative view of the heart of Burns country.

Across the River Doon the trackbed continues, now climbing, and passes under another road bridge at Longhill Avenue. Once a quiet country lane the road is now lined with houses. Again the earthworks were substantial, with a high embankment towering over the back gardens of the many houses now lining Longhill Avenue. There are views south to Newark Castle, on the southern slopes of Newark Hill. The privately-owned castle has been extended several times.

In the era of World War II, the scene was very different. The housing development so obvious today didn't start until the 1960s and most of the land was occupied by fields.

Doon viaduct in 2011, view looking west. *Author*

Ex-LMS class '2P' 4-4-0 40664 with the 1.48 pm service at Heads of Ayr station on 30th May, 1959. The steps and footpath on the left lead to Butlin's holiday camp.

Hamish Stevenson Collection

There was a prisoner of war camp at nearby Greenan Shore. During the war Italian prisoners were kept there but after the war German prisoners occupied the site. It was not an unusual sight to see prisoners being escorted to local farms to help out. By the end of the war morale among the Italians was not good, being fed-up with the weather, poor toilet facilities, no post from home and lack of parcels from the Red Cross. Frustration mounted and in a daring escape on Friday 15th December, 1944, 97 Italian prisoners, using wood procured from a truck delivering wood to the camp, dug a tunnel which emerged on the shore and escaped. It was the largest escape of enemy prisoners ever in the United Kingdom. However, it was more about protest than disrupting the enemy and most were soon captured, although four are still listed as missing because their recapture was never reported to the police. The local railway network was an obvious means of quickly leaving the area and in December 1944 you might have encountered some of the prisoners making their way along the railway. Four prisoners were recaptured, discovered in a gangers' hut near Dunure station and others at Holehouse Junction. Four were even found in the attic of an Italian café in the town of Ayr!

Housing estates now block some of the expansive view towards the island of Arran on this section, which made this route so scenically attractive. As the trackbed reached the Dunure Road it passed underneath a road bridge. This has been infilled although some of the masonry abutments remain buried in the embankment. To the left was Greenan Castle sidings (314183), mainly used to deliver coal or for loading potatoes when the potato specials were collecting the crop. Part of the loading bank remains.

From here the National Cycle Network can be followed back to Ayr and is clearly signposted. The cycle path passes Greenan Castle, perched on a hilltop overlooking Ayr Bay and the mouth of the River Doon. The castle, today a ruin, was originally a rectangular tower house which dates from 1603. Conservation work has been necessary to stabilize the structure and prevent its collapse which nonetheless is expected to happen someday. Following the path down from the castle Greenan Road is reached. Between Greenan Road and the shore was the site of the prisoner of war camp, now built over with no evidence of it remaining.

On the sea side of the Dunure Road the trackbed heads toward Craig Tara Holiday Park, formerly Butlin's Holiday Camp. The trackbed stops at the security fencing and the exploration must be continued once past the park. The holiday camp was built at the start of World War II, and was used a Royal Naval Training Camp, known as HMS *Scotia*, during the war before returning to its intended use at the end of the war. For many years the holiday camp's popularity ensured that the section of the Maidens & Dunure Light Railway between Alloway Junction and the camp remained open but by 1968 the service stopped and holidaymakers travelling by rail to Butlin's had to leave the train at Ayr station and use a bus or taxi to reach the camp. A station, Heads of Ayr, was built in the camp site, a second station to bear that name on the line. It consisted of a single long concrete platform with a concrete building on it. No remnants of the railway remain in the camp. However, on the western edge the trackbed can be seen on an embankment.

Walk 3.2 Heads of Ayr Station to Bracken Bay Cutting

Distance: 2 miles (***) return trip.
Start: Heads of Ayr Caravan Park, limited parking (284180).
Terrain: rough ground. Stout footwear recommended.
Facilities: Heads of Ayr shop (summer), or Dunure restaurant and shop, public toilets (seasonal) at Kennedy Park.
Further options: From Bracken Bay the path follows the route of the Ayr Coastal Path which continues to Dunure, a further two miles.

Heads of Ayr Caravan Park is located to the land side of the Heads of Ayr. The Heads of Ayr, a local landmark, and the remnants of an old volcano, rise on a grassy slope behind the caravan park to a steep cliff edge overlooking the sea. In the caravan park the loading bank, part of the sidings to the south of the station can still be identified in the park (284180), now ending with a curved brick wall, a modern addition. The station buildings and platform, having been modified in 1914 with a creation of an island platform, was then in a similar chalet style to others on the line, but with only one overhanging canopy on the seaward side.

The route taken by the trackbed is easily identified, as part of the Ayr Coastal Path, and can be accessed at the site of a missing bridge, with the concrete abutments remaining. Turn sharp left through a gate marked with the Ayr Coastal Path sign. It is about a mile between the caravan park and the Bracken Bay cutting.

The trackbed crosses fields on an embankment and can be followed as it twists towards a partly filled-in cutting at the top of the hill. Again bushes and trees conceal the extent of the earthworks required on this section with a steep embankment followed by the 40ft-deep Bracken Bay cutting which is filled in at the far end. An unsafe wooden bridge still straddles the Bracken Bay cutting.

Access bridge over Bracken Bay cutting on the Maidens & Dunure Light Railway.
Author

This is surely the most scenic part of a very scenic former railway and worth visiting for the views in all directions.

Beyond the cutting the trackbed disappears but there is the option of continuing along the Ayrshire Coastal Path which is clearly signposted and can be followed until the fishing village of Dunure is reached, a distance of two miles. The alternative is to retrace your steps and continue along the road until you reach the village of Fisherton a distance of 1½ miles along the A719.

Dunure to Culzean

At Fisherton village turn off the A719 at Station Road which leads down to the village of Dunure. A short distance down the Dunure Road is the road bridge over the old railway (264167) and the site of Dunure station located in a cutting (*). On the bridge, the blocked-off entrance to the station can be identified. The wooden stairway which led down to the platform has long since been removed. The site is very overgrown but the island platform can be spotted lurking under the vegetation. The buildings were similar in style to Alloway and like that station the goods yard and sidings were located above the cutting to the north. A similar style of shed to that used at Alloway, with a curved roof, was installed when the line opened. Housing now occupies the goods yard with the station master's cottage and railway staff cottages remaining. An early morning fish train ran from Dunure for many years, enabling the catch landed at Dunure to reach fish markets.

To the south of the station is a cutting which is now impenetrable. The road, however, can be followed downhill towards Dunure. Fisherton village has in recent years extended down the coastal road towards Dunure. Where the housing stops, Dunduff Burn flows under the road. Up the hillside the railway had already encountered the burn and crossed it by an impressive 70 ft single-span metal truss bridge with steel lattice parapets, at a height of 55 ft above the burn which can be seen from the road (*).

The route is now across farmland. The trackbed remains intact, and can be easily seen from the A719, passing behind the village of Dunure. Housing, built in the 1930s, now reaches closer to the former railway but there continue to be wonderful views towards Arran and beyond.

One guide book, *The Thorough Guide to Scotland, Part 3, Lowlands* published in 1903, described Dunure as a poor little hamlet on which much money had been wasted on the construction of a small harbour. One must wonder what whisky the writer had drunk the night before, because it had clearly befuddled his brain. The village has a picturesque harbour complemented by the ruins of Dunure Castle, once the seat of the local landowners the Kennedys, perched on a headland and the ruins have even been partially restored. While the writer couldn't have benefitted from the view from the railway, it wasn't built; surely he could have appreciated more of the considerable charms of this most pretty seaside village.

The trackbed continues behind Dunure climbing towards a transmitter mast on a hill to the south of the village. As the trackbed veers towards the road leading up from Dunure it slices through the hill in a deep cutting, to the west of Dunure Mains Farm. The drainage in the cutting has broken down and it should be avoided. The road bridge over the railway has been removed and infilled but the trackbed can be followed, the descending gradient quite apparent from the road as it snakes across the sloping fields which lead down to the sea. Dunure Mains was famous for the champion Clydesdale stallion known as the 'Baron of Buchlyvie' who sired many a foal. The railway played its part by bringing mares to nearby Dunure station. Between the embankment and the road was Dunure Mill, a late 18th century watermill, which on first sight because of its crosses, could be mistaken for a church.

From the road the low embankment is very clear, now fringed by bushes. On the coastal side the ground falls away, which must have given passengers the impression that they were high above the sea adding to the excitement of the journey.

Rejoin the A719. The trackbed now runs parallel to the road until Croy Bay. Ahead to the south perched on a cliff top are Culzean Castle and the lighthouse at Maidens, signposting the direction to be taken by the railway. Both road and railway veered inland on the approach towards Craigencroy Glen. The railway crossed the glen by a 90 ft-high viaduct with two central concrete piers supporting a metal truss. Only the abutments remain and are bricked off. The road can be followed round, and the road to Croy shore taken, to pick up the railway at Knoweside station (253127) (*) passing the 'Electric Brae' en route. The 'Electric Brae' (*), a local curiosity, is an optical illusion, where the road appears to descend towards Croy Brae but in fact the road is ascending. Beware of slow-moving traffic on this stretch. The same illusion was apparently experienced crossing the Croy viaduct by train.

Taking advantage of the good drainage along the trackbed is another caravan site, Culzean Bay, extending both sides of the narrow road leading down to Croy shore. The station was to the south, of the road which it crossed by a level crossing. Knoweside, in the lee of Knoweside Hill, had no station building, no signal box and only a small goods yard and a short curved platform with a water tank and small shelter on it. When a steam engine was filling up with water it would have extended across the road and blocked it. The crossing keeper's cottage sits close to the trackbed on the viaduct side. With no villages near it is difficult to understand why it was opened even as a request stop.

From here while the road (A719) veers east, the railway snaked south and within a mile reached the crossing of the Rancleugh Glen. Seven concrete piers some towering 124 ft above the burn remain and can be viewed from the road. The viaduct was similar in style to the Croy viaduct with approach girder spans and in the centre two metal trusses resting on three shorter central concrete piers. At 588 ft this was a long and substantial viaduct for a modest light railway. The concrete piers stand in mute testimony to a grand structure and the taller piers are visible from land and sea. The site of the viaduct can be visited by taking the minor road at Balchriston Lodge (264108) (*). Beside the viaduct was Balchriston Halt (254112) and level crossing. There were two cottages for railway workers. The building still exists in use as a house. There is no trace of the platform or the level crossing.

From here the railway entered the grounds of Culzean Castle, now Culzean Castle and Country Park. At the turn of the century visitors were permitted only to walk in the grounds on a Wednesday, shown round by the gardener. However, in 1945 possession of Culzean Castle was passed onto the National Trust for Scotland, by the fifth Marquess of Ailsa and the Kennedy family in part payment of inheritance tax. In 1969 the grounds were declared Scotland's first Country Park. Today the castle and grounds are extremely popular with visitors. Entrance is from the A719.

The Maidens & Dunure Light Railway cut through the grounds of Culzean. In the grounds was a station, Glenside (245102), which was initially intended as a goods depot to service the castle and grounds. Prior to opening the Marquis decided that the public could use the station but the family had a private waiting room.

Part of the old railway is retained as one of the pathways in the grounds. The section between Balchriston and the main gates of the country park is in poor condition and is not an official walkway. It is described for the sake of completeness.

From Balchriston Halt the trackbed entered Culzean Estate. For the next two miles the trackbed ran through the estate for the most part in a cutting. The first part between Balchriston and the entrance is frequently waterlogged and overgrown. The feature of interest, in this section, is the covered cutting passing under the Pennyglen Avenue. Not long enough at 42 yards to be listed as a tunnel, the covered cutting sits at an angle to the road and is double width but only ever was single track. Beyond the tunnel, the trackbed is overgrown but emerges at the Glenside Caravan Park. The loading bank remains beside the site office. The siding was to the rear of the station building. The chalet-style station building which had a private waiting room for the Marquis of Ailsa has been removed. From here the railway crossed Glenside Burn, and then under Glenside Avenue bridge, which has now been infilled. Today the area south-west of the former station has been totally changed to create a new entrance into the country park.

Walk 3.3 Kennelmount Picnic Area to Morriston Farm Road (Culzean Castle and Country Park)

Distance: 2 miles (***) return trip.
Start: The entrance road into the grounds winds round past the payment hut and leads to the Kennelmount picnic area (241097) on the left where the old railway walk begins.
Terrain: footpath, can be muddy underfoot.
Facilities: Admission charge, free for National Trust of Scotland members, full facilities in park including toilets. A very attractive and popular tourist site where you could easily spend a day.
Further options: Several other walks in park, map issued on entering grounds.

The trackbed is accessed beside the Thomaston Avenue overbridge. A steep set of wooden steps leads down to the trackbed which is in a deep cutting. The bridge is skewed with a brick lining at the head of the arch. The parapet and wing walls are of sandstone. From here the trackbed proceeds, now lined with trees, eventually emerging on an embankment. Some bridges over minor roads have been replaced by wooden structures. After a mile the Morriston Drive overbridge is reached. Concrete-lined, and with a roof similar to that of the Alloway tunnel, it has sandstone parapets. The overbridge is striking because of its confusion of angles caused by a combination of a dropping gradient and the skewed angle of the tunnel.

A short distance further on is another interesting bridge which crosses over the minor road from Morriston Farm, also at an angle. There is extensive sandstone with a skewed distinctive black engineering brick lining at the head of the arch.

This is an impressive stretch of trackbed, a testimony to the engineering skills of the builders and also blessed with views over the Firth of Clyde towards the southern end of Arran, Kintyre and Ailsa Craig and sometimes even as far as Ireland.

Beyond the farm road the trackbed is blocked by a section of overgrown cutting then by the Redgates Chalet Park. Walkers can retrace their steps or extend the walk by following the minor road down to Maidens, the next seaside village on this stretch of coast. The Country Park can be re-entered and a long circular route completed with opportunities for refreshments on the way.

The famous Scottish architect Robert Adam designed Culzean Castle, building started in 1777, and also the Home Farm. The approach to the castle, is through an archway designed to look like a 'ruin', and which appeared in the 1973 cult film *The Wicker Man* as the home of Lord Summerisle. Round the castle are terraces, conservatories and vineries and there are several tree-lined avenues making a visit to the park a very attractive 'day-out'.

Maidens to Girvan Junction

Continuing along the A719 the sandstone abutments of a railway overbridge (222079), again at an angle to the road, are soon reached on a dangerous bend in the road. Steps on the Culzean side lead to the site of Maidens goods station of which nothing remains. The passenger station was on the other side of the road.

Maidens is another delightful Carrick coast fishing village with a long history. It has prospered by its proximity to Culzean Country Park, and the Turnberry Hotel complex and golf courses. Many visitors pass through it and, enchanted by its charms, remain to walk along the harbour, breath in the sea air and enjoy the expansive views. The harbour was developed after the war when some of the hardcore from the airfield at Turnberry was used to extend the harbour.

The arrival of the railway brought to an end the delivery of dung or manure by sea. Dung produced on board cattle boats sailing from Ireland to various Clyde ports was loaded onto the barges which went out to the cattle boats moored off-shore and collected the dung produced on the trip. A local farmer at Maidens hired the barges and used the manure to fertilize the crop of famous 'Ayrshire tatties'. This happened at various points along the coast. The arrival of the railway allowed large quantities of dung to be brought in by train and also the 'Glasgow dung', the contents of the dry closets in the city. The dispersal of the dung from Glasgow was a problem to the city's authorities but the Ayrshire coast proved a good dumping ground. Maybe the railway should have been called the Manure & Dunure Light Railway!

Little now remains of Maidens passenger station apart (220078) from the double doors which once led to an underpass which passengers used to reach the island platform. Recent development of the site means that the trackbed at the station site has been cleared and caravans are now parked along it. The views from the station site over Maidens and Maidenhead Bay, and the local amenities, help to explain the popularity of the caravan sites in the vicinity.

Beyond Maidens are the remains of Turnberry Airfield. At the end of World War I a school of aerial fighting was created. Some of the grounds of Turnberry Hotel and golf courses were requisitioned by the military and three runways in a triangular formation were created along with numerous ancillary buildings, aircraft hangers etc. The railway played its part with an aerodrome branch and sidings built to provide transport in and out of the airfield. After each war, and particularly the second, much work was required to restore the grounds and golf courses, made more complicated by the nationalization of the railways in 1948. On 1st June, 1950 the hotel reopened with a partial reopening of the Ailsa Course. However, the railway was not reopened for passengers other than the short section which serviced Butlin's Holiday Camp.

The railway passed to the rear of Turnberry Hotel and was connected to it by a covered walkway which led into a conservatory and then the hotel building itself. The development of Turnberry was one of the largest hotel projects in Scotland at the time and a bold initiative by the Glasgow & South Western Railway to attract additional business to the Carrick coastline. Viewed from the sea the hotel is perched on a low ridge, with the rolling Ayrshire hills behind. Long and not overly high, its white render finish and red tiles catch the evening sunlight to dramatic effect. Between hotel and sea stretches the Ailsa golf course complete with a picture perfect lighthouse, all familiar to those who follow the British Open Championship. The site is a haven for golfers and those who could afford the unabashed luxury which is the trademark of the Turnberry Hotel resort. Direct train services from London showed the section of the market that the railway company was trying to attract. Today the hotel is still listed in the top hotel complexes in the world, a fitting tribute for a vision that was not shared by all G&SWR shareholders.

The architect for the Turnberry Hotel, James Miller, was a major influence on Scottish railway architecture, but whose work was more often linked with the Caledonian Railway.

While the route taken by the railway through the grounds can be traced, for many years only a section of the platform edge remained of the station but even this has now been removed. The covered canopy and supports was sold to Dumbarton Football Club in 1957 and re-erected at one end of the ground behind the goals, presumably known as the 'Railway End'. With Dumbarton FC having now moved to a new ground from Boghead Park even this link has been lost.

South of the station the railway crossed over the A77 and continued south towards Girvan passing through rolling fields with the ever-present Ailsa Craig dominating the seaward view and between the road and the beach are some of

Grangestone Halt, looking towards Girvan, on 20th September, 1965.
Hamish Stevenson Collection

Girvan Junction, with the divergence of the Maidens & Dunure, the Turnberry line, on the left. Ex-LMS '2P' class 4-4-0 No. 40645 heads a southbound passenger train in June 1958.
W.A.C. Smith/Hamish Stevenson Collection

the famous 'tattie fields' which provide the flavoursome early crops of Ayrshire potatoes and whose transportation generated much needed income for the Maidens & Dunure Light Railway. Turnberry Holiday Park (207034) is reached which now occupies the site of Dipple sidings which fanned out to the west of the trackbed. An extra siding was added to serve the Dipple tileworks. The caravans extend north and south of a road bridge over the line. The sidings also served Dowhill Farm. Confusingly the hamlet of Dipple lies further south.

Closer to Girvan the trackbed edges towards the A77 and the coast. The alginate or seaweed factory is located on the coastline at Dipple and just south of it the trackbed, near Dunnymuck Farm, crosses, first a minor road then Drumuskin Burn, by a double-arch skewed concrete bridge. (*) Shortly after the trackbed becomes squeezed between the road and hills and becomes overgrown and impassable.

Travelling south on the A77 the Grangestone industrial estate dominates the view to the left, often with thousands of whisky barrels stored outside of the William Grant & Sons Distillery complex, part of the industrial estate. The industrial grain distillery was built in 1963 to provide extra grain whisky for the Grant's blend and in 1966 a small malt distillery was opened producing single malt whisky known as 'Ladyburn'. It closed by 1975, it was claimed, so that the space could be used to expand the grain distillery. Some, however, claim that the real reason was that it was not very good. Bottles of the malt are now rare and expensive, if not as rare yet as a train on the railway. In September 2007 a new malt distillery was opened on the site and will be known as 'Ailsa Bay' single malt whisky.

The expanding Grangestone Industrial Estate was partly built over an earlier factory which during World War II was constructed to produce munitions to help the war effort. Operated by ICI munitions factories were scattered over a wide area of south-west Scotland, ensuring that if one building was destroyed by explosion the others would not be affected. The factory was linked to the M&DLR and within the factory grounds there was a further narrow gauge rail system for internal use. Some workers were conveyed to the complex by rail and Grangestone Halt was built, to accommodate them, on the nearby Ayr to Stranraer line to the east of a bridge where the B741 crosses over the railway.

On the southern edge of the industrial estate there is a final glimpse of the former railway as a short section of embankment veers south-west towards Girvan Junction where it joins the Ayr to Stranraer line on the outskirts of Girvan.

From Alloway Junction

Beyond Alloway Junction and the crossing of the A77 bypass the line climbs past both Ailsa and Ayr Hospitals. Ayr Hospital opened in 1993. The psychiatric hospital had been opened in 1868 and was then known as the Glengall Asylum. There was a short siding, known as the Glengall siding, from the railway into the Ailsa Asylum as it became known. Goods, mainly coal, were brought into the hospital each week by the railway and also visitors on occasion. From the Ayr Hospital car park the route taken by the siding into the hospital grounds can still be identified.

The railway climbs, passing Mount Oliphant Farm with its connections to Robert Burns and then behind Pleasantfield Farm is Dalrymple Junction where the railways to Dalmellington and Maybole part (*see map page 74*). At the junction was located briefly Maybole Junction station, which was only open for three years from 1856 to 1859. The station had three platforms and a goods station. From 1861 the junction was known as Dalrymple Junction.

Dalrymple Junction to Dalmellington

From Dalrymple Junction, 11 miles from Dalmellington station, the next railway landmark is the Dalrymple or Burnton viaduct (372153) (*) made of stone from the quarries at Dunaskin. The 16-arch masonry viaduct with semi-circular arches remains an impressive local landmark crossing the Purclewan Burn and the B742 at a maximum height of 83 ft. Now railings extend the length of the viaduct due to Health & Safety requirements but in the past with the viaduct straddling a district boundary the railings only were required on one half and marked the district boundary. From the viaduct the railway climbs steadily for the next two miles.

A view looking towards Ayr, from the train as it crosses Dalrymple viaduct on 4th April, 1964. Railings only extend halfway across the structure. *Hamish Stevenson Collection*

The Nanny Line

A few hundred yards beyond the viaduct is Potterston Junction. The junction facing in the direction of Dunaskin gives a clue to the reason why this branch was built: it was a coal line to feed the furnaces. Known as the Coylton line it operated from the 1860s initially taking coal from Carbieston pit near Coylton and extended to the Sundrum pit in the 1870s.

The DICo. had a dispute with the G&SWR over taking coal from its pits to its ironworks. The DICo. wanted to use its own haulage all the way, including over the G&SWR line, but the railway company would not allow this, wanting to retain the business for itself. The railway placed restrictions on the type of engine that DICo. could use on its line hoping to stop the proposal. Ever resourceful, however, the DICo. ordered a new engine to comply with G&SWR restrictions and got its way.

One of the earliest drivers on the Coylton line, Thomas Rutherford, was known by the strange nickname of 'Nanny' and in time this became associated with his engine (number 10) and many locally still refer to the route as the 'Nanny Line'. The engine was nicknamed the 'Coylton Nanny' and was retired in 1918 and replaced with a more modern engine.

Today the Nanny line can be traced from the Potterston Junction (377152), where the route curves away from the Dalmellington line, only with difficulty. The route disappears in Potterston Wood before emerging to cross a minor road, the site of the first level crossing (382158), close to Purclewan Mill, where there was an unreliable water supply for thirsty engines, and heading towards the A713. In 1931 a concrete road bridge was built to replace another level crossing, just four years before the line closed. On the eastern side of the A713 the route crossed marshy ground before cutting through Martnaham Woods and skirting to the south of Martnaham Loch. Close to the eastern edge of the loch was a water pump. For engines travelling to Dunaskin this was the last opportunity to fill up the tanks for a long climb.

A further level crossing was reached across a minor road, at the eastern edge of the loch (405177), before the railway curved south of Raithhill Farm, the site of some early ironstone pits, before reaching Carbieston Mains Farm, where Carbieston pit was located.

From Carbieston Farm the trackbed curved towards the A70 Ayr to Coylton road. The railway passed under the A70 then crossed open fields, passing Meadowhead Farm, with short sections of the embankment still remaining, before curving to the right towards Sundrum pit. A roads depot now occupies the site of Sundrum pit beside the B742.

This was an important mineral line and showed the determination and effort made by the Dalmellington Iron Company to harness local mineral reserves. The Sundrum pit closed in 1933 and the Nanny Line in 1935.

Potterston Junction to Holehouse Junction

Just over a mile south of Potterston Junction was Hollybush station (393149), closed since 6th April, 1964. Hollybush station had a single platform and the

Hollybush station, looking to Ayr on 4th April, 1964. *Hamish Stevenson Collection*

sidings at the station were used by the local farms and the nearby Skeldon woollen mills which harnessed the power of the River Doon. The station is now a private residence.

The journey continues south passing under the A713 and running parallel to the road in a cutting before both road and rail curve away from each other. The railway crosses the valley of the Boreland Burn on a section of high embankment. Where rail and road merge Holehouse Junction, named after a local farm, is located. Holehouse Junction (407136) was an exchange platform at the start of the line to Rankinston and was originally known simply as Holehouse and then renamed Holehouse Junction in 1937. Situated in the 'vee' where the two lines merged it had no public entrance. A signal box positioned high on the embankment was required to keep sight of the trains. There was a waiting room for passengers transferring from one line to the other. The Rankinston branch formed a north-facing junction with the Dalmellington line.

Rankinston Branch

This six mile route was a useful addition to Ayrshire's growing railway network, giving access to coal pits along its route and to the Ayrshire & Cumnock line, while also providing an alternative route to Ayr. There were some suggestions, when it was opened, that it would provide a shorter route for importing iron ore from Whitehaven in Cumberland when local supplies ran out although there is no evidence that this option was ever used. The mine at Littlemill, near Rankinston ensured that the eastern end of the line remained open until the 1960s.

Sections of this route can be traced but conditions underfoot can be difficult and with the viaducts fenced off no walk is recommended.

The first 1½ miles, from Holehouse Junction, were reopened as access to Broomhill opencast coal disposal site between 1998 and 2001. The rails have now been lifted and the garden of a newly-built house has already encroached on the trackbed. The exchange platform at Holehouse Junction has been removed. The trackbed can be accessed before Holehouse Farm, from the A713, and heads east on the hillside through a mixture of cuttings and embankments.

The concrete loading bay for the opencast pit marked the end of the reopened section. Coal was loaded here from the Broomhill opencast immediately to the south on Broom Hill.

The trackbed continues towards the reed-lined Kerse Loch but between Kerse Loch and Knockshinnoch Farm the trackbed abruptly disappears east of the loch and the conditions underfoot deteriorate.

The trackbed can be rediscovered to the west of Knockshinnoch Farm, where the route crossed over the B730. The section of embankment before the road have been removed and with it any traces of Cairntable Halt (432140), opened in 1927. The halt was opened to serve a local mining community. A cairn exists, a short distance west from the former railway beside the B730 to commemorate the location of Cairntable village, another of Ayrshire's lost mining communities. The rail bridge over the B730 has also been removed.

The trackbed then passes through a waterlogged cutting crossed by overbridges, before approaching a single-arch bridge over the Bow Burn.

Ahead, still leaving a scar, not yet healed, are the remnants of the Littlemill Mine. It changed hands from the original owners, the Colyton Coal Co., being taken over by Bairds & Dalmellington Ltd and was then extensively redeveloped by the National Coal Board from 1952. The fifth and last shaft led to extensive surface workings and multiple sidings mainly to the north of the line. Like many mines, Littlemill, known locally as the 'Drake', had its problems. The redeveloped pit closed in 1974, after only 20 years, having expected to remain in production for nearer 40 years. The headgear for shaft No. 3 was taken to the Prestongrange Mining Museum in East Lothian. Earlier, in 1938, an explosion at the Ashentree section, near the bridge over the Bow Burn had killed four men and injured six.

'Pugs', usually in pairs, and known as the 'twins' had to haul the hutches up from Belston Junction, travel beyond the mine buildings before being shunted down into the sidings. The substantial abutments of a bridge over the line remain. This was used by the local farmers to reach the hillside beyond.

The last stretch, towards the station has been infilled and landscaped for use as playing fields. From here the track once passed through a cutting to pass under a road bridge to reach Rankinston station.

The village of Rankinston lies at right angles to the railway perched high on the hillside, 635 ft above sea level, reached by a steep road from the hamlet of Littlemill. The opening of the Littlemill pit caused an expansion of the village to over 800 at the turn of the century and the pit's closure caused a decline to around 200 at the present time.

The road to Rankinston climbs even higher up the slopes of Ewe Hill to the south before stopping. On this stretch was located the severely-graded branch to the Rankinston ironstone and anthracite mines operated by Merry & Cunninghame of Glengarnock, which linked to the Holehouse branch to the east of the station site.

In such a location, and with a pitch on the side of a hill, it is not surprising that the local football team was once known as the 'Rankinston Mountaineers'. Formed in 1876 their moment of glory came in 1912 when they reached the final of the Mauchline & District Cup but lost to the mighty Auchinleck Talbot 0-4. On some occasions, when football teams from the Doon Valley, visited,

Cairntable Halt looking towards Rankinston *circa* 1920s. Notice the people walking along the line. *Hamish Stevenson Collection*

Rankinston station looking towards Belston Junction in 1951. *Hamish Stevenson Collection*

carriages which took miners to their place of work in nearby mines could be used to take supporters onto the plateau above the Dunaskin ironworks and close to the grounds of rivals like the 'Rankinston Mountaineers'. There was a timetabled passenger service to Ayr from Dalmellington via Rankinston, Belston Junction and Annbank. The journey took about 1¼ hours compared to almost half an hour for the more direct route to Ayr via Hollybush.

Rankinston, on the southern edge of Ayrshire has extensive views over the county, Arran, the Clyde coast, the North Ayrshire hills and to the east Cairntable and the Lanarkshire hills. Meanwhile, planes approaching Prestwick Airport frequently pass overhead.

The site of the station, opened on New Year's Day 1884, is found opposite the playing fields and is now a car park (452145). The station consisted of a single platform, to the north of the line, with a simple wooden building and was reached by a fenced path leading down from the road.

A detour around the abandoned Rankinston Bowling Club leads to the five-arch Rankinston West viaduct over the Water of Coyle. Health & Safety requirements has led to the well-preserved, sandstone-faced viaduct being fenced off. The viaduct was previously used as part of a local pathway. A short distance on is the nine-arch Rankinston East viaduct, similarly fenced off.

From the Rankinston East viaduct the trackbed lost height and curved north-west towards Sinclairston, initially through a deep cutting and then on an embankment passing Poquhairn pit, which was opened in 1911, modernized in the 1950s but closed in 1962. Once visible for miles around, with its name spelt out in white bricks on the side of the bing (spoil heap) the pit was beset by problems and closed earlier than planned.

The railway trackbed continues to lose height as it passes through the village of Sinclairston.

At Belston Junction (481176) (*) the Rankinston branch joined the A&C line.

Rankinston West viaduct in 1996 with Rankinston village in the background. The station was next to the viaduct on the village side. *Author*

Patna station on 30th May, 1959, looking towards Dalmellington. *Hamish Stevenson Collection*

Waterside station and signal box looking towards Ayr on 30th May, 1959.
Hamish Stevenson Collection

From Holehouse Junction

Beyond Holehouse the climb at last becomes easier and the railway finally comes in sight of the River Doon just as it is about to enter the Doon Valley and pass Smithston Farm, the focus of the earliest proposals to build a railway into the valley. There was a short branch from here serving the Summerlee Iron Company's Kerse pits.

The summit of the railway is just before the village of Patna. The village was originally located on the far side of the River Doon but has expanded on both sides of the river and road with the relocation of villagers from nearby Waterside and Lethanhill. The station in Patna opened along with the railway but closed in 1897, with a second station built almost immediately to the south separated only by the goods yard. The station was on the left of the road after you enter the village. Modern housing has eradicated all signs of the station.

From Patna the railway ran along the valley floor towards the Dunaskin ironworks. The ironworks were named after Dunaskin Farm but the railway confused matters by naming their station at Dunaskin, Waterside after another local farm.

The station building at Waterside (438086) (*) remains beside the track, a crumbling sandstone building, once part of a large and busy industrial site. To the rear of the station there is a distinctive external spiral staircase. It was here that the DICo.'s extensive rail system connected with the Dalmellington Railway.

Dunaskin to Dalmellington

The sheer scale of the ironworks at Dunaskin (*) is breathtaking. The furnace bank towers 70 feet over the site, with coal and limestone brought up inclines before being fed into the furnaces from above. Limestone, iron ore, latterly imported from Spain, and uniquely coal were mixed. Coal could be used instead of coke, because the local black band ironstone was rich in carbon, a strong reason for siting the ironworks in this remote valley. When the furnaces were in operation they must have lit up the valley at night and have been seen for miles around and with the roar of the furnaces also heard all through the valley. The eight furnaces have long been removed, iron production ending in 1921, but even when they were present they were in turn dwarfed by the twin chimneys, at 143 ft and 160 ft, which effortlessly dominate the valley. After the closure of the ironworks, it was the coal pits that sustained the valley's economy and Waterside was used as a marshalling yard.

Bairds & Dalmellington Ltd looked for opportunities to develop the coalfield, also built a coal washing plant, near Waterside. With increased demand for bricks, brickworks were constructed around the furnace area and incorporating the original blast engine house. Extracting coal and making bricks continued during the war before the National Coal Board took over shortly after the war.

The National Coal Board complex at Dunaskin received coal from many local pits. The Dunaskin Central Washer, a coal preparation plant continued in

Waterside station looking towards Dalmellington. Notice the slag heap to the right.
Hamish Stevenson Collection

NCB Andrew Barclay 0-6-0T No. 17 passes the coal washer at Waterside in September 1974.
Andrew J. Arnot

operation until 1976. There were many exchange sidings between the NCB and BR at Waterside and even today Scottish Coal still own the final two miles of the route from Waterside to the Chalmerston railhead.

The Dalmellington Railway passed in front of the former ironworks, through a deep cutting. The approach to the ironworks from the road, both from the north or south, was up a steep road followed by a sharp turn crossing a bridge over the Dalmellington Railway. The entrance bridge was shared with a rail link, which continued over the road by another bridge taking slag to the slag heap in a field beside the River Doon. The bridge over the road has been removed. At one time the slag heap was twice as high but some was removed to use as the foundation for the Ayr bypass. The slag heap is now listed.

South of the works the railway crossed over Dunaskin Burn. The bridge is still in use as part of the mineral line to Chalmerston. Just north of the bridge, in the 19th century, a single-cylinder steam engine worked the incline to the furnaces. Further up the narrow confines of Dunaskin Glen were brickworks, dating back to the opening of the ironworks, and a tramway extended even further up the valley to clay pits. There is a lot for the industrial archaeologist or the just downright curious to explore.

All around the area are many disused railways, mineral lines which fed the furnaces or tried to meet the general demand for coal. All the coal pits have now closed and extraction of coal is only by opencast.

An attempt to preserve the ironworks and ancillary buildings as an industrial museum was attempted with the opening of the Dunaskin Heritage Centre. Sadly this closed in 2005 when funding was withdrawn. However, part of the site is now occupied by the Ayrshire Railway Preservation Group (ARPG) who are breathing new life into the old works, restoring old industrial railway stock and offering 'steam days' for young and old to savour a taste and smell of the railway experience. A visit is a good way to explore the heritage of the site. Their website gives details of 'steam days'.

Dunaskin site, the home of the Ayrshire Railway Preservation Society. *Author*

Two recent views of Drumgrange incline. Lethanhill village is beyond the top of the slope but not in view. *(Both) Author*

The ARPG have built a new station as a terminus for their 'steam rides'. Steam workings in the area lasted until 1978 and an engine shed constructed in 1964 at Waterside may well have been the last engine shed purpose-built for steam in the country. Fortunately the ARPG are now using it to maintain and operate their collection of industrial 'pugs'.

Within the complex were several tramways and mineral lines, to feed the furnaces. The line then continued to Dalmellington with several branches to coal mines along the route. Today Scottish Coal operates a branch to the Chalmerston Opencast coal terminal which deviates from the original line to Dalmellington within the grounds of the former ironworks.

Walk 3.4 Dunaskin to Lethanhill

Distance: 2.5 miles – round trip (**).
Start: Beside former visitor centre (440084).
Terrain: Mostly paths but rough terrain on hill. Stout footwear recommended. Weather can be extreme in winter and change quickly. Be prepared. For safety reasons access to Lethanhill may be restricted in the future, due to the operations of the nearby Dunstonhill Surface Mine until the end of 2013. Access may be arranged by phoning Scottish Coal (01292-532510 or 01259-733360)
Facilities: nearest shops/cafes at Dalmellington 2.5 miles away, no public toilets unless there is a 'steam day' operated by Ayrshire Railway Preservation Group when there are café and toilet facilities available (admission charge).

From the former visitor centre (440084) which is found to the left having crossed the bridge over the railway walk up by the metal fence until you reach a path, beside a railway embankment, with the exposed girders of a railway bridge ahead.

To the right the path, a former railway trackbed, leads to the sidings above the site of the furnaces. Coal could be fed into the furnaces from the furnace bank. Return to the railway bridge. Under the bridge a path leads to Arddoon House, which was the former manager's house.

Turn back to the railway bridge and take the grassy path to the north The tree-lined path offers views over the Dunaskin site and of the Doon Valley. Reach a gate and carry on. The countryside is now more open. To the right are some brick remains associated with the Drumgrange pit. To the right the Drumgrange incline starts. Ahead the mineral railway continued, crossing the Drumgrange Burn to eventually reach further coal pits including the Houldsworth pit. The village of Patna can be seen to the north.

At the foot of the incline are the brick abutments of a former rail bridge over it. The Drumgrange incline has a gradient of one in six and was used to bring ironstone down from the plateau above, where there were no less than 37 ironstone pits, to be taken to the furnaces. The first incline to be constructed had two sections with a short level stretch connecting the two, which must have been worked by horses.

Later a new incline, on the same site, was constructed capable of handling heavier traffic. The later incline had a double set of rails with pulleys set between each pair of rails for the support of the rope. It was often referred to as the Burnfoothill incline and was in use until 1933. As loaded wagons descended, usually empty wagons were hauled up and this approach was known as 'self-acting'. Sometimes coal was taken up in the ascending wagons for the stationary pit engines on the plateau and to supply the villages at the top.

As you climb you will notice to the left there are now water-holding pits for an opencast surface mine. There is a fence down each side of the incline and you should remain within the fenced area. Keep climbing until you reach two thick brick buttresses between which a five foot iron drum was once suspended. The operator worked a handbrake which controlled the drum. Inevitably there are tales of runaway wagons smashed to pieces further down the hill.

Beyond the former brick buttresses is a wood in which are found the ruins of Lethanhill. To the left of the wood is the Lethanhill war memorial and also a nearby white plaque which reads:

1851 to 1954
LONG LIVE THE HILL

Within the woods are the ruins of Lethanhill, a miners' village. Burnfoothill was further north and has been lost to the opencast pit. Mineral railways passed through the village and around it. When the village was occupied there were few trees and the houses must have been brutally exposed to the weather. Between the two villages there were over 200 houses. After, a time, the people of the two villages simply called the area 'The Hill'. A railway, but no road connected 'The Hill' to Benquhat, sometimes spelt Benwhat, another village constructed to the south. The people from the plateau were eventually rehoused in Patna or Dalmellington but never lost their bond with their former villages. Today wreaths are still lovingly placed at former homes and an annual remembrance service is also held at the war memorial. A walk through the silence of the wood past the houses impresses how different life was for many in the past – how hard and demanding without the comforts that we now expect. You cannot help but admire the fortitude of those who coped on this windswept plateau. May 'The Hill' never be forgotten. Probably with a changed mindset you return down the incline and back to Dunaskin.

Memorial to those who lived and worked on the 'Hill'. *Author*

Drumgrange incline. The brick buttresses once supported an iron drum, 2012. *Author*

WALK 3.5 DALMELLINGTON RAILWAY: FROM DUNASKIN TO DALMELLINGTON

Distance: 2.5 miles (**).
Start: A713 south of entrance to the former ironworks and behind the bus shelter (446082) opposite the Chapel Row miners' cottages. The trackbed is overgrown, it is around 50 years since the branch closed but there are no major obstacles to block the route.
Terrain: Rough ground which can be muddy underfoot.
Facilities: See walk 3.5.

Initially the trackbed is separated from the existing mineral line by a fence before the mineral line veers away south-east towards the hills and the site of the opencast coalfield.

Bridge No. 26, with pillars constructed of bricks is passed and gradually the line pulls away from the road. The two Dunaskin chimneys are such a prominent feature that you could never get lost on this walk. To the right is another notable feature, the River Doon which snakes along the valley floor. There is a marked contrast between the largely industrial east side of the valley and beyond the River Doon Farm land used for grazing dotted with occasional farm buildings.

A missing bridge at Laight Farm, removed to improve access, proves no obstacle. At the Laight Crossing, on the nearby coal line, ash was dumped from the fireboxes of the steam engines and accumulated alongside the trackbed.

The trackbed continues passing under a stone arch bridge which is followed by a deep cutting. Ahead, on this short route, lies the small town of Dalmellington. It's surprising that the ironworks was named after a place 2½ miles away.

Dalmellington was built above what was once a flood plain before the River Doon was tamed when the Galloway Hydro-electric Scheme was constructed in the 1930s. A latter addition to the landscape is Bellsbank, a housing scheme built to provide housing for the people of Benquhat village who lived in the plateau

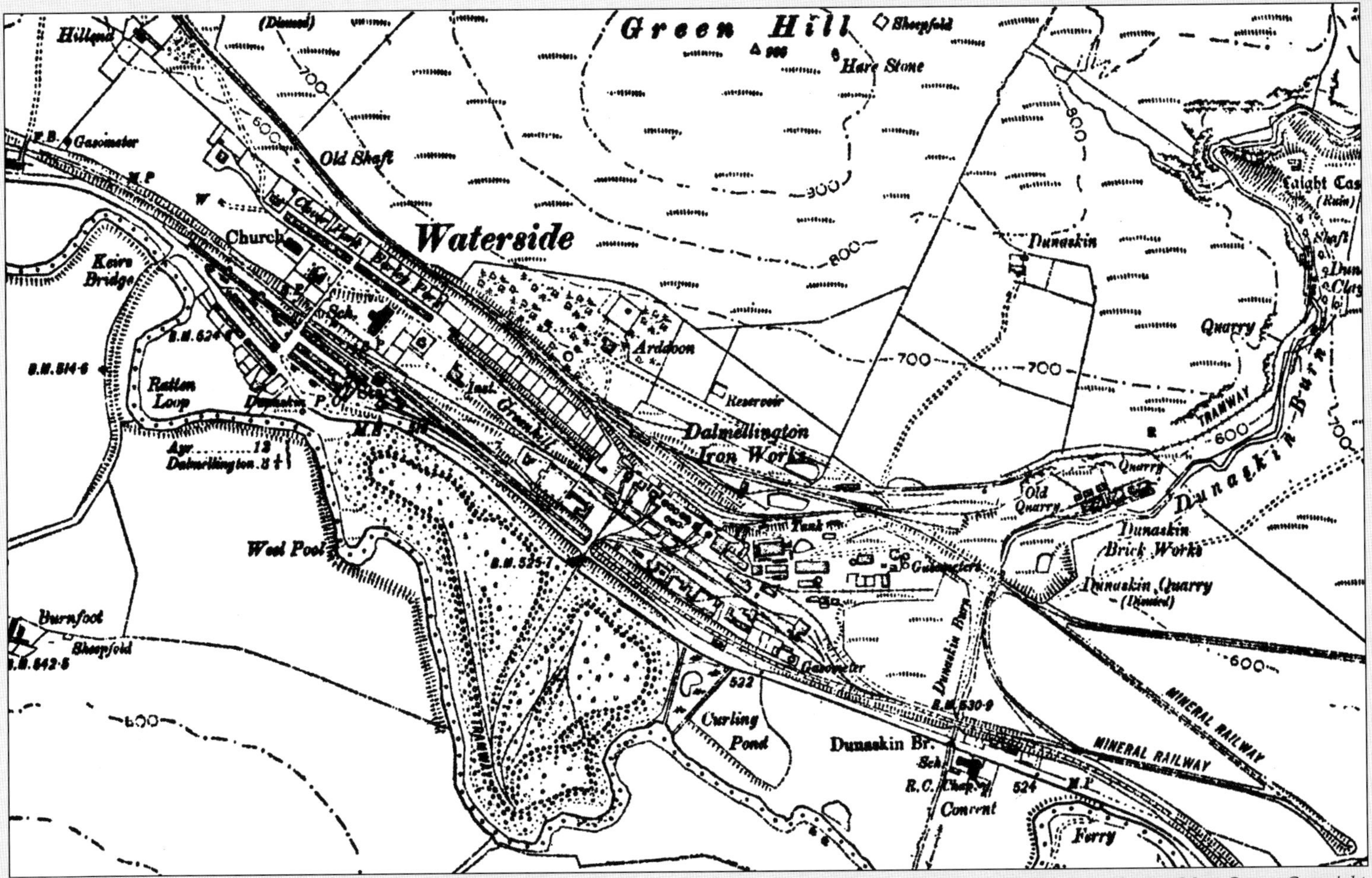

The railways around Waterside and Dunaskin.

Reproduced from the 6", 1911 Ordnanace Survey Map, Crown Copyright

Dunaskin viewed from the slag heap, 100 years later. The furnaces have gone but many of the original buildings remain. *Author*

Dalmellington station in 1905 looking towards the dead end. *Hamish Stevenson Collection*

above Dunaskin and for miners brought down from Lanarkshire, when their mines closed. The houses sit to the west of the road perched above the River Doon.

Dalmellington is the last town before the Galloway Hills, and sits beside the Southern Upland fault line. South of Dalmellington the road starts a twisting climb through a narrow valley passing Loch Doon with ever increasing views of the Galloway Hills. In the past travellers often rested before the journey into the wilds began.

Before the arrival of the Dalmellington Iron Co. almost a tenth of the population was involved in weaving using wool from the thousands of sheep grazing on nearby hills. Two woollen mills were operating in the town, one which initially supplied yarn for carpets manufacture in Kilmarnock and the other producing blankets and plaids. All this changed with the discovery of coal seams and carbon rich black stone in the surrounding area when the outside world then became interested in this quiet valley.

The trackbed veers south-east away from the road on the approach to Dalmellington. The access road to the Chalmerston opencast workings cuts across the trackbed. Beyond the road is a further section of cutting and shortly afterwards a bench seat is located at the side of the track. A pleasant walk has been created incorporating the trackbed. Beside the track, especially to the west are several small lochs, some created by old mine workings causing subsidence.

Dalmellington or Sillyhole Moss was a formidable barrier with early track builders floundering as branches and stones, used as foundations and tipped into the marshy ground, sank overnight leaving the engineers no further forward. The Sillyhole Mines were some of the first to be exploited to supply the furnaces but due to flooding were closed by the late 1860s.

Across the trackbed at this point, from the 1930s was a mile-long overhead cable system which carried coal from the Bogton mine (to the west of the A713) to the coal washing plant at Minnivey (to the east) which operated until the

1950s. Another aerial cable system continued east from Minnivey to Chalmerston. After the cable system was dismantled it found a new home at Butlin's Holiday Camp near Ayr where it carried visitors from the camp entrance to the chalets below.

A missing railway bridge over a burn requires a short detour to a nearby road bridge. Sillyhole signal box was located here and the signalman's cottage, now much extended, remains. The trackbed is now a well-worn path leading into Dalmellington past the football ground of Craigmark Burntonians, the local junior league team, but the path stops abruptly at the Doon Valley Leisure Centre, then by Doon Academy. Beyond them was the site of Dalmellington station, now occupied by an industrial estate.

In the 1890s plans were presented in Parliament for a railway to connect Muirkirk, Mauchline and Dalmellington which would have reached Dalmellington from the north-east and created a second station in the town. Coal, as usual, was the impetus behind the scheme but the proposals were abandoned after the sudden death of its promoter.

The plans of the Ayrshire & Galloway Railway to reach Galloway were not practical although the line was surveyed, the route planned initially through Ness Glen and by Loch Doon. Indeed for a few years a line was laid to provide access to Loch Doon at the end of World War I. This was a grand scheme to build a School of Aerial Gunnery beside Loch Doon with moving targets on a monorail system. The locals with experience of the boggy ground around Dalmellington knew that it would never work and they were proved right The rails were lifted, they had been supplied from a Welsh line, and the scheme was abandoned with a lot of money wasted.

The Dalmellington branch was a valuable industrial route taking the extracted coal from mine to factory, furnace and home and before the closure of the ironworks taking away the pig iron. The passenger service was also important allowing people to travel to Ayr and beyond, but declined with competition from the buses. It was the arrival of the railway that brought so much activity to the valley and changed it forever. The owners certainly benefitted but it was a hard life for the miners charged with extracting the coal and conditions for their families were not easy. So the railway was probably a mixed blessing to the upper valley of the River Doon.

Maybole Junction to Girvan

Closed stations abound on this route but at least the line is open (*see map page 26*). From Maybole Junction the line passes Dalrymple station (348156) and then Cassillis station (329132), both closed in 1954, and both are now privately owned to reach Maybole station (298101). South of Maybole, Kilkerran station (297044) and Dailly station (261024) both closed in 1965. There was a halt at Bargany (247014) known as the Bargany Colliery Halt to serve miners working at the Bargany Pit which was operational in the 1920s. Closer to Girvan Killochan station (221006) closed in 1951. Grangestone Halt (199996), discussed in the section on the Maidens & Dunure Light Railway, was closed in 1965.

Killochan station, looking towards Maybole on 20th September, 1965.
Hamish Stevenson Collection

A more recent (2011) view of the former Killochan station. The waiting room is now used as a garage.
Author

Bargany signal box, 15th July, 1963. *Hamish Stevenson Collection*

It is reckoned that over the centuries there were as many as 110 pits extracting coal from the small isolated coalfield around Dailly and along the Girvan Valley towards the sea. Several of the pits survived into the 1970s, although the Killochan pit, also known as Bargany pit, ceased operations in 1967. There was a coal washing plant at Killochan which treated coal from the other pits along the valley. Famously a coal seam near Dailly went on fire in the 18th century and is still warming some of the fields around it even today.

The first station in Girvan, north of the River Girvan, closed in 1893. The river was then bridged and the present station brought into use.

The G&SWR built a short branch down to Girvan harbour where coal from the Bargany pit was loaded onto ships bound for Ireland using a coal chute. This only lasted until 1918; three years after the Killochan Coal Co. went into liquidation. Part of the route can be followed from the abutment of the former railway bridge over the River Girvan (185984) to the harbour side a distance of about 100 yards. (*) To the north of the river was the site of Girvan goods station in a loop of the Girvan Water. In a few hundred yards the railway crossed the river twice. Girvan had an engine shed which closed in 1940.

South of Girvan but still in Ayrshire are Pinmore (203921) and Pinwherry station (194873) on the former Girvan & Portpatrick Railway which were both closed in 1965. The 542 yard Pinmore tunnel, north of Pinmore station, and the 10-span Kinclair viaduct, north of Pinwherry station, are only some of the highlights on what is a steeply-graded route through a largely barren landscape.

LMS Fowler '3F' class 0-6-0 No. 615 on shed at Girvan.
W.A Camwell/Hamish Stevenson Collection

Pinmore station, looking towards Girvan. *Hamish Stevenson Collection*

Chapter Four

Railways to the East of Ayr

The G&SWR's main rival in Ayrshire was the Caledonian Railway, and competition between the two companies was intense as they sought to back proposals for new lines in Ayrshire and gain an advantage over one other. However, Ayrshire was the natural territory for the G&SWR and they had already a considerable presence in the county, by the 1850s, through their existing routes. The network operated by the 'Sou'West', while not complete, was starting to reach the mineral rich areas of Ayrshire but others were keen for a slice of the action and to fill in the gaps.

In the mid-19th century there was a growing demand for railway routes in an era of 'railway mania' with communities, large and small, wanting the prestige of a local station and every pit and ironworks also seeking a rail connection. The land to the east of Ayr was ripe for development with landowners anxious to develop the mineral deposits of the Ayrshire coalfields to supply iron furnaces and export coal. The railways, with steam locomotion, were well placed to service these industries and could provide a faster route to the ports than the waggonways. With a developing railway network other markets could also be reached both in Scotland and further afield in England. So there was no shortage of interest in the possibility of new railway routes, especially a railway eastwards from Ayr through the coal rich lands of Ayrshire around Annbank, Cumnock and Muirkirk.

One proposal to develop a route across the county was the Ayr & Douglas Railway whose Prospectus was published in 1864. Strongly supported by local land owners and businessmen, including James Baird the iron and coal magnate, the 40 mile route was intended to exploit the mineral reserves in the area, shorten the journey to Edinburgh, Carlisle and other places to the east and south, and develop goods and passenger traffic. The proposed route would have linked with the G&SWR north of the River Ayr and branches to the harbour and mineral rich estates along the route would have been built.

The route would have proceeded from Ayr to Coylton, Sinclairston, Ochiltree, Cumnock, Muirkirk and Douglas where it would have linked up with the Caledonian Railway. It would have been single track but with the possibility of doubling if required. The route had been surveyed, local clients were enthusiastic and returns promising. It sounded attractive but then a Prospectus is intended to be. The lure of Robert Burns and the Clyde coast was also mentioned but the intent was to carry coal and other minerals. The G&SWR and the Caledonian Railway were invited to tender for the business and the Directors of the fledgling company no doubt hoped to benefit from the railway companies vying with each other to secure the business.

The Ayr & Douglas Railway never became a reality like many other similar proposals. The G&SWR had other plans and within six years the G&SWR had further extended its grip on the county, filling in some of the gaps, by constructing the Ayr to Mauchline branch, opened in 1870, to create an

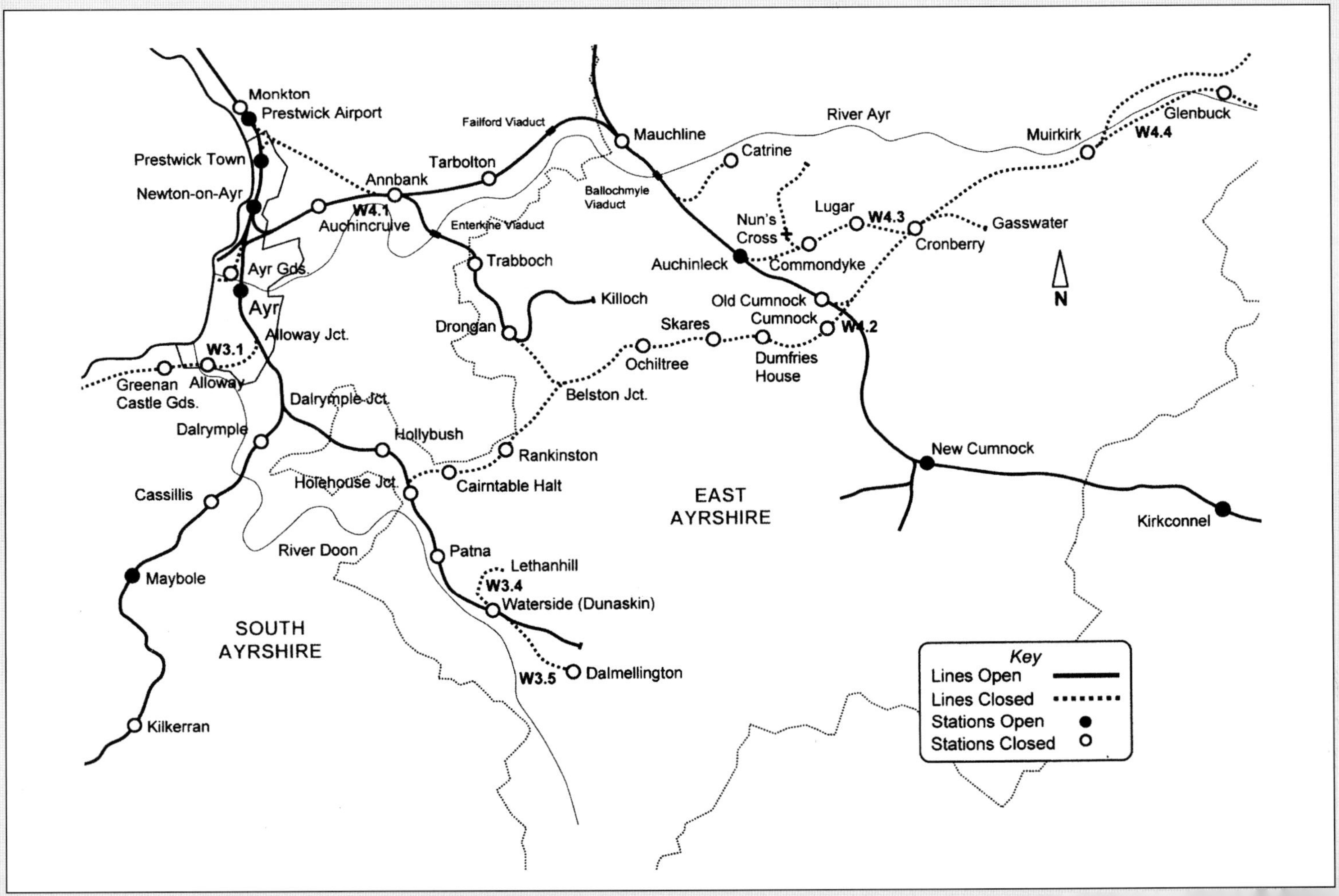

Monkton
Prestwick Airport
Prestwick Town
Newton-on-Ayr
Failford Viaduct
Tarbolton
Annbank
W4.1
Auchincruive
Enterkine Viaduct
Mauchline
Ballochmyle Viaduct
River Ayr
Catrine
Muirkirk
W4.4
Glenbuck
Lugar
W4.3
Nun's Cross
Gasswater
Cronberry
Commondyke
Auchinleck
Trabboch
Ayr Gds.
Ayr
Killoch
Old Cumnock
Cumnock
W4.2
Skares
Drongan
Alloway Jct.
W3.1
Ochiltree
Dumfries House
Greenan Castle Gds.
Alloway
Belston Jct.
Dalrymple Jct.
Dalrymple
Hollybush
Rankinston
New Cumnock
Holehouse Jct.
Cairntable Halt
Cassillis
EAST AYRSHIRE
Kirkconnel
River Doon
Patna
Lethanhill
W3.4
Maybole
Waterside (Dunaskin)
SOUTH AYRSHIRE
W3.5
Dalmellington
Kilkerran
N
Key
Lines Open
Lines Closed
Stations Open
Stations Closed

important cross-country link between Ayr and the Nith Valley line south to Carlisle. Coal could now be exported more easily to markets south of the border. This route is still open but only for freight and only after several close brushes with closure. The cross-country line started at Newton Junction in Ayr and joined the Nith Valley line at Mauchline Junction just north of Mauchline, a distance of just over 11 miles. There were stations at Auchincruive, Annbank and Tarbolton which are all now closed.

A branch from the Mauchline route the A&C line, another important cross-country line, was also opened by July 1872. There is some doubt over what the initials stood for. Some people thought that the A&C stood for Ayr and Cronberry, Cronberry being where the route joined the Muirkirk branch, or even Annbank & Cumnock but the official title was the Ayr & Cumnock line. Along with a short spur from the A&C to the Nith Valley line the three routes were known as 'The Ayrshire Lines'.

Branching at Annbank, four miles from Newton Junction, the Ayrshire & Cumnock Railway veered south-east towards Drongan and then east towards Cumnock. From Drongan it took a similar route to that proposed by the ill-fated Ayr & Douglas Railway passing under the Nith Valley line, where there was eventually a junction, and heading out onto the moors at Cronberry. Here there was another junction, this time with the Muirkirk branch, which had opened in 1848. Three or four trains a day were sufficient for passengers and at first two went as far as Edinburgh, but at 3½ hours for the journey, were never popular.

The network extended 'spider-like' across the Ayrshire countryside. The Rankinston branch joined the A&C at Belston Junction to the south-east of Drongan (*see Chapter Three*). In 1892 there was a short three-mile branch built, the Monkton and Annbank branch, which left the Glasgow to Ayr route just north of Prestwick at Monkton Junction, close to the present location of Prestwick International Airport railway station, and connected to the Ayr to Mauchline route just west of Annbank at Mossblown Junction. Later a south-facing junction was added at the Prestwick end. The route meant that freight trains could bypass Ayr and later it served several coal pits along the branch. It had no public passenger service.

All these connections were invaluable serving the burgeoning coal industry, and the iron industry, and generated profits for the G&SWR. Short branches were made also to many pits along the network. Coal was king and the Ayrshire coalfield was a kingdom packed with black diamonds.

Sadly for the miners and the mining communities the conditions and rewards were not shared equally. Squalor, malnutrition and disease often confronted the many small isolated communities, miners' rows, built close to the coal pits and eking out an existence. The inequalities between coal pit owner and worker were immense, no wonder that socialism grew so strongly in Ayrshire. Keir Hardie, who helped create the powerful Ayrshire Miners' Union, fought for improved conditions and later became a founding member of the Labour Party. Even today when all the deep coal pits have closed the memory of harsh conditions has not been forgotten.

Passenger services linked isolated communities, although often stations were far from the communities they purported to serve. It's a proud boast, however, that even at small stations, such as Trabboch, it was possible to take the train to

Edinburgh, travelling on a mixture of G&SWR and CR lines. It is also true that such services were not direct or successful.

Beyond Cronberry the railway had already reached Muirkirk close to the Ayrshire border with Lanarkshire, when the A&C linked up with it. Muirkirk with its iron industry benefited greatly from the railway. Pack horses and carts quickly replaced by steam-powered engines which could easily transport tons of coal. Now just along the valley was Douglas and that was Caledonian country. Here the two railway companies could not avoid each other and we will return to that confrontation shortly.

At the turn of the century a further branch was built from the Nith Valley line to the small village of Catrine with its cotton mills. At 1½ miles in length it was not a major addition to the network. Cotton mills had been established in 1787, harnessing the power of the River Ayr and at one point the mill was the biggest manufacturing factory in Ayrshire. Within 40 years of its opening over 900 people were employed. By the time the railway arrived in 1903 the industry was well-established and many surrounding villages wove the yarn produced. The 50 ft diameter Catrine big wheels which powered the works were a tourist attraction, considered to be the largest in the world, and lasted until 1947. The head of water required to turn the wheels was created by damming the River Ayr near its source at Glenbuck (*see the Muirkirk to Glenbuck section later in this chapter*). The locals welcomed the railway having long felt isolated, and complaining that their industries were held back by lack of a connection. The railway station closed in 1917, due to wartime conditions, but was reopened soon after before closing finally in 1943. Freight traffic and the occasional 'special outing' continued until 6th July, 1964.

The cotton trade outlasted the closure of the railway and in 1950 a new mill was built. The old mill was destroyed by fire in 1963. The new mill lasted only until 1968.

Close to Catrine is a more durable railway structure, the iconic Ballochmyle viaduct, on the main line, one of several impressive viaducts between Cumnock and Kilmarnock. The gorges formed by rivers flowing from east towards the sea demanded a high price, to be crossed, in engineering skill and architectural design.

Exploring the Railway Heritage

The Ayr and Mauchline Line

When the Mauchline branch opened, the line started at Newton Junction, next to Tam's Brig, before passing through farm fields en route to Auchincruive. By 1879 Ayr locomotive shed, with two sets of three roads, was constructed beside Tam's Brig and a triangular junction created on the site of which Newton Junction was the most northerly.

Along the Mauchline line within Ayr industry such as chemical works, forges, carpet factories, and boot and shoe manufacturers grew close to the railway, some with rail sidings. In time more farmland was absorbed as Ayr expanded and in the 1950s council housing estates were built beside the route. Today the line passes derelict factories, more housing estates and retail parks reflecting the decline of manufacturing and heavy industries.

The railway passes under the Ayr bypass, in a deep cutting, just north of the Whitletts roundabout, largely unnoticed before reaching the site of Auchincruive station (373241) in St Quivox. Only part of a loading bank and abandoned sidings remain. The sidings were at times operated by Esso for the MOD but are now abandoned with the sign that reads: 'Stop. Locomotives not to pass this point' now being redundant. The sidings were once used to stage a 'nuclear accident' to test the response of the emergency services to wagons carrying nuclear fuel. The station buildings were close to the rail bridge over the narrow road in the village of St Quivox.

Around half-a-century before the Mauchline branch was constructed waggonways served several pits around St. Quivox and it was noted that: 'One hundred wagon-loads a day were conveyed to the port along a railway, from the coal mines in the parish of St. Quivox.' There were coal pits all around the area. In contrast the scene is now of agriculture.

Walk 4.1 Waggonway Trail

Distance: 3 miles return trip (***).
Start: The car park for the start of the walk can be found by taking the B742 from Whitletts roundabout and turning first right. The car park is clearly signposted and is on the right. From the car park walk further along the road towards Oswald's bridge (388231). To the left within the grounds of Auchincruive Estate is Oswald House (originally known as Auchincruive House and dating from 1767), the former home of the Oswald family. The former car park beside Oswald House is now closed as the area is being redeveloped. The Waggonway Trail starts at the bridge and is signposted with red arrows.
Terrain: Rough stout footwear recommended.
Facilities: Nearest facilities Ayr or Annbank, no public toilets.

Within sight of St Quivox is the Auchincruive Estate, parts of which were operated by the Scottish Agricultural College (SAC) for many years. There are remnants of old waggonways all around the estate. They were largely worked out by the early 1870s when a dispute between the coal operators, George Taylor & Co., and the Oswald family finally closed the routes. No direct connection was made with the Ayrshire lines, although some of the pits to the north of the river, around Annbank, may have used the routes to take coal away. Most of the SAC has now moved closer to Ayr and is part of the Craigie Campus of the University of South West Scotland.

From the car park cross Oswald bridge, built in 1862 as part of the estate, and the waggonway trail is immediately on your left beside a house. Opposite is a memorial cairn, erected by the Burns Federation in 1929, to commemorate the lives of William Wallace and Robert Burns, two of Ayrshire's most famous sons, both with links to this area. Robert Burns walked to Auchincruive and heard

Brockle Wood on the Auchincruive Estate in 2012. This view shows an abutment of the Auchincruive Waggonway bridge over River Ayr. The waggonway continued over the viaduct to reach Annbank. *Author*

Oaklea tunnel in 2011, on the Auchincruive Waggonway, looking towards Ayr. It passes under the road to the west of Oaklea Farm. The original name of the tunnel is unknown but it is now associated with the name of the farm. *Author*

there the stories of William Wallace and his battles for freedom against the English and how he hid from the English in the woods around the cairn. It is believed that Burns got the inspiration to write *Scots Wha Hae* on a visit to the woods.

Before starting the walk there are two short interesting detours. Firstly a short distance around the bend in the road, just before Oaklea Farm, the road crosses a bridge (388229) over an old waggonway. The skewed arch tunnel is partly filled in but the stonework is in good condition. (*) The waggonway continued through a cutting until it reached the River Ayr about 200 yards south of Oswald bridge. From the Oaklea tunnel the waggonway ran east to two small pits. Another branch headed north initially parallel to the road and eventually merges with the Waggonway Trail but this section of waggonway cannot be followed and you should return to the signposted trail.

Secondly by following the River Ayr Walk (signposted) south of Oswald bridge the remnants of the stone abutments can be found to each side of the river bank. When the river runs low the bases of two stone piers can still be seen (*). This was one of the earliest rail bridges across the River Ayr.

The River Ayr loops round the land that the Waggonway Trail crosses in a deep gorge hewn out of the soft sandstone. The trail is tree lined for most of the way with views across to Oswald Hall and of the River Ayr in the gorge below. What a contrast to the times of the waggonway when horses and men strained to fill coal wagons and start the journey down to the coast, while, on the far bank of the River Ayr, the Oswald family lived in luxury on the proceeds. Unemployed miners even helped construct the steep hanging gardens on the west bank in the 1830s. The waggonways must have been familiar to Robert Burns but he never wrote about them.

The initial part of the waggonway trail, beside the house, was not part of the old waggonway system. The old waggonway merges with Waggonway Trail shortly after the house, emerging from a cutting on the far side of the house. The trail then enters, by a wooden gate, what is now a tree-lined cutting known as Cutting Wood. Controlling wagons and horses must have been difficult on the gradient and would still have been difficult in the 1860s when it appears that steam engines were being used. In 1865 a young man was killed, further down the route, by slipping as he stepped down from the engine and got caught up in the wheels. His legs were mangled and he died a few hours later. The engine and wagons were returning from Annbank which is to the north of the River Ayr.

The trail continues beside the river leaving Cutting Wood and entering Pheasant Nook Wood. The waggonway then bridged the River Ayr at Brockle Wood (400234). The sandstone abutments remain along with one of the piers. The stone work was impressive and must have been expensive to construct but once over the river more coal pits near Annbank could be reached and the coal shipped back to Ayr. The bridge was an early example of the efforts made by railway builders to access more coal pits.

The trail then continues round by Wallace's Seat, leaving the former waggonway, where Wallace hid from the English. High above the river the view from Wallace's Seat can be enjoyed with a dramatic and dangerous drop

Monkton station, looking towards Troon, in 1956. *W.A.C. Smith/Hamish Stevenson Collection*

The site of Monkton station in 2012. The siding is used to deliver aviation fuel for Prestwick airport a short distance to away. *Author*

to the river below. The trail returns to the start close to Oswald bridge. Other trails are signposted and Oswald's Trail which is on the other side of the river can be used to explore other parts of the waggonway system. On the Annbank side of the river were located the Enterkine pits. This section of the waggonway was in operation from around 1865 and continued to be worked into the 1870s with coal then feeding into the A&C line.

Auchincruive Station to Mossblown Junction (and the Monkton branch)

Beyond Auchincruive station the railway passed Mossblown Farm where the short three-mile branch, known as the Monkton and Annbank (M&A) line joined it at Mossblown Junction. The only part of this route still visible is a section of embankment crossing a field on the left of the Ayr bypass when travelling south from Sandyford roundabout. The Ayr bypass and the expansion of Prestwick International Airport have combined to remove other traces of the route. Close to the north-facing junction at the Prestwick end of the branch was Monkton station (349276). There are still sidings at the former station site used to deliver aviation fuel to Prestwick airport.

The route opened on 3rd March, 1893 and offered freight an alternative route avoiding Ayr, if required, and giving direct access onto the Glasgow line. By 1897, near Mossblown Junction but on the M&A branch, the first two Auchincruive pits, owned by George Taylor, were sunk with a third shaft added in 1910. There was a platform for use by miners known as Mossblown Junction Halt at Mossblown Junction but there are no recorded dates when it was in use. Halts like this did not have an advertised service and were not open to the public. In 1916 William Baird & Co. took over the ownership of the pits. The pits closed in 1960. To those travelling along the Ayr bypass after it opened, the reek from the coal bing permeated the car and travellers learned to hold their noses. Today the bing is landscaped and looks a natural part of the environment. A kink in the B742 opposite what is now the former Sandyford foods factory was the location of the multiple sidings. The factory itself used some of the former pit buildings.

Towards the Prestwick end of the branch the Auchincruive Coal Co., owned by William Baird, obtained a lease to dig for minerals. It was in 1910 that the Glenburn pits, known as Auchincruive 4, 5, 6, and 7, were sunk. Shortly afterwards houses were built for the miners although some had to travel from further afield. The Glenburn pit extended beneath Prestwick Burgh and also out under the sea and was not abandoned until 1974. There was a Central Workshop located at the Glenburn site and also for three years it was West Ayr National Area Coal Board headquarters.

In Prestwick there are few remaining links with the railway other than a bridge over the former route. The Glenburn miners' village has been demolished and the area is occupied by the Shaw Farm Industrial Estate. Further east a runway has been constructed over the former trackbed.

Annbank station in the 1930s, with Drumley pit in the distance; Mauchline route to left with Ayrshire and Cumnock line to right. *Hamish Stevenson Collection*

The site of Annbank station in 1997. *Author*

Mossblown Junction to Annbank Station

From Mossblown Junction, a few hundred yards east, was another platform for use by miners known as the Auchincruive Colliery Platform which was open from 1898 to 1926. The railway then continues in a cutting until it reaches Annbank station (404248) located at the junction where the A&C line leaves the Ayr and Mauchline route. The first name given to the station, before the line opened was Bogend station after a local farm. Several of the stations, on the A&C, were initially named after local farms until the final name was decided. The station had four platforms, two on the Mauchline line and two on the A&C. There was a goods yard, with a possible fifth platform on a goods loop and sidings to the south of the line. The station buildings like the others on the A&C were simple wooden structures with Annbank station having a canopy over the platform. Located close to the vee of the junction was a large coal bing, the waste from the Drumley pit, now much reduced in size and landscaped. Some of the waste material from the bing was used for the foundations of a runway extension at Prestwick airport. The platforms on the edge of the vee merged to form a large triangular area of platform. Overlooking the scene, on the western approach to the junction was Annbank Junction signal box perched on the hillside, accessed by an exposed flight of steps, with exposed rodding and cabling running down to the track. At the start of the A&C route there was another signal box. At one time this was a busy junction and still sees traffic on both routes today. Today the signalling is reduced to a ground frame.

Around Annbank station a mining community developed and the community became known as Mossblown. Annbank village is a short distance to the south on a hillside.

Ayrshire and Cumnock Branch

South from Annbank Junction there were more pits to the left (Enterkine pits No. 9) with sidings above the level of the railway trackbed. (The Enterkine pits were also known as the Ayr pits.) Part of the Annbank brickworks, survives as a private residence. The track then passed under two bridges. The first bridge was at the foot of the hill which leads up to the village of Annbank. Between the two bridges on the left hand side, opposite the entrance to Enterkine Hotel, was the Weston Bridge Halt (410237), used by commuting miners around the 1920s and 1930s.

South of the second bridge the railway crosses an embankment to reach Enterkine viaduct (418230), also known locally as the Crawfordston viaduct. This viaduct, consisting of 14 stone piers, is one of Ayrshire's hidden railway gems best viewed from Gadgirth bridge on the B742 Annbank to Coylton road. There are nine piers on the Annbank side, one in the river and four on the other side. At 90 ft its tall central piers, built for double track, tower over the river. It was strengthened and redecked in 2008. It was only ever used for single track and the girders on the unused section of the deck are exposed. There is a reported 'sway' on the bridge when trains cross over. On both sides trees mask

Enterkine viaduct in 2011. It crosses the River Ayr on the former Ayrshire & Cumnock route.
Author

Drongan station looking towards Cumnock on 28th December, 1966.
Hamish Stevenson Collection

the sound of approaching trains and walkers, passing on the River Ayr Walk which is located underneath the bridge, can be startled by the sudden rumbling noise heralding the arrival of a coal train.

Once over the River Ayr more coal pits were encountered at Springs (425228) where a minor road crosses over the railway. For a time Annbank brickworks were located to the west, Ayr Coal pit No. 7 to the east, with sidings and a tramway which also ran east to a quarry. The site of the sidings is now occupied by a small housing estate.

More coal pits followed at Drumdow, where there was a miners' halt, opened, it is thought, between 1922 and 1928 and at Trabboch where just south of the road bridge on the road to Drumdow Farm, there was a small station which opened on 1st July, 1896 (434218). The station building was again of a simple wooden design with a single platform. The bridges had been built for double track and since the line was only single track a store was built into the arch on the platform side.

Trabboch village was built in the 1880s to accommodate miners working on the newly sunk Trabboch pit. The houses were very basic with no sanitation or inside running water. The pit closed in 1908 and Drumdow pit in 1910. The station, however, lasted until 10th September, 1951. By then the miners' rows had been demolished and subsidence had created two new lochs. The former local primary school building is now a community centre but few other buildings remain to indicate that there was a village in the area. The people from Trabboch were relocated to Drongan.

The railway crosses the A70 Ayr to Cumnock road about two miles east of Coylton, at Coalhall, and reaches Drongan station, opened around 1875, beside the B730 (446190) a mile south of the rail bridge. A more substantial station built of stone and with a single platform and sidings to the south, it lies just to the north of Drongan village and must have been named after Drongan estate because no village of that name existed when the station was opened. Even today the former station lies slightly to the north of the village. Most of the village was built after World War II to accommodate miners working at Killoch, Barony and Littlemill coal pits and those decanted from isolated communities such as Trabboch. The station buildings remain as a private residence with the platform having been removed. The station house was at the rear. There was a sheltered waiting room but no protection on the platform from the weather. South of the station was another coal pit, Shields Main.

Also south of the station, but to the east, there was a later addition to the A&C when the short branch to Killoch Colliery, one of the National Coal Board's super pits, was opened in 1959, a year before the pit started production. A signal box which had been lying in storage for many years was assembled to work the branch. This caused problems because, whilst in storage, it had become infested with flies and had to be fumigated shortly after being erected.

Killoch Colliery became the first in Scotland to produce over a million tons in a year but geological problems meant that the known coal reserves could not be fully exploited. It closed in 1987 but the rail link remains and coal is collected from local opencast pits around Ayrshire, and sent to the Killoch railhead for washing, screening and grading before being sent by train to power stations like

Ochiltree station looking towards Cumnock *circa* 1950. *Hamish Stevenson Collection*

Skares station looking towards Cumnock *circa* 1950. *Hamish Stevenson Collection*

the Drax power station in Yorkshire. The branch loops through 180 degrees before passing under the A70 Ayr to Cumnock road to reach the railhead.

From the junction the rails of the former A&C line have been lifted but the story of links to coal pits along the route continued. Between the abandoned junction and Drumsmodden Farm there are few signs of the trackbed. However, near Drumsmodden Farm the A&C and the Rankinston branch merged at Belston Junction. The junction site is easily identified from the road (480176) from the entrance road to the farm.

Belston Junction (*) was an isolated location but was well-known to train drivers using Ayrshire's web of lines. There was a signal box and a water tank and a Belston Junction Halt (481176) which was known to be in use around 1904 but no other details are known. There was also a loop on the Rankinston branch which was probably required to ensure safe workings on the branch to position the engine and guard's van correctly. In addition the loop was used by the daily passenger train from Rankinston to Ayr via Annbank which was required to reverse at the junction. Coal, of course was transported in all directions from many local pits: to the coast for export, to the furnaces at Dunaskin when they were in operation and east to Cumnock and beyond.

Near the farm was Drumsmodden mine and miners' rows. The mine opened by the Dalmellington Iron Co. was unsuccessful and closed in 1904. The coal was apparently of excellent quality but problems in exploiting the seams meant an early closure.

To the south of Belston Junction and stretching towards Cumnock are many opencast pits. This is the way that the black diamonds are now mined in Ayrshire, where coal remains an important industry with coal lorries delivering the coal to the Killoch rail head.

East of Belston Junction the trackbed can be followed until a minor road is reached with more branches, at one time, connecting to coal pits to the south. From here the outlook for walkers is poor but many interesting railway sites remain. The A&C once crossed the minor road branching from the B7046. A mile further on the trackbed crossed the Burnock Water (504173) (*) by an 11-arch masonry viaduct. The trackbeds on both sides of the viaduct have been trampled on by cattle and conditions underfoot are very difficult. Beyond the viaduct it is only a short distance to Ochiltree station (510190), which was similar in design to that of Drongan station.

The station sits beside the minor road linking the B7046 to the A70 Ayr to Cumnock Road. Ochiltree is over 1¼ miles to the north which must have given some extra business to the carters. The provisional name for the station was Barwharrie, after a local farm. Ochiltree was a small mining and farming community. The village is situated between the Killoch and Barony mines which have both now closed.

East of Ochiltree station the next railway station, 1½ miles to the east, was at Skares (529190) which didn't open until 1901 and was the last station to open on the line. South of the station was Whitehill pit, the first shafts being sunk in the 1890s. The village of Skares, built by the Bairds in the 1870s, was a mining village with the miners' rows lasting until the mid-1960s. Skares village is on the edge of opencast workings and has survived the demise of the deep mines.

The station site at Skares is now occupied by two houses. The road bridge over the railway remains. Part of the bridge was adapted as a store for lamps etc., like Trabboch, when the station was operational. There were sidings to the north.

The trackbed then crosses the seven-arch Dykes or Skares viaduct (533190) (*) close to the station site. The minor road in front of the station site turns south and passes under the most westerly arch. Like other viaducts on the line it has been well maintained.

Close to the viaduct was Dykes Junction which connected the railway to the Whitehill pit and then further south-west the Skares or Hindsward pit which closed in 1925 but operated as a private mine between 1969 and 1988. Between the two pits was a branch to the east to a stone quarry. The start of the branch to Whitehill continued east and continued beyond Dumfries House station down a steep gradient to a short reversing siding ending beside a farm track, and then a climb towards the coal pit. Several engines did not cope with the steep gradient and ended up on the farm track.

South of the Skares viaduct, on the road from Dykes viaduct, there are the abutments of a bridge over the road. This was part of the mineral railway to Whitehill pit.

Nearby is the Whitehill Colliery Woodlands (532182) (*), a series of woodlands walks on the Whitehill pit bing. The walks provide excellent views over the surrounding countryside. Beside the bing was a brickworks whose buildings were demolished in 2000.

Within ½ mile of Skares station was Dumfries House station (539192) (*). In the Ayrshire map published in 1872 its name was shown as Grimgrew station, after a local farm, but this again was never an operational name. The station was connected to the A70 Ayr to Cumnock road by Station Avenue. To the north of the A70 Station Avenue continued to reach Dumfries House, the estate of the Earl of Dumfries. The estate was purchased by William Crichton, who became the First Earl of Dumfries in 1635. Dumfries House was completed in 1759, by the architect John Adam, brother of the more renowned architect Robert Adam.

Through marriage to the Marquis of Bute, the estate was owned by the Marquis of Bute. The family chose to live on the island of Bute. In 2007 the estate was put on the market and saved for the nation by Prince Charles. The station would have been used by the family but was also used by the mining community.

Unusually the platform was located in a deep cutting with the station houses at the top of the cutting. Steps and a path led down to the trackbed. There were also two station cottages. The buildings remain but the cutting has been infilled.

This was the third station in just over a 1½ miles and with Dykes Junction the area was a very busy railway hub.

Beyond Dumfries House station the trackbed is in a very poor state and little remains of it between here and Cumnock. This was the first section of the line to be abandoned. In this section were sidings at Knockterra to serve Knockterra and Glengyron pits.

The Cairn Road (starts at 553173) which leads into Cumnock, over the bypass, from the south-west provides goods views over Cumnock, the Glaisnock

Dumfries House station. Between the station buildings and the trees was Station Avenue which led down to the gates of Dumfries House Estate. The station cutting has now been infilled. *Hamish Stevenson Collection*

viaduct on the A&C line and its continuation under the Kilmarnock to Carlisle route. There is a short section of landscaped embankment on the left just over the Cumnock bypass, but nothing else remains as you follow Cairn Road into Cumnock. The station site was beside the cemetery, which is on the right. Cumnock (A&C) station was shown on early maps as Shankston station. In later days it appeared fairly basic with a simple brick building and a single platform on an embankment overlooking the cemetery. Heading east there was a rail bridge over the road which has now been removed. This section was often used to store disused coal wagons.

Across the road at Wylie Crescent, close to the fire station, there has been a recent housing development replacing older flats. Almost hidden behind these houses is Glaisnock viaduct.

WALK 4.2 GLAISNOCK VIADUCT TO LOGAN JUNCTION

Distance: 1.25 miles return trip 2.5 miles (***).
Start: From Glaisnock Road, then Wylie Crescent, close to Fire Station.
Terrain: Public path.
Facilities: Cumnock shops, cafes, public toilet at Tanyard, Cumnock.

Glaisnock viaduct (574195) is now used as a footpath. Unusually for viaducts on this route local residents can use it to cross the Glaisnock Water. There is a tarmac path, street lights and a railing on the stone parapets. Built for double tracks, the 13-span, slightly curved masonry viaduct is a local landmark and at 75 ft it provides good views over the town. It is also known as the Barshare viaduct, sometimes the Cumnock viaduct or even the Deil Stone viaduct due to a legend that a large stone nearby has the mark of the devil's hooves on it.

Glaisnock viaduct, Cumnock, now hemmed in by housing. The Nith Valley line is to the rear. *Author*

Steps lead up to the viaduct and at the other end it passes to the south of Barshare housing estate built at the end of the 1950s. This was an experiment in trying to design an estate with a variety of styles and wide paths and houses at right angles to roads, with some timber houses and insulated aluminium roofs. The trackbed then reaches the abutments of an old road bridge over the railway before it reaches a missing bridge, easily circumvented, prior to approaching the Nith Valley line, which it passes under. Just beyond the bridge is Logan Junction where there was a spur from the A&C to Cumnock Junction on the Nith Valley line.

This was a very valuable spur. A loop on the Nith Valley line, at this point, enabled railway traffic to go north or south. Coal traffic could head south to Carlisle or north to Hurlford, near Kilmarnock.

Beyond the abandoned spur the route reaches a gate beside a road. The next section beside Logan is overgrown and difficult but east of the houses the trackbed can be walked. Returning to the start provides different views, looking west, including the head gear for one of the shafts at the Barony pit, a mute memorial to the miners' efforts.

There is another viaduct on the line before the A&C reaches Cronberry Junction. Glenmuir viaduct (599214) (*) over Glenmuir Water is fenced off. The tall seven-span segmental masonry arches overlook a narrow valley where the Glenmuir Water passes under the western end of the viaduct. It joins the Bellow Water and thereafter becomes the Lugar Water. The A70 continues east, now heading for Muirkirk and beyond. Lugar consists of housing mainly on the north side of the road, which replaced earlier miners' rows, along with the football ground of Lugar Boswell Thistle, the local football team with a literary connection in their name. James Boswell was the son of Lord Auchinleck and accompanied Dr Johnson on his famous journey around Scotland, before the age of the train. Culture and football 'gang thegither' as Burns might have said!

Lugar ironworks was located on a plateau to the north side, served by sidings from the Muirkirk line, also on the north side of the Lugar Valley. The valley played an important role in the industrial revolution, being the birthplace of William Murdoch. He was born at Bello Mill, Lugar in 1754 and early in his career worked for James Watt, whose improvements to the Newcomen steam engine helped create the industrial revolution. Murdoch, when working for Watt, built in his own time a steam road vehicle and built his own steam carriage. Watt would not let him proceed with his ideas believing that this was not the way ahead. Murdoch used the steam carriage and can claim to be the first person in Britain to use such a mode of transport. However, it was experiments with producing a gas which could be burnt to provide illumination, coal gas, which was the idea for which he is most famous. Some of the early experiments were carried out in a cave in the Lugar Valley near Bello Mill house (597216).

The trackbed continues through a cutting and eventually passed under the A70, although road realignment has removed the bridge. It is only a short distance along another cutting before the former railway reached the site of Cronberry Junction (606225) where it joined the Muirkirk Railway.

The journey along the Ayr and Cumnock line is a story of exploitation of coal reserves, of communities developing to serve pits and a railway built to take the coal to where it was needed. Many of the geographical scars created by the coal industry are now healing or are covered up, the communities have moved on while the linking steel thread, the now abandoned trackbed, which connected all the disjointed points gradually fades from memory. There were many noble people who worked their living in often harsh conditions and some who made profits on their backs but all contributed to a chapter in Ayrshire's history when coal was king.

Annbank to Mauchline Junction

East of Annbank station, the next station on the line, which is closed, is Tarbolton (440250). The trackbed veers north-east passing over the B743 close to Failford on what was once the Montgomerie lands and where, before it burnt down in 1969, there was a very fine mansion house known as Montgomerie Castle. There is a very elaborate railway bridge, designed to complement the mansion house, over the road, consisting of a single elliptical arch (455262) (*) and detailing on the arches. The rail bridge is listed Grade B.

This is followed almost immediately by the Failford viaduct (457263) (*) which has nine semi-circular arches. In four of the arches the surface area between the arches has been replaced with brick. The viaduct crosses a wooded valley.

The railway then continues north-east before turning south-east towards Mauchline Junction. Between Mauchline Junction and where we pick up the tale of abandoned railways south of Kilmarnock in Chapter Five, are the 680 yards Mossgiel tunnel, and located just north of the tunnel, the Mossgiel tunnel Platform, followed by a siding to the Mauchline pit, which closed in 1966 but stayed open as a coal preparation plant until February 1974. There was also a

Tarbolton station in 1996. *Author*

Catrine, looking towards the buffer stops. *Hamish Stevenson Collection*

small goods siding at Garrochburn, closed in 1965, which was used for farm traffic and also as a coal siding for coal traffic from Mauchline pit. The railway also crossed the Cessnock Water twice en route to Kilmarnock.

Turning south the railway passes Mauchline station (497265) which is closed. The former goods shed is found in the small industrial estate with the former station buildings at the entrance to the estate. To the north of the station there is still an operational signal box. South of Mauchline was a siding which served Ballochmyle Quarry with its famous distinctive red sandstone and then the railway crossed Ballochmyle viaduct (508254) (*) with its long semi-circular central arch of 181 ft. The central arch is flanked on each side by 35 ft spans. The viaduct is 163 ft above the River Ayr. I wonder if Tom Cruise ever saw the good folk of Catrine as he clung onto his computer-generated train as it hurtled across the viaduct in the film *Mission Impossible*. The viaduct can be reached by following the River Ayr Way from Catrine.

Catrine Branch

Much of this short branch line has been lost. The section between Brackenhill Junction, where the branch left the main line and the A76 which the branch passed under has almost disappeared. Turning off the A76 and taking the B713 the trackbed can be seen on the right. Near Whiteflats Farm the railway had crossed the Bogend Burn. The abutments of the bridge and the single pier remain. The trackbed is then lost in a wood. If the first road on the right on entering Catrine is taken, the line of the trackbed can be spotted, now a path. To the left of the road in splendid isolation are the refurbished parapets of a bridge over the former railway (*). The cutting, which had become an eyesore, has been infilled and two stone semi-circular seating areas created to improve the area by the Catrine Environment Group.

Ahead now down a slope was the station site now occupied by Catrine Games Hall. There was a signal box on the approach to the station. The station building had a canopy extending over the platform with glazed side partitions. There was a single long platform with sidings and goods shed to the left. The station sat on an elevated position above the village and was flanked by a row of tall trees to the right. Beyond the trees was the tall chimney, now removed, of the Catrine Mills.

In 1909 the folk of Catrine were awakened by the sound of an explosion. Burglars, intent on what they thought was a cash-filled safe at the station, were over generous with the explosives and blew up most of the station.

Auchinleck to Cumnock

Auchinleck station reopened in 1984 but Cumnock (Old) station has remained closed. However, Auchinleck and Cumnock stations were only two miles apart, so one station is possibly sufficient to serve both communities. Given the local rivalries between the two towns, certainly on the football field, it was probably not a popular decision in Cumnock. Close to Cumnock (Old)

Station (577204) is another fine viaduct, the Lugar or Templand or sometimes the Bank viaduct (574206) (*) which has 13 semi-circular arch spans and towers 175 ft above the Lugar Water. Obscured by wooded hillsides it is often unnoticed but is another fine example of how railway engineers conquered Ayrshire's valleys in constructing their routes. Cumnock (Old) station site is now occupied by a residential home and the goods yard has been cleared.

Auchinleck to Muirkirk

The line from Auchinleck to Muirkirk was an important line bringing in business for the G&SWR from the many coal mines along the route and reaching Muirkirk with its ironworks. The 10½ mile branch was authorized along with the Glasgow, Dumfries & Carlisle Railway Act of 1846. Further short branches served the Lugar ironworks on the plateau above the valley of the Bellow Water and on the other side of the valley from the A&C line. At Cronberry Junction on the Airds Moss the two routes met. The Bellow Water flows south-west across the southern edge of Airds Moss and the River Ayr along the northern edge. In between is a bleak landscape scarred by numerous pit workings. Beyond Cronberry there was a short branch to serve the barytes mines near the Gass Water Burn.

The trackbed then passed under the A70 and keeping to the south of the River Ayr reached Muirkirk. There were stations at Commondyke, Lugar, Cronberry and Muirkirk. There was a passenger service of four trains on weekdays and extra at the weekends. The passenger service lasted just over 100 years closing in July 1950. The National Coal Board (NCB) operated the line between Auchinleck and Cronberry until 1976, withdrawing traffic from the Lugar ironworks sidings earlier in 1970.

For a while there were plans to reopen the line from Auchinleck to a surface mine at Powharnel, near Cronberry but these have now been abandoned.

To the east of the railway bridge across Main Street in Auchinleck lies the start of the disused branch to Muirkirk. At the junction was a two-road engine house which ceased to be used when the new shed at Muirkirk was opened in 1879. There was also a mineral line branching at Gilmilnscroft Junction 500 yards to the east, along the Muirkirk branch, which headed north.

Apart from the trackbed the area is now built-up, surrounded by housing estates. On the left to the south of the station is Coal Road which crosses the trackbed by a plate metal bridge. The trackbed edges out of Auchinleck keeping to the south of the road, with views to the south-west including the Nith Valley line heading towards Cumnock. The route skirted fields passing south of Fore Rogerton Farm before entering a wide cutting with stratified rock faces and crossing over the Auchinleck Burn high on an embankment.

This was once an area with several small communities clustered around coal pits. Today some of the remnants of the coal pits remain and there is an ever changing pattern of surface mines extracting still more coal and reshaping the countryside in their aftermath. Signs of the pithead communities are less obvious. Darnconner to the north and Birnieknowe and the Commondyke, close to the trackbed, were once bustling with their own schools, stores and churches. Most of these communities even had their own football teams like Commondyke Celtic. The names of these 'ghost villages' are now associated with farms. A visitor a century ago would have experienced a very different environment.

One remnant which stands out in the landscape, to the north as the trackbed approaches a road bridge, is a red sandstone cross (577223) (*) beside a crumbling embankment. The embankment once linked to the Muirkirk branch and led to a mine. There is a sad story behind the cross since it tells of a nun accidentally killed when struck by a steam train. The inscription reads: 'At a distance of eight feet in front of this spot, the Rev Sister Laurienne was accidentally killed on the 8th August 1888'.

Sister Laurienne, from St Patrick's church and convent, the site now occupied by a new house a short distance to the west, was looking for a lost pupil and strayed onto the railway. It is believed that she was recovering from an illness and had just returned to duties and was probably in a frail condition.

The local communities at Birnieknowe and Commondyke were shocked and some blamed the engine driver who had the unfortunate name of Goodfellow and who was known as a staunch Presbyterian. Birnieknowe and Commondyke were

Nun's Cross near the site of Commondyke station in 2010. *Author*

Commondyke station looking towards Auchinleck. *Hamish Stevenson Collection*

The site of Lugar station looking towards Muirkirk on 12th May, 1962. Lugar Iron Works sidings were to the right. *Hamish Stevenson Collection*

largely Catholic communities and passions were inflamed. Johnnie Goodfellow, a driver from the Muirkirk shed, had to go into hiding for a few months.

Commondyke station (577222) (*) is located just before the road bridge over the trackbed in Birnieknowe Glen. A crumbling brick platform is all that remains. On the day of Sister Laurienne's funeral thousands attended and the station was probably never busier. Sadly the station site is now strewn with rubbish.

The next stretch of trackbed is through a shallow tree-lined cutting, with conditions underfoot difficult.

The route emerges onto Airds Moss beside a loch. The Craigston Burn empties from the loch downhill towards Lugar through a deep gorge. Lugar station (589222) was located to the west of the loch and before the start of the Lugar ironworks sidings. A path leaves the trackbed at the site of the station but there are no remnants left.

When operational the Lugar ironworks, which opened in 1845, were situated on the valley floor, before being taken over by Bairds in 1856. Bairds moved the ironworks to the plateau above the Lugar Valley. Chimneys belching fumes and the roar of the furnaces must have made conditions in the valley below, where the workers and their families lived, unpleasant. A network of mineral lines criss-crossed the moors feeding coal and ironstone into the ironworks from the north.

There was a junction close to Lugar station which led down the western edge of the gorge towards the ironworks. At one time there was a railway bridge over the Craigston Burn to a coal mine, with a coal bing still evident. Once inside the works there were sidings to each furnace and a multitude of lines. The main mineral line into the site continued through the site and passed under a sharp bend in the road, Peesweep Brae, which led up from the valley. This was possibly a reversing siding.

The ironworks were closed in 1928 and the subsequent removal of the chimneys and blast furnaces, along with extensive tree planting, have transformed the scene masking the scars of the past. For a while the NCB headquarters and workshops used the site but this site is now occupied by East Ayrshire Council Offices and an industrial estate. Only a few rails remain embedded in the ground.

After Lugar the railway descended through a cutting curving towards Cronberry. At a junction, where a coal line split from the Muirkirk branch, is an unusual brick signal box (600225) (*) with a curved roof. The three-arch rail bridge over the Bellow Water and minor road to Cronberry has recently been demolished. The route taken by the coal line, if followed, reaches the road. The mineral line headed east to reach Cronberry Moor pit which closed in 1957 but operated for almost 40 years.

Cronberry is isolated on the moorland close to the A70 on the Airds Moss. It was built in 1862, by Bairds, to provide housing for miners and their families working on local coal and ironstone pits. The miners' rows lasted until the mid-1960s with the residents being moved to Logan. Recently there has been some private housing built. The Glasgow Rangers and Scotland football captain Eric Caldow belonged to Cronberry.

Cronberry No. 4 signal box with its unusual curved roof. *Author*

Mosshouse viaduct being demolished in 2008. The village of Cronberry is beyond the road bridge. *David S. Rutherglen*

WALK 4.3 CRONBERRY TO LUGAR STATION

Distance: 2 miles (circular route) (**).
Start: Park at Cronberry and walk north along the road until the former level crossing gate for the mineral line is reached (100 yards), where the level crossing on the mineral line was located.
Terrain: Can be muddy underfoot. Stout footwear recommended.
Facilities: None locally. Nearest shop Lugar, nearest public toilets at Tanyard, Cumnock.

Walk up towards the brick signal box and continue west towards the site of Lugar station. The details have been given in the proceeding text. Walking in from this direction avoids the poor conditions underfoot which exist east of Commondyke station site. The views over Airds Moss, the scars left over from the closed coal pits and the sense of remoteness make this walk interesting. The journey can be continued down to the site of the former ironworks at Lugar.

The railway having crossed the Bellow Water then met the A&C line at Cronberry Junction. Just to the east of the junction was Cronberry station (608226). There was a signal box at the western end of the station which controlled Cronberry Junction. The station building was a simple wooden affair and nothing of it remains. A footbridge linked the station to the village of Cronberry across the river. There is evidence of several mineral lines in this area leading to pits such as the Cairnhill pit.

The junction for the Gasswater branch (612230) was also next to Cronberry station and then passed under the A70 and led to a barytes mine and coal pits, but little of this now remains. Mining for barytes, known as barium sulphate, started in the area towards the end of World War I. Barytes has many uses, among them, in paper making and as a white pigment in paints and the railway was used to dispatch the ore south to England. There were rows of houses alongside the road but only the primary school survives as a private residence.

Cairnhill pit near Cronberry with Andrew Barclay-built 0-4-0ST (Works No. 2368 of 1955) in action on 19th June, 1968. This locomotive has been preserved by the Ayrshire Railway Preservation Group. *Hamish Stevenson Collection*

On the moors to the south of the A70 Muirkirk Road are the remnants of many other mines and disused trackbeds.

To the east of Gass Water is the opencast coal pit at Powharnel producing about 600,000 tonnes a year. Previously there had been a short-lived coal mine at Powharnel, opened in 1952 by the NCB and which closed in 1959.

Where the trackbed crosses the Bellow Water, in 1867 there was an act of sabotage by persons unknown which led to the derailing of a train, which toppled into the stream and resulted in the death of two people.

To the north is a memorial to a prominent Covenanter, the Revd Richard Cameron who was killed at this spot in what was known as the Battle of Airds Moss on 22nd July, 1680, a period known as 'The Killing Times'. The Covenanters opposed any interference from the Stuart kings in the running of the church and this led to conflict.

The trackbed continues east often parallel to the A70, Muirkirk Road before passing under the road. To the south are hills and to the east Cairn Table, a popular destination for walking groups, rises to over 1,900 ft with views from the summit as far as Ben Lomond and the island of Arran. However, an extension of the Powharnel surface mine has removed the trackbed on this stretch and the sidings at Wellwood, a coal disposal point which served yet more coal pits and lasted until 1961. The trackbed is best left until Muirkirk.

Muirkirk to Glenbuck

It was the blood-coloured iron ore known as haematite, discovered in the 1700s, which changed this area around Muirkirk or Garan as it was then known. Initially the ore was sent by pack ponies to Ayr and then to Bonawe in Argyllshire, where there was a plentiful supply of wood for conversion into coke, the ore was smelted into pig iron and then returned to the area, for conversion into wrought iron. This second process required bellows operated by water power and the source used was the River Ayr. The first ironworks closed down but mining for the ore continued.

The next development of industry in the area was the British Tar Co. which used coal deposits for conversion into tar, lampblack (fine soot) and varnish and was located at Springhill to the south of the area we now know as Kames on the old drover's road from Muirkirk to Sanquhar.

During 1787 Muirkirk received an inspection by Glasgow businessmen checking out if coal, iron ore and limestone could be profitably extracted. The result was that, despite fears over whether or not there was sufficient iron ore, a single furnace was set up and the first iron produced in 1789. A new road north to Strathaven was completed the following year providing an additional route for the finished iron to reach buyers.

John Loudon McAdam, famous for his contribution to road engineering and whose name is still associated with the 'Tarmcadam' finish, bought out the local landowner owner of the British Tar Co., in 1790. For the next eight years, before his departure for England, he was involved in the construction of roads around Ayrshire, although he didn't use the finish associated with his name at that time. Part of the reason for his departure was a dispute with Muirkirk Iron Co. over the quality of coke he provided to them. His son took over the management of the struggling British Tar Co. but the venture eventually failed. A cairn commemorating John Loudon McAdam (695256) is to be found on the site of the former tar kilns just to the south of Kames. His nickname of 'Tar McAdam' was more due to his ownership of the British Tar Co.

The year 1790 also saw a canal being dug between the iron furnace and Waukmill to the east of Muirkirk which, in the age before the railways, enabled coal and limestone to be transported more easily to the furnaces but the finished iron and the coal, at that time, still had to be carted to markets.

There were more discoveries of coal in the vicinity of Muirkirk but then to the west of Muirkirk at Wellwood there was a major discovery of iron ore. Unfortunately for the Muirkirk Iron Company they didn't own the rights and the landowner initially refused to sell the rights. Gambling that he wouldn't build rival furnaces they built more furnaces. The gamble paid off, the landowner leased the mineral rights and the future of the ironworks, the first in Ayrshire, was assured.

Around this time an ironworks was also established at Glenbuck, a small village three miles to the east, near the source of the River Ayr. The iron rails required for the construction of the Troon to Kilmarnock line were produced here.

Sometimes the ironworks ran into financial difficulties but they survived and were eventually taken over by Bairds in 1856, not long after the railway arrived in Muirkirk from the west. Chemical works were added in 1883 to utilize the waste gases from the furnaces to produce ammonia, pitch oils and other products. Gas lighting was introduced in the furnaces, before any other industrial premises in Scotland enabling continuous production.

However, by 1901 the iron ore deposits were exhausted and ore had to be shipped over from Spain. Spanish labourers were attracted to the ironworks and their families housed in the area. All this involved higher costs which eventually made the ironworks unprofitable. By 1923 they were closed. The coal pits continued to provide employment until the 1960s. In 1957 there was a tragic accident at the Kames pit (the pit was known as Kames without the extra 'i'), on the western approach to Muirkirk, when an explosion caused by a build-up of methane gas occurred and 17 men died. Sadly they were not the last to die and six more died before the mine closed in 1968, the same year as the ironworks were finally demolished.

Muirkirk is no longer an industrial town. At the turn of the 20th century its population was 5,670 and a century later it is down to under two thousand. The iron furnaces and the miners' rows to the south of the River Ayr have gone. Furnace Road still twists towards the Kames Institute with its clock tower. The first station in Muirkirk, which was in operation between 1848 and 1896, has now been converted into a motor sport race track. The building on the platform, now modernized and a café on track days, was part of the original station building which later became the station master's house when the second station opened.

The site of the second station 400 yards due east is now occupied by a road haulage contractor. It was jointly run by the CR and the G&SWR.

The engine shed was between the first station and the institute and was unusual in that railway houses were very close to it. The engine shed was a sub-

Muirkirk engine shed on 26th March, 1949, with the Kames Institute to the right.
Hamish Stevenson Collection

shed of Hurlford and at one time 12 engines were housed here but this steadily declined. The first shed opened along with the branch was a two-road affair but in 1879 after the arrival of the Caledonian Railway a new four-road shed was opened in which the Caley found some space. The four-road shed was rebuilt and reduced to a two-road shed in 1950 and closed finally in 1964 when the station and rail link was finally severed. Mineral sidings to the Kames pit fed into the station area from the north-west.

The iron furnaces dominated the scene between the station and Muirkirk were finally demolished in the 1960s. Also on the south side of the River Ayr were many miners' rows. The 'Southsiders' were considered to be an even closer community living 'cheek-by-jowl' but a community that was gradually lost and many were moved to the housing estate at Smallburn as it developed on the western approach to Muirkirk.

Walk 4.4 Muirkirk to Glenbuck

Distance: 4.5 mile or 9 miles return trip (need transport organized to collect walkers at the Glenbuck end or retrace your steps). (***)
Start: Walkers Car Park near Kames Institute, signposted from village.
Terrain: Walk follows the River Ayr Way (red markers) Weather can be extreme in winter and can change quickly. Be prepared. Stout footwear recommended.
Facilities: Shop, garage, bars in Muirkirk, no public toilets.

The walk starts at the Walkers' car park beside the Kames Institute and opposite the car race track which was the site of the original Muirkirk station. Construction of the Kames Ironworks Institute and adjoining church was started in 1903 by the furnace owners to cater for the spiritual and leisure needs of the Southsiders. The institute had a library, billiards room, function suite and baths. There was a 3*d*. weekly charge to use the library and reading room but it was well-supported by the miners and their families. After its closure it was used for a time as an outdoor centre and then an adult learning centre. Its prominent clock faces, some cynics believed, were to ensure that no one had an excuse to be late for work. The church was demolished in 1952.

The route then passes the site of Muirkirk's second station which is occupied by a road haulage company. The station had buildings on both platforms each with a canopy overhanging the platforms and glazed side partitions. On the approach to this station there was a footbridge brought from Darvel station in the Irvine Valley and erected at Muirkirk to replace a level crossing at which a young girl had been killed while trying to cross the line.

After a few hundred yards the walk eventually reaches steps that lead down onto the trackbed of the railway. This is a significant moment because for the first time, in the long journey east from Ayr, you are stepping onto a trackbed once belonging to the Caley. It was at Muirkirk station that the Glasgow & South Western Railway and the Caledonian Railway met. The CR had built a line through from Douglas, in Lanarkshire, to Muirkirk in 1874. Both companies jostled at Muirkirk, as we shall shortly find out, to encroach on the other's territory. The G&SWR wanted access to the Douglas coal field which started near Glenbuck and the CR wanted to reach the Ayrshire ports and take business away from the 'Sou'West'. This indeed was frontier territory and both railway companies were very territorial.

However, at the beginning of the walks the former CR trackbed is not closely followed. The route taken does, however, show the plethora of old tracks in the area. Also to the right of the path are the marshy remains of the Muirkirk canal. The CR trackbed is also to the right and as you emerge onto a road, at a gate, where you turn left, the abutments of a railway bridge on the former CR line can be seen. The River Ayr Walk follows the road down towards the Crossflat bridge over the River Ayr. Before the bridge the road joins another minor road. Turn onto this road and walk up the hill away from the bridge.

A short distance up the hill between two sets of bridge abutments, is a gate which leads onto the River Ayr Walk. The walk then reaches the former CR trackbed and heads east towards Glenbuck. The first bridge carried Baird's Railway, a mineral line over the road, while the other abutments supported the railway bridge which carried the CR track.

To the east the piers of Auldhouseburn viaduct (708278) can be seen crossing the valley and the River Ayr. This viaduct formed the start of a line which branched from the Caledonian route and has a central role in a curious railway story.

Towards the end of the 19th century the CR built a 'new line' as the people of Glenbuck called it from Auldhouseburn Junction next to the Auldhouseburn viaduct across the valley and turning east through the hills to reach Glenbuck. The Mid Lanark, Spireslack & Muirkirk Railway, as it was officially known, connected with the Muirkirk & Lesmahagow Junction Railway, opened in 1883, in the hills behind Glenbuck thus ensuring a through route into the Lanarkshire coalfield.

The Auldhouseburn viaduct did not, however, just cross the River Ayr. At the southern end the viaduct crossed over the Muirkirk canal which ran between Muirkirk and Waukmill to the east. The canal linked the iron furnaces to a supply of coal and limestone. The brick-lined, partially-skewed, tunnel built to allow the canal to pass under the 'new line' still remains. The next section of the

Muirkirk (Old) station looking eastwards with the ironworks in the background. The station was moved about a quarter of a mile east in 1896. *Hamish Stevenson Collection*

Muirkirk (Old) station site in 2012, looking westwards, now part of a motor sport race track. *Author*

Muirkirk (New) station looking eastwards on 26th March, 1949.
Hamish Stevenson Collection

viaduct crossed Baird's Railway, a mineral line which reached as far as Glenbuck. The piers of the viaduct south of the river remain but on the far side of the river the piers are now reduced to a heap of crumpled masonry demolished by sappers' explosives during World War II training exercise. The piers to the south were spared as the sappers were called away.

The 'new line' to Glenbuck required a major investment in two other viaducts beside the Auldhouseburn viaduct. The second viaduct was the brick-built Ponesk viaduct, over the Ponesk Burn, of which nothing remains, now lost in an

Auldhouseburn viaduct, seen here in 2012, passed over a canal which once connected Muirkirk to local pits.
Author

expanding opencast coal field. The third viaduct which lay behind Glenbuck, the Glenbuck viaduct, crossed the Stottencleugh Burn which runs through Glenbuck. The three stone piers of this tall viaduct remain for the moment while the rest of Glenbuck is being lost to opencast operations.

What is surprising about this short four-mile branch was that while fully signalled and completed, no trains ever ran on it. Some sources suggest that one inspection train did use the route but this is not confirmed. The junction signal box beside the Auldhouseburn viaduct remained for many years before the signalling equipment was removed after World War II with the brick base still remaining.

Locals claim that old mine workings made the foundations of the Auldhouseburn viaduct unsafe and that repairs were going to be too expensive. Given the many mines in the area this is certainly possible. Others, however, suggest a more complicated scenario for the trains not running on the line - it was down to manoeuvrings between the G&SWR and the CR.

The G&SWR knew the price of transport and, by the mid-1890s, many Ayrshire users were unhappy with the railway company's charges. The CR having already reached Muirkirk had promoted a line continuing through Ayrshire, which was supported by Ayrshire business men, but the Bill was lost due to an election. The Bill was again put before Parliament, this time with the short branch to Spireslack included, but the G&SWR reduced its charges, worked hard to win back the support of those promoting the Bill, and as a consequence the Bill was lost for a second time.

The CR did receive assent, however, for another Bill in 1896 which again included the Spireslack branch, along with several other lines in Lanarkshire, one of which would allow the Caley greater access into Ayrshire by linking Strathaven to Darvel. The Bill even allowed the G&SWR access when all the lines were completed. The building of the Lanarkshire & Ayrshire Railway through north Ayrshire to Ardrossan, a few years earlier, does show how desperate the CR were to gain access to Ayrshire and its ports so this might be seen as an attempt to build bridges (or tracks) between the two companies. The G&SWR, however, never gained access because while the lines were built the Spireslack branch was never opened thus denying the 'Sou'West' running rights into Lanarkshire. Also near Stonehouse in Lanarkshire a triangular junction was never completed, again to thwart the 'Sou West's' attempts to enter Lanarkshire. It is a story to gladden the heart of those who love conspiracy theories. However, it is more likely that it was the geological faults that ensured the route from Muirkirk to Spireslack never opened.

The River Ayr Walk passes the viaduct and continues east along the Caledonian trackbed towards Lanark. On the far side of the valley the Mid Lanark, Spireslack & Muirkirk Railway can be seen for a short distance. The former trackbed had continued over the road and turned towards Lightshaw Farm which is surrounded by trees. There is a short section of a substantial embankment, beyond the farm and then the opencast coalfield. In the complicated arrangements of lines a tramway from the Lightshaw pits to the north passed under the 'new line' and reached the River Ayr which the tramway crossed by two bridges. On the south side there were sidings, part of

Baird's Railway and the canal at Waulkmill. The cornerstones of the former mill are all that remain.

To the east of the farm and in the lee of the 'new line' there is a standing stone, cast there, according to local legend, by the devil angered by the sight of John Brown, a local covenanter, praying in the field.

There is an ever-changing scene on the northern flank of the valley as the coal is ripped out of the ground with the progression of the opencast coal fields towards Glenbuck.

Meanwhile the CR mainly on a low embankment on the southern flank also approaches Glenbuck as part of the River Ayr Walk. There are several missing bridges over streams, on this stretch, but the walkway provides paths around any obstacles.

The remains of the platform of Glenbuck station (744286) are found close to where the former CR trackbed and the River Ayr Walk separate. The River Ayr Walk should then be followed to its start beside Glenbuck Loch.

Situated in a narrow glen Glenbuck Loch was created by building a dam to hold back the water where the infant River Ayr began. At six o'clock each evening sluice gates were opened and the water released to flow downstream and power the mill wheels at Catrine when they were working.

The space in the valley is restricted and a causeway was required to take the railway across the loch. Access to the village of Glenbuck is not possible until opencast operations have finished.

Beside the bridge over the Stottencleugh Burn is a memorial plaque to the legendary Bill Shankly, manager of Liverpool Football Club. His tough upbringing in the mining village prepared him for the vagaries of football management and an inbred ability to motivate footballers. His brother Bob was also a very successful manager. He led Dundee Football Club to the Scottish

Glenbuck station looking eastwards on 6th July, 1957. The remnants of the platform remain today with the trackbed being used as part of the River Ayr Way.

Hamish Stevenson Collection

League Championship and to the semi-final of the European Cup in the early 1960s.

Bill Shankly never played for the local football club, the wonderfully named Glenbuck Cherrypickers. By the time he was of age, in the early 1930s, the club were folding due to lack of support. He played initially for the Cronberry Eglinton.

There are several views on how the 'Cherrypickers' got their unusual name. One of the most likely was that people who graded the coal, selected or cherry picked the different grades. Like many stories about Glenbuck the truth is lost in the mists of time. Glenbuck, like many isolated mining communities was tight knit, people bonded together by the harsh living conditions.

By the early 1930s the ironworks had long been closed and also the mines. The last pit to close was the Grasshill pit in 1933. There was no work left to support the community. People drifted away.

When the coal operations are completed the land will be landscaped and the Shankly memorial plaque moved back into the village, Bill and others, however, will no longer recognize the place.

The 'old line', behind Glenbuck over the Douglas Moors from Coalburn lasted until 1952 serving mines further east. There was no station, on this line, at the Glenbuck end.

Cumnock to New Cumnock

Just before New Cumnock is Bank Junction with a branch which splits to reach both the Knockshinnoch Washery and the coal loading point at Greenburn. The coal loading point serves local surface coal mines. The route to the surface mine at Greenburn used an old railway trackbed and even incorporated a former timber rail bridge over the River Nith with the deck being raised and concreted. Coal was sent to power stations and fireclay was extracted for brick production. There were many deep mines in the area in the past and an old waggonway which extended all the way west to Beoch and Pennyvenie pits close to Dalmellington.

Knockshinnoch became the focus of the world's attention on Thursday 7th September, 1950 when 129 miners were trapped underground at the Knockshinnoch Castle pit with 116 of them scrambling to comparative safety and 13 being cut off. Reporters flew in, from the *New York Times*, *Time* and *Life* magazines to report on the drama. Coal was being extracted too close to the surface causing a large section of ground to cave in, flooding the mine workings. Rescue efforts were initially hampered by poisonous gases but on Saturday breathing apparatus reached them and by Sunday morning 116 men were rescued with only 13 fatalities. The attention of the world shifted and Ayrshire folk were left to pick up the pieces, as usual.

South of Bank Junction is New Cumnock station and then the railway leaves Ayrshire and enters Dumfriesshire. On the border between the two counties more scenes were filmed for *Mission Impossible*. Tom Cruise was added later.

Chapter Five

Railways Around Kilmarnock

Much to the frustration of the townsfolk of Kilmarnock the first railway into Ayrshire from Glasgow bypassed Kilmarnock choosing a route through the Garnock Valley, then along the coast to reach Ayr. However, Kilmarnock was already served by the Kilmarnock & Troon Railway, a railway of historic significance, and soon by a branch from Dalry which in time continued south to Carlisle. A further branch along the Irvine Valley and eventually a direct route from Glasgow by Barrhead, along with the transfer of the G&SWR's workshops, meant that Kilmarnock had at last become a railway town. With the development of Andrew Barclay's Caledonia works, locomotive builders to the world, Kilmarnock could claim to have made a significant contribution to railway history.

The Kilmarnock & Troon Railway

At the turn of the 19th century Troon was a small hamlet surviving on fishing and salt making and, like many ports on the Ayrshire coast, part of a thriving black economy with Troon having a particular reputation for brandy and rum smuggling. The Fullartons, the local landowners, had prevented development of Troon harbour and this was enshrined in an Act of Parliament but the family line was dying out and the Fullartons were in debt.

William Henry Cavendish Bentinck, the Marquis of Titchfield, a member of a well-known and powerful family (his father was Prime Minister) married Henrietta Scott the daughter of a local landowner. Through the marriage he gained control of her family's valuable coal-bearing estate around Kilmarnock and began to look for ways to market the coal. Later in 1805 the Marquis purchased the Fullarton estates around Troon and successfully introduced a new Act of Parliament to allow him to change the status of Troon harbour. His purchase of the Fullarton Estates made him the largest landowner in Ayrshire and, with the passing of the Act, the potential to export coal from his estates was made viable by developing Troon harbour. The Marquis became the 4th Duke of Portland in 1809 on the death of his father.

The small promontory jutting out into the Firth of Clyde, which became Troon harbour, was soon transformed. By 1811 the Duke had started to develop the harbour although it was almost a further 20 years before the inner and outer harbours were completed. Houses were constructed for workers and the small town of Troon started to grow with 'feus' (leases) being offered by the Portland Estate for house building. The development of the harbour was driven by the Duke's ambition to export coal to Ireland, through Troon, and to stop using the port at Irvine a few miles away. The Duke was aware of the considerable mineral resources on his land, between the coast and Kilmarnock, and had initially considered constructing a canal between Troon and Kilmarnock.

This map is applicable to Chapters Five and Six

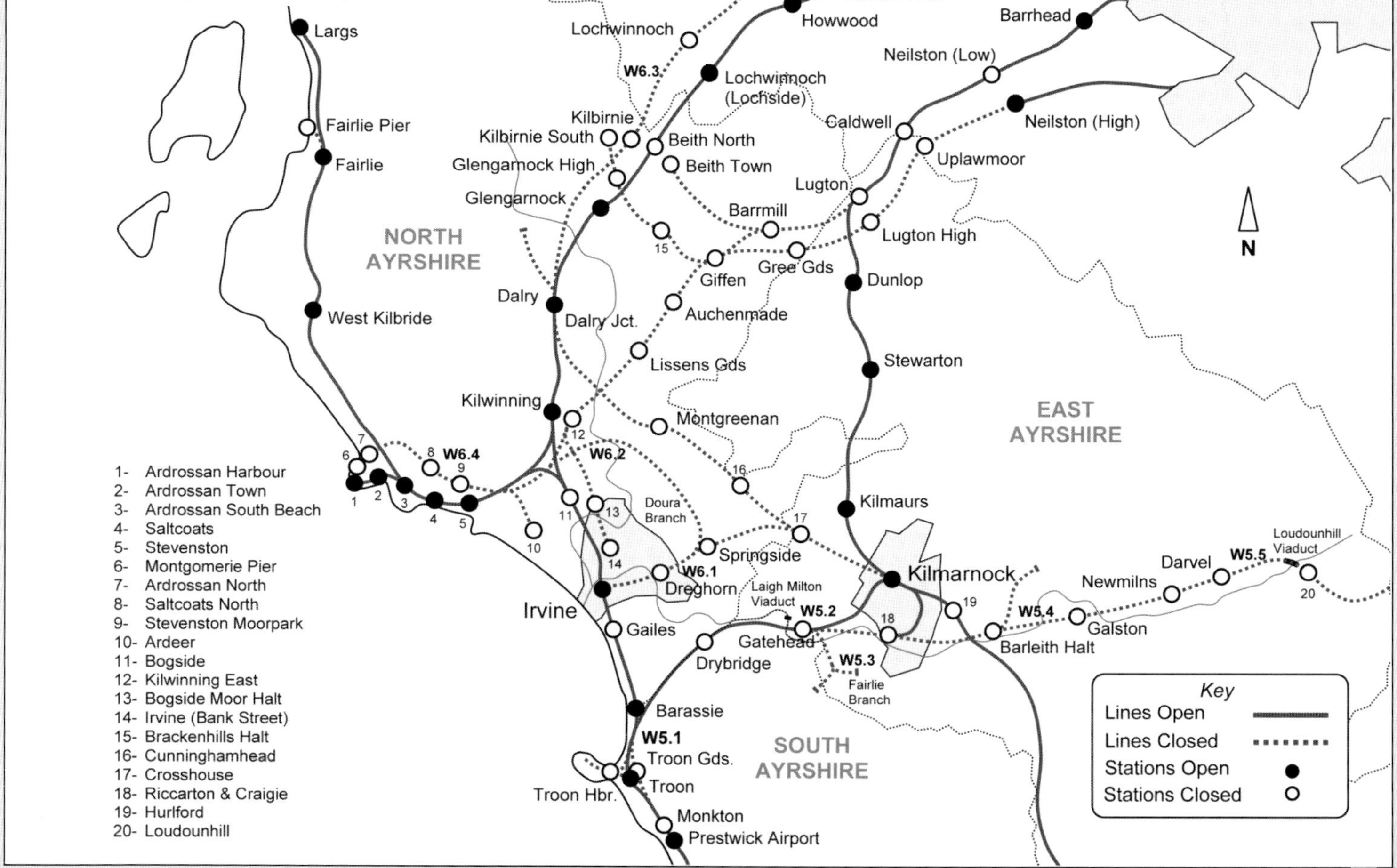

Indeed a survey had been completed but the required Bill was never passed. The alternative was to build a railway, a bold step, with few precedents anywhere at that time. In a historic development, on 27th May, 1808, the Kilmarnock & Troon Railway became the first railway in Scotland to be authorized by an Act of Parliament. The Act was necessary because the railway crossed the land of several different landowners.

William Jessop was chosen as the railway surveyor due to his experience in developing similar railway routes in England. He was a partner both in the firm of Benjamin Outram & Co., whose family company were pioneers in early canals and tramways, and also in the Butterley ironworks, which produced fish-bellied cast-iron rails, seen as an advance in railway technology. Jessop had helped Thomas Telford with the construction of the Caledonian Canal, where many temporary plateways had been required often for short distances between quarries and the canal. This, however, was a much larger project on a scale not yet seen in Scotland - a motorway compared to a minor road.

So with his background and experience Jessop was an obvious choice to survey a route between Troon and Kilmarnock. At just over 10 miles between the harbour at Troon and Kilmarnock the line rose just 80 ft or under eight feet a mile. With only one viaduct, crossing the River Irvine, the route was not too problematic although the crossing of Shewalton Moss, up to 40 ft deep in places, proved awkward and difficult to drain.

Two tracks were laid to four foot gauge. Typical of early plateways, the cast-iron rails were three foot in length; 'L-shaped' and each weighed 40 pounds. They were produced at the Glenbuck ironworks. The rails were laid with the flange of the rail on the inside and the plate on the outside, a reversed 'L'. In theory they could be laid with the plate on the inside, or the outside like the Kilmarnock & Troon Railway. The rails were then laid on blocks of stone which served to spread the load over the ground. About 70,000 stone blocks were required and most of the stones were sourced from local quarries and were about 14 inches square and six to eight inches deep (a cubic foot). Each stone had a hole drilled in it which was filled with an oak plug. The rails were produced with a niche at each end and when two rails were pressed together a hole about one inch in length was created which was placed over the plug of wood in the stone, and a nail driven in. The rails were also broader at each end to ensure more contact with the stones and higher in the middle, 'fish bellied', for additional strength along the length of the plate and to keep the wheels flat on the track. Men were employed to sweep the rails, before the horse-drawn wagons, and keep them clear of ballast and stop the ballast catching on the wheels which would have made hauling the load harder. The space between the rails was filled up almost to the top with stones to reduce the chance of the horse tripping on the stone blocks. Frequent crossover points were made along the track to allow horse-drawn wagons to overtake each other if required. What was being created could be likened to a 'motorway' in comparison to the rutted and potholed tracks which passed for roads at the time. Coal could now be transported smoothly to the coast with less effort and more quickly. Importantly, wagons and carriages did not require adaptation to use the line if their gauge was four foot.

The Duke of Portland recognised that his substantial coal deposits around Kilmarnock would provide a generous return on an investment of around £40,000 for the construction of the railway and over £100,000 for the development of Troon harbour. The Duke provided almost all of the capital for the railway with only three other minor shareholders.

Thirty years after opening there were around 12,000 journeys a year carrying 130,000 tons of coal. Those in Kilmarnock saw even greater benefits with the potential to export goods produced in the town and import goods from abroad. There was also the added attraction of travel to the coast. One early commentator, Aiton, marvelled at the Duke of Portland's foresight and enterprise, in developing the railway and a harbour at Troon, stated 'that Kilmarnock may be considered, in Ayrshire, as Manchester is in the county of Lancashire', but added, 'that a railway was more effective than a canal'.

The line took just over four years to build and its progress was followed with interest by the local population, it was history in the making. Most of the day-to-day management was left to Thomas Hollis, the site manager probably due to the increasing ill-health of William Jessop which meant that he could no longer be actively involved.

Eventually on 6th July, 1812, over 200 years ago, a railway between Troon harbour and Gargieston near Kilmarnock was opened, although one of the tracks was operational earlier than this date.

In the wider world Napoleon was about to invade Russia, President James Madison of America was asking Congress to declare war on the United Kingdom and Prime Minister Spencer Perceval has just been assassinated in the lobby of the House of Commons. In Ayrshire a revolution in transport was gathering pace with little fanfare.

Early Passenger Services

The first notification in the *Air Advertiser* of the new railway was the notification of the passenger service, which featured only in an advert inserted by William Paterson. The advert appeared on 25th June, 1812 with the service starting on Saturday 27th June before the official opening of the railway.

No mention had been made in the Parliamentary Act of the line carrying passengers. Like many railways in Ayrshire the line's economic justification was coal, but this did not seem to have been a problem to the proprietors who had accepted an offer from a local businessman, William Paterson, to run a passenger service even before the line was completed. Since the Act did not allow the railway company to levy passengers the solution was to charge tolls in the same way as coal and goods traffic. The toll was worked out on the weight of the passengers - how many passengers it took to weigh a ton! The K&TR never operated its own passenger service.

The passengers were to be conveyed by a horse-drawn carriage, and it was the first passenger service in Scotland to use a railway, beaten in the United Kingdom only by the Oystermouth, later Swansea & Mumbles Railway, which had conveyed passengers on a horse-drawn waggonway system in 1807.

The Kilmarnock terminus was close to Kilmarnock House, owned at that time by the Duke. With the terminus not yet completed the initial passenger service ran from Gargieston, an area now incorporated in Kilmarnock, which lies to the south of Dundonald Road (A759) but in 1812 was to the west of Kilmarnock.

The passenger service on the K&TR initially used two horse-drawn carriages both known as the *Caledonia* which charged 1*s*. 0*d*. per journey or 1*s*. 6*d*. return. The passenger carriage was described as a box with small windows all round with a door which was at one end. The 'box', possibly yellow in colour, sat on four cast-iron wheels. The journey would have been bumpy, the first 'carriage springs' did not appear until the 1830s. There were also no brakes, although at a speed of three miles an hour this was not a significant problem, with the driver jumping down and pushing against the carriage if a quick stop was required. Twelve passengers were carried inside, but those who chose to cling to the frame were charged a lower fare for this dubious privilege. The driver's name on that first historic journey was William Wright, sometimes spelt Wight. The service ran three days a week: Tuesday, Thursday and Saturday. The *Caledonia* left Kilmarnock (Gargieston) at 9.15 am and returned from Troon at 6 pm. The journey took up to two hours including a comfort stop for man and beast at Drybridge. Two months later, in August 1812, according to another advert in the *Air Advertiser* the service had been reduced to twice a week, now leaving Gargieston at 8.15 and returning from Troon at 4 pm. By 1st May, 1813 the Kilmarnock terminus was being used for passenger services.

The carriages raised a lot of interest and some local boys and girls used to follow them and chant:

The Caledonias, down they come
From Kilmarnock to the Troon;
A shilling up and a shilling doon,
Hey Caledonia!

Troon was referred to as 'The Troon' by the locals, possibly being derived from the Gaelic, 'An t-Sron', meaning 'the nose'. The passenger terminus in Troon was then, a coal lye, in front of the Portland Arms Inn, on the same site as the Anchorage Inn is presently located, where the passenger wagons, conveniently for the innkeeper, stopped. Some passengers did not wait to reach the Portland Arms and got off earlier at another pub, the Bottle and the Glass, to slake their thirst.

It was from such modest beginnings that railway passenger services developed throughout Scotland. There were no platforms or station buildings. A ticket office could have been anywhere, even a local tavern, and the first adverts in the *Air Advertiser* stated that tickets could be bought at the Angel Inn, Kilmarnock. Some claim that the K&TR did eventually have a ticket office, which would probably have been another first.

In the second year the fare went up, some railway practices began early, and soon after Mr Wright purchased one of the *Caledonias*. Soon a rival business started using a carriage called *The Boat*, which was no more than an open wagon. Later, in 1824, Mr Paterson sold the second *Caledonia* to a Thomas Cuthbertson and he competed with Mr Wright for business. In October 1830 a

Mrs Jean Brown was given permission to run a jaunting car on the line which suggests that the passenger service was operating for most of the year. The good folk of Kilmarnock were being the first people in Scotland to be offered the opportunity to have a day out at the seaside. A new type of tourism was emerging. The railway was a success and already showing the potential to transform society.

The introduction of steam on the Kilmarnock & Troon Railway

The Duke of Portland's wish to innovate was relentless and he ordered from George Stephenson a steam locomotive, for £750. *The Duke* was the first locomotive built for a customer outside the Killingworth Colliery where Stephenson was working at the time. The engine arrived on-site probably in 1816. The engine was named *The Duke* but it is not known whether after the Duke of Portland or to commemorate the Duke of Wellington's recent victory, over the French, at Waterloo, which was still being celebrated all over the country. Given that Stephenson's first steam locomotive was called the *Blucher* after the Prussian general at the battle of Waterloo then it seems possible that *The Duke* was named after the Duke of Wellington.

The engine was described as having six wheels. The front and rear wheels were turned by long connecting rods while the middle wheels were turned by a chain. On the centre of each axle was a wheel with teeth, on which an open chain revolved, keeping the valves in their place.

The problem was that if the surface was uneven, and horses did churn up the surface, making it uneven, then the toothed wheels dug into the rough surface, bending the teeth wheels and the rods. This problem was seemingly difficult to resolve.

The major concern was that *The Duke* was also too heavy for the track and this added to the vibration created which damaged the plates, which being of cast iron were too brittle. The demand for replacement plates increased after the engine was introduced and this was first noted around 1816, hence the theory that *The Duke* arrived in that year. The replacement rails were mainly sourced from the Kilmarnock Iron Foundry.

Thousands gathered, at a safe distance, to witness *The Duke* travelling along the track, after all until now to the people of Kilmarnock, steam engines had been stationary. A moving steam engine was a wonder to behold. The engine was thought to have been scrapped in 1838, although a silver model of it, a silver wedding present in 1914 to the then Duke of Portland, still exists.

The Duke of Portland and the Glasgow & South Western Railway

The arrival of the Glasgow, Paisley, Kilmarnock & Ayr Railway created even more opportunities for the enterprising Duke of Portland. The Duke of Portland did not, however, always enjoy a good working relationship with the GPK&AR or its successor the G&SWR and as a consequence was keen to encourage competition with the Caledonian Railway to drive down prices. Too few wagons and high, some might say extortionate rates, and a poor train service soured the Duke's relationship with the G&SWR.

As early as 1845 the Caledonian Railway was examining a possible route from Muirkirk to Ayr. This proposal was backed by the Duke of Portland and his third son Lord Bentinck who both wanted to encourage the CR to alter its route and enter Ayrshire through the Irvine Valley to reach Kilmarnock where his coal bearing land was located. With the coal pits in the Irvine Valley and around Kilmarnock the Duke hoped that this would ensure the expansion of the harbour at Troon with a steady flow of coal traffic along the 'Caledonian route' to the coast. The Duke even considered selling the Kilmarnock & Troon Railway to the CR as part of a deal.

This vision never materialized and the next year the GPK&AR, the precursor to the G&SWR, leased the Kilmarnock & Troon Railway from the Duke for 999 years, although this did not initially include Troon harbour, which the Duke's family retained until 1901 when it was vested in the G&SWR. Part of the lease agreement allowed the route to be altered to standard gauge and adapted for traction engines. The line was closed from 20th July, 1846 until 1st March, 1847 to allow the improvements to be made. The G&SWR eventually bought the line in 1899 and the K&TR was wound up.

The original Troon harbour station was replaced, on the same site, for the reopening of the K&TR in 1847. With a junction established at Barassie between the K&TR and the GPK&AR, trains for Troon Harbour and Troon station (GPK&AR) were now divided or joined up at Barassie. Previously the GPK&AR had crossed over the K&TR at Barassie.

The GPK&AR station in Troon had been opened earlier in 1839 and eventually this station became the goods station when the Troon Loop line was built.

From an early date, 1818, there was a four-mile waggonway from east of Drybridge station south-west ending south of Gatehead. The branch was built for Sir William Cunningham of Robertland to serve his coal pits. Surprisingly the gauge was narrower, at 3 ft 6 in., than that of K&TR so there cannot have been a direct link between the two waggonways. Cunningham's route was always horse-drawn and fell into disuse when the Fairlie branch opened. No trace of the route remains. There was also a mineral line to the north which crossed the River Irvine.

A branch line from the K&TR, known as the Fairlie branch and named after the local estate, served several coal pits and opened in 1849 after the G&SWR had taken day-to-day control. Fairlie Junction was to the east of Gatehead and the branch crossed the River Irvine. Several other mineral lines also fed into the K&TR.

Stations at Drybridge and Gatehead were ready for the line's reopening but did not appear continuously in the timetable until 1859. For two periods between June 1848 and May 1850 and then October 1853 until June 1859 the stations did not appear in the timetable.

The 4th Duke died in 1854 and was succeeded by his second son, the first son having died before his father. The 5th Duke was an eccentric who increasingly lived the life of a recluse, but who had inherited his father's interest in railways.

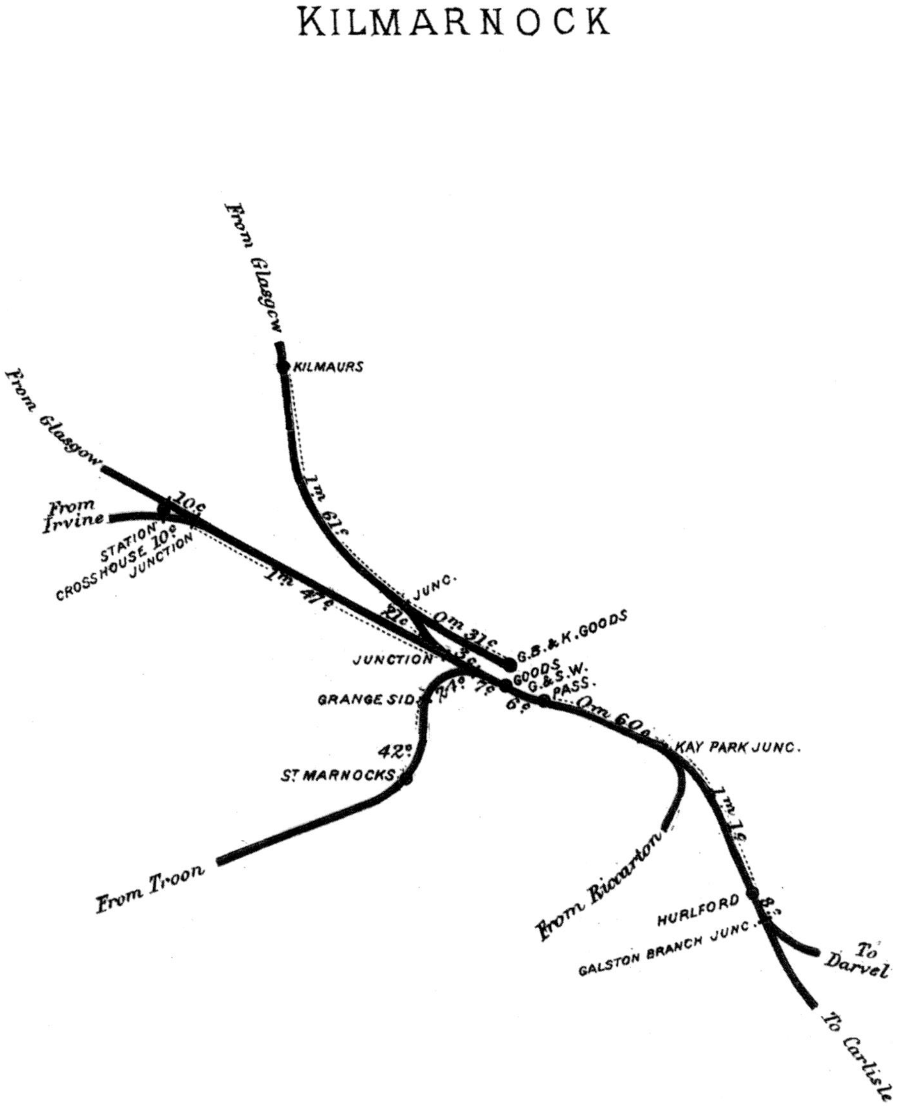
KILMARNOCK
From Glasgow
KILMAURS
From Glasgow
From Irvine
STATION
CROSSHOUSE 10c
JUNCTION
10c
1m 61c
1m 47c
JUNC.
0m 31c
G.B.& K. GOODS
JUNCTION
GOODS
G.& S.W.
PASS.
GRANGE SID
6c
0m 60c
KAY PARK JUNC.
42c
ST MARNOCKS
From Troon
From Riccarton
1m 1c
HURLFORD
GALSTON BRANCH JUNC.
To Darvel
To Carlisle

1914

By 1862 the growth of the coal traffic through Troon harbour was troubling the 5th Duke since Troon harbour was now facing stiff competition from the development of Ardrossan harbour, further north, operated by the Earl of Eglinton. Furthermore the relationship with the G&SWR had not improved since the death of his father with disputes ending up in arbitration and delaying dividend payments. With an Act passed to authorize the CR to build a route to Muirkirk the Duke, like his father, saw a chance for his businesses to attempt to persuade the CR to alter their route to take in Kilmarnock and then on to Troon. Financial inducements were prepared to encourage the CR and the Duke of Portland and his agent Captain Boland certainly hoped to ditch the 'Sou'West'. The move stalled, however, when Captain Boland, who had been a fierce critic of the G&SWR's business approach, abruptly changed tack, or should that be track, and suddenly refused to speak against the G&SWR claiming that there were no problems after all. Such a complete turnaround scuppered the case against the G&SWR and not unexpectedly the agent paid for his change of mind by losing his position with the Duke.

Kilmarnock

The Bill authorizing the GPK&AR also provided for a branch between Dalry and Kilmarnock, something that helped to placate the people of Kilmarnock and the branch line from Dalry was duly opened on 4th April, 1843.

Three years later the Glasgow, Dumfries & Carlisle Railway was authorized, which passed through Kilmarnock, and so the town was to become part of a main route to the south, which eventually opened in 1850. After initially missing out Kilmarnock had become a railway centre.

With the building of the route from Kilmarnock to Dumfries and beyond, southbound traffic faced a long haul via Kilmarnock and Dalry. Pressure again built for a more direct line and with improvements in engine design this became more feasible. After another long battle with the Caledonian Railway, who also wanted to reach Kilmarnock, a joint line called the Glasgow, Barrhead & Kilmarnock Joint Line was opened by June 1873. Southbound passenger traffic now used the joint line, which was nine miles shorter. A lot of the freight traffic, however, still used the Kilmarnock to Dalry branch with its easier gradients. There was also a local passenger service on the Kilmarnock to Dalry branch.

The arrival of the railway brought change. The K&TR was diverted from its existing terminus near the centre of Kilmarnock, and the track deviated north, from the St Marnock's mineral depot, before veering north-east to reach the GPK&AR line, from Dalry, to the west of the present Kilmarnock station. A new station had been built in Kilmarnock for the arrival of the GPK&AR but was soon replaced in 1846 by a station a few hundred yards away but situated on the still developing Glasgow to Carlisle route; thereafter the second station became the goods station with the two-storey sandstone building being incorporated into the new station until it was demolished in 1995. Kilmarnock station has a prominent position in the town at the top of John Finnie Street. The station's tall slender red sandstone Italianate tower added as part of alterations

Kilmarnock station from the south end. Ex-LMS '2P' class 4-4-0 No. 40665 waits in the bay platform in the 1960s. *Hamish Stevenson Collection*

Kilmarnock station from the south end in 2012. The Johnnie Walker buildings to the right have now been demolished. *Author*

in 1878, and a floral clock on the embankment between the station and the road are both well known local landmarks. The floral clock has been recently revamped. The canopy supports above the platforms still have the 'G&SW R Co' name incorporated into their design. The K&TR terminus had been located almost at the bottom of what was to become John Finnie Street but the street, a later development, was not built until 1864.

An engine shed was established in Kilmarnock shortly after the arrival of the railway in 1843 to the west and north of the station and later a turntable and a further shed was added by 1857. The early sheds were replaced later by a single shed, with four roads, with space for about a dozen engines with further expansion not possible in the confined space. With the Kilmarnock area providing increasing business for the G&SWR and no more space for expansion, in February 1873 it was decided that the company should move to a new site over two miles away at Hurlford, close to the junction for the Darvel branch, where there were no restrictions on space.

With insufficient space at the G&SWR's workshop in Cook Street, Glasgow, Kilmarnock benefitted with the transfer of the workshop to Kilmarnock. The G&SWR Kilmarnock works opened in 1856 in the space to the left of the Troon branch on its curving approach to the main line. For a while carriages and wagons were also serviced at the site but pressure of space caused the carriage and wagon works to be moved to Barassie in 1902.

The industrial age favoured Kilmarnock and the inventiveness and engineering skills of men like Andrew Barclay and Thomas Kennedy brought much attention to the town and, for a while, wealth. Andrew Barclay had a knack of understanding and adapting machinery, starting with looms for weaving carpets, then designing and building steam engines. He patented improvements to gas lighting equipment but had to sell the patent as he required the money to survive after an unfortunate accident had almost killed him. However, in 1859 he produced his first locomotive and the company eventually became famous all over the world, including building fireless locomotives. Andrew Barclay even found time to help Thomas Kennedy to improve the design of his first water meter. Investments in ironworks overstretched Barclay's finances and almost brought his company down as did the money required to support his hobby - building a giant telescope to observe the night sky. Despite financial problems the company survived until it was bought up in 1972. The company has had several owners since 1972 including TELFOS Holdings and was known as Hunslet-Barclay then Brush Barclay. Presently the company, which still has premises close to Kilmarnock station, is operated by Wabtec Rail Scotland. Brodie Engineering, which refurbishes railway stock, also has premises near to Kilmarnock station at Bonnyton Industrial Estate.

Glenfield & Kennedy Ltd was another important Kilmarnock company, known all over the world for its water valves and was founded by Thomas Kennedy in 1865. Kennedy merged with a local company, the Glenfield Iron Co. in 1899, as both companies realised that a merger made sense. The merger was a success and Glenfield & Kennedy, or the 'Glen' as the company was known locally at one time, employed over 2,500 people and like Barclays did much to

Ex-LMS '2P' class 4-4-0 No. 40662 on a Kilmarnock to Darvel train waiting to leave platform 4. Kilmarnock shed and part of the Johnnie Walker plant are in the background.
Hamish Stevenson Collection

Riccarton & Craigie station looking towards Kilmarnock. *Hamish Stevenson Collection*

substantiate the claim that the town was Ayrshire's industrial capital. In the early 1970s, however, profits and demand for their products fell and in June 1977 the works, located to the south of the town, closed, although like Barclays they have been acquired by a series of companies. Known firstly as Biwater Valves Ltd they are now operating as Glenfield Valves. Other local industries like weaving and carpet manufacturing, also once important, have now disappeared from the town. Carpet manufacturing became established due to innovation introduced by another local man Thomas Morton and manufacturing of shoes, by Saxone, was also established in the town

Another famous Kilmarnock businessman was Johnnie Walker whose range of blended whisky was developed at his grocer's shop in Kilmarnock. The square bottles with the slanting labels and motto 'born 1820, still going strong' is also renowned around the world. Now part of the Diageo Group the bottling plant at Kilmarnock has been moved to Fife breaking the link of this iconic whisky brand with the town, much to the frustration of locals. The former red brick Johnnie Walker's bottling plant overlooks Kilmarnock station, a forlorn symbol of a great past which no one in Kilmarnock will now want to toast.

Immediately east of Kilmarnock station the railway crosses the 23-arch Kilmarnock Water viaduct and shortly after Kay Park Junction is reached and the start of the Riccarton Loop which joins the Gatehead and Hurlford lines at Bellfield Junction. The Gatehead & Hurlford line, a late addition to the railway network, opened in 1902. It left the K&TR at Thirdpart Junction and passed, when opened, to the south of Kilmarnock. Today the section of the Gatehead & Hurlford line to the south of Kilmarnock is lost to the A71 Kilmarnock to Irvine road (Kilmarnock bypass). Most of the Riccarton Loop, which opened in 1904, remains serving the Scottish Fuels Depot, near Riccarton. There were further sidings, at various times, connecting to the Glenfield works sidings which served the Glenfield & Kennedy engineering works and sidings to the gas and electricity power stations, now demolished, which earned revenue for the railway. Also located on the Gatehead & Hurlford line was Riccarton & Craigie station, built for a passenger service but the station never had a regular service, apart from the occasional 'specials' and was used as a goods station. The station had an island platform and a glass-paned overhanging canopy and certainly looked as if it was intended for use by passengers. The station closed in 1965. The oil depot occupies what was once the goods yard and the station site is now beneath the elevated road bypass close to Campbell Street.

Riccarton, not to be confused with the iconic Riccarton Junction deep in the Scottish Borders, was once a small village separated from Kilmarnock to the north by the River Irvine. With the expansion of the nearby Glenfield works in Kilmarnock the village grew rapidly.

The additions to the rail network around Kilmarnock were useful. The Riccarton Loop meant that trains bound for Troon did not have to reverse at Kilmarnock station. The loop was also useful when the viaduct over the River Irvine was damaged by floods in 1932 and trains were diverted via Kilmarnock. At busy times trains could use the Gatehead & Hurlford line to bypass Kilmarnock and special trains coming along the Irvine Valley to the coast could also use it to avoid delays. It was mooted that the G&H line would enable coal

Barleith Halt, Hurlford looking towards Kilmarnock in 1959. *Hamish Stevenson Collection*

The site of Barleith Halt in 2012 with Hurlford to the right and the former Johnnie Walker warehouse to the left. *Author*

from the Lanarkshire pits to reach the harbour at Troon and avoid congestion at Kilmarnock. However, by the time the route from Strathaven in Lanarkshire opened the Rothesay docks in Glasgow were becoming operational and the opportunity was largely lost. East of Bellfield Junction the G&H line veered south-east, passed under the railway from Kilmarnock to Carlisle (south of Barleith) and joined the route to Darvel at Mayfield Junction.

The Riccarton Loop does have one sad footnote in history. Kilmarnock suffered from only one bombing raid during World War II. It is believed that that German bombers spotted glowing embers from a steam train, near Kay Park Junction, dropped bombs on the area and killed four people in the town's Culzean Crescent. In 2010, nearly 70 years after the raid a memorial plaque, on a bench, was unveiled in the street.

Kilmarnock to Hurlford

Continuing from Kilmarnock the route crossed the seven-arch Hurlford viaduct over the River Irvine. Hurlford station was the next station on the main line. Opening with the route in 1848 the station closed on 7th March, 1955 and no remnants of the station, which was located just south of the road bridge (A71) over the railway line, remain. There were sidings to serve Portland ironworks and local coal pits near Hurlford station. Fireclay deposits found near Hurlford, close to the River Irvine, were used to make glazed facing bricks for buildings.

South of Hurlford station was Hurlford Junction, where the Darvel branch left the main line at the start of its journey along the Irvine Valley. In the vee of the junction was the Hurlford locomotive shed. The locomotive sheds at Hurlford were at the centre of the G&SWR's operations in Ayrshire. Initially planned for 40 engines, just prior to World War I it had an allocation of 92 engines. Beside the sheds were offices, stores and accommodation for workers. The site also included a coaling stage for fuelling locomotives. Mineral sidings, busy with the traffic from local pits, formed an important part of the Hurlford operation. Barleith Halt, a wooden platform for use by workers living in the railway village, was opened on the Darvel line. The station was opened around the turn of the 19th century and closed on 6th April, 1964. From 1933 until 1944 it was renamed Barleith. No trace remains with the site having being cleared.

Along with the Beeching cuts and the loss of passenger services and the concentration of coal production at super pits in Ayrshire, like Barony and Killoch, the importance of the Hurlford shed waned and it was closed on 3rd October, 1966. The sheds were demolished, the sidings removed and travellers on the train would now be unaware of the existence of the site. Johnnie Walker built warehouses for storing whisky on the site and at one time the warehouses were served by railway sidings. The warehouses are now used as a distribution centre.

Loudounhill viaduct on 12th May, 1962. *Hamish Stevenson Collection*

Loudounhill viaduct approach with Loudoun Hill in background 2012. *Author*

The Irvine Valley

The railway system also expanded along the Irvine Valley and eventually in 1905 a through connection was made from Darvel to Strathaven in Lanarkshire. The Irvine Valley with its coal deposits and towns of Galston, Newmilns and Darvel famous for their weaving and textile industry provided more business. Passenger services along the Irvine Valley usually ran from platform four next to the Johnnie Walker bottling plant.

Beyond Darvel there was a gap in the railway network between Ayrshire and Lanarkshire. Again the 'Sou'West' and the Caley faced off, each anxious to enter the others' territory and gain business but they eventually agreed to joint working with each taking six month turns to operate the route. The 11-mile gap was completed, by the Caledonian Railway, including the construction of the impressive 13-arch Loudounhill viaduct, to the east of Darvel, and the section within Ayrshire. Business never flourished, with part of the railway eventually being used to store wagons waiting to be broken up.

Exploring the Railway Heritage

The Kilmarnock & Troon Railway

It is worthwhile taking the opportunity to travel along the Kilmarnock & Troon Railway and to watch out for the places mentioned. The section of the line still in use starts at Barassie station and finishes at Kilmarnock station. The 'Kilmarnock platform' at Barassie has been removed. Passengers using the line need to get on at an earlier station en route.

Troon

Troon is an attractive seaside resort, within easy commuting distance of Glasgow. The rail link allows residents to commute the 30 miles to Glasgow and encourages visitors attracted by a day at the sea or to play golf. There are beaches to the north and south of the harbour and a seasonal ferry link to Larne in Northern Ireland. The inner harbour is now a popular yacht marina, a centre for leisure pursuits.

There is little left to link with the railway network which once extended round both sides of Troon harbour. The harbour station (315311) and the engine shed opposite were located close to the eastern edge of what is now the Troon Marina (former inner harbour) and the roundabout at the entrance to the ferry terminal, opposite Templehill and the Anchorage Hotel, where there is now a grassy knoll. The railway sidings to each side of the harbour forked at this point. The Troon railway terminus, before the harbour was developed, was referred to as 'the Point' and was located where the Ballast Bank, a hill created by the dumping of ballast from boats using the harbour, is now situated. Usefully the

Ballast Bank provides the harbour with protection from south-westerly winds gusting up the Firth of Clyde.

Despite the G&SWR taking over the running of the K&TR, Troon harbour was not part of the arrangement and the harbour company used its own engines until the 1860s. There was an earlier engine shed operated by the Portland Estates near Templehill. The engine shed, which the G&SWR inherited at the harbour, however, may have been of later construction. It had two arches and its engines were used in shunting at Troon and Irvine harbours and along the K&TR. The 'Sou'West' took over the operation of the harbour in 1901. The Troon engine shed closed in 1935 and no trace remains of the station or shed. Later in the 1960s, at the end of the steam era, engines, some very famous, were brought to the harbour area to be broken up. From 1860 until 2000 Ailsa-Troon shipbuilding yard occupied part of the harbour and there were sidings to serve the yard. The large shed belonging to the shipyard, a local landmark for many years, has now been demolished. The branch lines to the harbour were all closed by the end of 1973.

When the Troon Loop line was built in the early 1890s, the railway was brought closer to the town and the harbour, although most of the land to the east of the new station was undeveloped. The new Troon station, designed by James Miller, to great critical acclaim, is still an attractive landmark (*). The single-storey buildings on each side of the line were timber-framed with external rendering and connected with steel-framed awnings, with a covered footbridge. The 'seaside' design as it was described appealed to the up and coming seaside resort, which was becoming popular with commuters and golfers visiting the many fine local courses. The station buildings with timber framing and external rendering still remain but the elaborate steel-framed awnings and a covered footbridge have been modified, a consequence of electrification. The station on its elevated position is a local landmark with four access roads, two on each side, leading up to the station concourses.

Troon Harbour The famous LMS 'Duchess' Pacifics arrived from Carlisle in December 1964 for scrapping. *Hamish Stevenson Collection*

A spur was built from just south of the new station (Troon Junction) to the harbour, completing a triangular junction with the K&TR and the loop line, which eased the flow of freight traffic to the harbour. The course of the spur can be detected from the elevated view, provided from Troon station, as there is a line of more recent buildings curving towards the harbour following the route of the spur.

The original GPK&AR route which became known as the Troon Avoiding Line closed to passenger trains in 1966, except for the Glasgow Central to Stranraer Harbour service, and eventually closed completely in 1982 due to the remodelling of Barassie Junction. The line continued as a long siding from just north of what was Troon goods station (Troon Old station) to Barassie Junction. The tracks remain in this section. Close to Barassie Junction was the site of Barassie carriage and wagon works.

Walk 5.1 Troon Avoiding Line - Lochgreen Junction to Barassie Junction

Distance: 2 miles – one way (***).
Start: beside the railway bridge over the disused railway line on the B749 Craigend Road (335299). The route is signposted as part of National Cycle Route 7 and is also part of the 19 mile Ayrshire Coastal Route between Irvine and Ayr.
Terrain: Tarmac footpath.
Further options: on reaching Barassie Junction the walker can retrace their steps or return by Beach Road along the sea front to the harbour. Troon station is clearly signposted from the harbour. From the station head south and turn left onto Willockston Road which leads back to the pathway.
Facilities: Troon has many cafes, restaurants and bars, public toilets at The Tower Hotel, Beach Road, Church Street and St Meddans Street, Troon.

Looking south, at the start, is Ayr Bay with the Carrick Hills as a backdrop and the golf courses of Royal Troon, another Ayrshire golf course used for the British Open Championship. Also to the south is the site of Lochgreen Junction where the avoiding line merged with the present railway.

Follow the signs and once on the disused trackbed turn and pass under the road bridge over the route. Ahead is a tarmac path following the line of the trackbed. To the right is Lochgreen Golf Course and to the left are the back gardens of houses. The Ayrshire Polo Club ground filled the increasing gap between the two rail tracks before houses were built on the site. The avoiding line was double track and useful to ease congestion on the Troon Loop. The morning Glasgow Central to Stranraer Harbour express would hurtle along this stretch much to the enjoyment of trainspotters.

The trackbed passes the end of Willockston Road, named after former barracks in the area, and approaches the next road overbridge at Dundonald Road (A759). There are now three more golf courses to the left, Darley, Fullarton, both like Lochgreen run by the local council, and Troon Welbeck - golfers' paradise. To the right is the local cemetery protected by high stone walls.

Troon Avoiding Line looking towards Lochgreen Junction in July 1982.
. *Hamish Stevenson Collection*

Troon looking towards Lochgreen Junction in 2012. *Author*

Troon Old station. The footbridge to Marr College is in the background with the dome of Marr College to right. *Hamish Stevenson Collection*

The trackbed passes under Dundonald Road with the road bridge also having been doubled in width. Immediately to the left after the bridge was Troon goods station (332312), the site of the original station in Troon, before the loop line was built. The original buildings on the left of the trackbed remain albeit modified, and are now a private residence partly obscured behind a wooden fence. The buildings on the right of the former trackbed have been demolished. Sidings to the west of the goods station have been replaced by part of a small housing estate.

Beside the trackbed is the entrance to Marr College. The green coppered dome and fine stone buildings of Marr College, the local secondary school, are a local landmark. The funds for the school were left by Charles Kerr Marr to the people of Troon for the building of a school. Marr had been born in Troon but had worked elsewhere, mainly in London, and was involved in the shipping trade. Legal difficulties concerning the bequest delayed the opening of the school until September 1935. Construction work on the school, however, started in the 1920s and a railway siding was added at the Troon goods station to bring quarried stone to the building site. To improve access to the school an elaborate footbridge was built over the railway in 1933. In 1953 British Railways had cause to complain that some of the concrete cladding was falling from the footbridge onto the line and was creating a hazard for trains on the avoiding line. The footbridge was eventually demolished in 1977 at the time that a possible electrification of the route was being considered. The building of Marr College encouraged people to move to Troon and led to further housing developments in the town.

Beyond the site of the former goods station are the Barassie sidings which extend for about a mile. The footpath now runs beside the sidings. Slowly the number of sidings increase as Barassie Junction is approached. Originally this section was part of the avoiding line. In 1902 the G&SWR moved its wagon building and repair facility to Barassie. They were busy for many years but gradually went into decline, losing the wagon building shop and then finally in 1973 they were closed. The sidings were used as an engineer's base when the Ayr line was being electrified in the late 1980s. Barassie Junction, where the sidings meet the main line, is located just before a road bridge over the railway.

Barassie looking towards Glasgow on 29th July, 1982. *Hamish Stevenson Collection*

Barassie in 2012 with the Kilmarnock line now singled and many changes to the station site. *Author*

Kilmarnock Road (B746) which crosses over the railway offers views to the north towards Barassie station which has a vee-shaped platform. The now-singled railway line to Kilmarnock branches to the right and the Glasgow line heads north. Road realignment has moved the road south of the station. The vee shaped platform is now denuded of the buildings which once occupied the northern end. A lawn and shrubbery once occupied most of the triangle. One night the turf was lifted, it is believed by a railway employee for his use in his own garden, and a full investigation resulted. Beyond the station is Kilmarnock Barassie Golf Club.

On 4th February, 1898 there was a collision at Barassie Junction and seven people died and eight were injured when due to driver error a passenger train and a goods train collided head-on. The momentum of the collision caused the wagons and carriages to smash into the tenders and pile up.

Barassie started as a railway community around the junction and became known locally as 'New Kilmarnock' because those, who in Kilmarnock could afford it, enjoyed a commute to the coast and built a house by the sea. A walk back along Beach Road shows many examples of grand houses. Later Barassie grew as a consequence of extensive housing development.

Beach Road leading to North Shore Road

Returning by Beach Road is a pleasant walk along the promenade with views across the Firth of Clyde to Arran and towards the harbour. To the left there is a footbridge over the line. From here looking south the junction of the main line with K&TR can be seen. The trackbed of the harbour branch has been largely built over.

Barassie Station to Kilmarnock

On 10th February, 1974 the Barassie-Kilmarnock line was reduced to single track and worked as one section. Grange, St Marnocks and Shewalton Moss signal boxes were closed with ground frames being provided at the last two to permit access to sidings. In 1976 the level crossing gates at Gatehead were replaced by unmanned lifting barriers. Drybridge and Gatehead stations closed on 3rd March, 1969.

From Barassie Junction the line passes between Kilmarnock Barassie golf course and a housing estate before passing under the A78. Shortly after there is a half-mile siding, opened in 1988, leading to the Caledonian Paper Mill. The paper mill specializes in glossy paper finishes and as a consequence there was a weekly train supplying china clay from Cornwall, one of the longest regular freight journeys in the UK; but the Cornwall clay mine has now closed and the clay is imported from Belgium. No timber is delivered by rail.

The next section which takes the trackbed across Shewalton Moss is very straight and the trackside is mostly tree lined. The Hillhouse whinstone quarry to the right of the track was rail connected when the quarry commenced operations in 1907. A rail bridge still crosses the road to sidings beside the railway but the sidings have been disconnected.

Drybridge station looking towards Kilmarnock on 25th July, 1963. *Hamish Stevenson Collection*

Gatehead station looking to Kilmarnock on 29th September, 1966. *Hamish Stevenson Collection*

The site of the demolished Shewalton Moss Litter Factory and the Shewalton Coup which has now been closed, lie to the left. There are several sidings remaining but with saplings growing through the track the sidings have not seen recent service. Rubbish was dumped at the site for many years, often brought by rail. Some of the sidings had no buffers and trains reversing along the siding faced the hazard of wagons dropping off the end of the track. It is believed that a number of wagons met this fate and could not be retrieved.

In what is an industrial area the trackbed continues past the Olympic Industrial Estate, part of the former Monsanto nylon textile factory, and once a major employer in the area, which closed in 1980. The site was partially built over RAF Dundonald and one of the aircraft hangers of the former airfield remains. To the south is Dundonald Castle, perched on a hill, the favourite residence of King Robert II with most of the tower remaining. The castle dates back to the 14th century and has been recently restored. Nestling beneath the castle is the village of Dundonald.

Drybridge station was located to the west of the B730 and some of the station buildings remain along with most of the platforms. To the east of the bridge were sidings to the north of the line. Tradition claims that the hamlet got its name because it was the first bridge in Ayrshire not to cross a river, hence a 'dry bridge'.

The trackbed continues crossing the River Irvine and reaching Gatehead, where there was a station and signal box with only part of the platform, to the west of the unmanned level crossing, remaining. Gatehead had many local pits and even a distillery which closed around 1840. Robert Burns hid at Old Rome, just across the river from Gatehead, from Jean Armour's family, who were searching for him because he had made her pregnant.

As the train crosses the present five-arch River Irvine viaduct, en route to Gatehead, an older viaduct can be seen to the north. This is the original Laigh Milton viaduct, opened in 1812, the oldest surviving multi-span bridge in Scotland and one of the oldest surviving multi span bridges in the world.

Walk 5.2 Laigh Milton Viaduct

Distance: 0.5 mile – round trip (***).
Start: Car park beside the ruined Laigh Milton Mill (384373).
Heading towards Kilmarnock, take the first minor road on the left, once past the unmanned level crossing in Gatehead. Follow the minor road past a farm on the left until a car park is reached.
Terrain: Can be very muddy. Stout footwear recommended.
Facilities: Restaurant and shops in Gatehead. No public toilets.

The four-arch viaduct (383369) crosses the River Irvine on 44 ft-span freestone segmental arches at a height of 25 ft above the river. It is about 270 ft in length and 19 ft across. The viaduct was closed in 1846.

By 1992 the first viaduct was in a poor state with the first arch sagging (Troon end) and the head of the next arch had become misshapen. There were also a number of cracks on the stone work. The Laigh Milton Viaduct Conservation Project was formed to raise funds to preserve the viaduct from collapsing. The Directors bought

Laigh Milton viaduct in 2011. *Author*

Laigh Milton display of waggonway rails on restored viaduct 2011. *Author*

the viaduct for £2 and were successful in raising over a million pounds. The contract was awarded to Barr Construction Ltd and restoration completed within budget. For all railway enthusiasts this was a wonderful outcome.

During restoration when the deck was lifted the space between the outer walls was found to have been infilled with boulder clay. The outer walls were found to be acting as gravity retaining walls, also gaining some lateral support from the bull-nosed buttresses above the pier.

Iron railings have been added and a short section of rails in the original style has been laid on the viaduct with interpretative boards. Beyond the western end of the viaduct is evidence of coal workings. The Fairlie coal pit No. 3 was located here with sidings from the K&TR. The coal workings required a further shift in the trackbed and the building of the present viaduct.

The present viaduct, built in 1865, is ½ mile upstream and between the two was another viaduct, wooden in construction, with a short section of embankment leading from its eastern side the only visible remnant. This viaduct replaced the first one when the railway was converted to standard gauge in 1846-1847, when the first viaduct proved unsuitable for conversion. The present viaduct, the third one, effectively removed a loop in the railway.

Further down stream from Laigh Milton Mill, on the same bank, is Craig House, which has been restored from its previous ruinous state and converted into luxury apartments.

To the east of the viaduct there were mineral railways running north to Gatehead Pit and Thornton Pit, the latter being just to the west of Crosshouse.

Laigh Milton detail of plate joint. *Author*

Gatehead to Fairlie Junction

To the east of Gatehead there were connections to further coal pits. The Fairlie branch veered south and crossed the river to serve several coal pits. The lands are still owned by the Cunninghame-Fairlie family.

The abutments of the railway bridge over the River Irvine remain as does much of the trackbed. Two railway bridges over a minor road south of Gatehead and over the B751 remain. The trackbed ends abruptly after crossing the B751 near Templeton Farm (395346). (*) There is a section of embankment to the north which disappears once the bridge is crossed. There is some suggestion that the trackbed was planned to be continued to reach other mines but that this was abandoned. There were also a number of pits in the immediate vicinity. From the Fairlie branch there was a branch to the east passing to the south of the small village of Earlston and continuing further east to Shortlees with links to coal pits.

WALK 5.3 BLACKSYKE TOWER-EARLSTON TO THE B7038

Distance: 1.5 miles (***).
Start: A public footpath follows the line of an old waggonway, latterly part of the Fairlie branch, from the southern end of Earlston (407353) to beside a garden centre on the B7038 (former Ayr Road). The path crosses Caprington Golf Course, so beware of golf balls!
Terrain: Conditions underfoot can be muddy.
Facilities: Garden centre with a café at the far end of the walk. No public toilets.

The public footpath sign at the southern end of the Earlston shows the start of the path. The footpath turns south-west after a short distance and continues to the edge of the golf course. Ahead is a ruined tower.

On the approach to the tower is a limekiln with an arch at each end, with a rectangular metal grate, in each, set at the back. There is a ramp to the top of the limekiln enabling coal and limestone to be fed in from the top.

A few yards after the limekiln is Blacksyke Tower (416323), this is also known as Caprington Tower or sometimes Lusk's Folly. There were several other buildings around the tower. The tower itself is the ruined remains of a three- or four-storey square plan industrial building. There is a telegraph pole fixed to the projecting chimney flue and turret.

The tower has always attracted interest and people have been intrigued by its purpose. Some consider it a folly, made out to look like an historic ruin. To the north but hidden behind trees is the home of the Cunninghame family, Caprington Castle, who still live in the castle. In times past they would have been able to survey the land from the castle and the number of pits being developed on their land. A 'ruin' or folly, concealing industrial premises, would have been more attractive to the residents of the castle than industrial workings and the thinness of the stone walls supports the theory that this was not an ancient building. The building is grade C listed.

So what was the purpose of the building? Many believe that the building was an early signal box, one of the first. Beyond the tower there were several branch lines leading to coal pits. The tower, however, predated the railway. Another suggestion is that wagons of coal passing the tower could have given tokens in at the tower so that coal loads could be tallied. Something similar could have operated on the Doura branch close to Eglinton Country Park (*see Chapter Six*).

However, the tower was built to house one of the oldest Newcomen-type atmospheric beam pumping engines. It was built by the Carron Iron Co. in the 1770s and in the early 19th century was installed second-hand at Caprington Colliery where it worked for 95 years pumping water from the coal pit. The Caprington pit closed around 1924. A cast-iron beam replaced the original wooden one in 1837. The engine had a 30 inch bore and a stroke of 54 to 60 inches in a 96 inch-long cylinder. The engine was given to the local museum in 1901 and then transferred to the Royal Museum of Scotland in 1958. It was only when the Museum of Scotland was opened in 1998 that funds were found to restore the engine and it's now part of an exhibit at the National Museum for Scotland.

Beyond the tower are hedges which almost seem to point in the direction of former branch lines. The end of the walk on the former Ayr Road (B7038) is beside a garden centre.

Blacksyke Tower, seen in 2011, which housed a Newcomen engine to extract water from nearby pits. *Author*

Fairlie Junction to Kilmarnock

The former K&TR continues north of the river and passes Moorfield Industrial Park, on the approach to Kilmarnock. Thirdpart Junction the start of the Gatehead & Hurlford line was at the western edge of the industrial park. Moorfield Park was also the location of the Massey-Ferguson tractor and combine harvester factory, attracted to the Kilmarnock area after the war and which once employed 1,500 people but closed in 1980, another severe blow to the local economy. At considerable expense a siding was built to the plant but was never used because there were no wagons capable of carrying the combine harvesters.

The railway then passes under two new bridges, the second being the A71 Irvine bypass and enters Kilmarnock. The Gargieston temporary terminus was a short distance after the railway passed under the Irvine bypass, to the south of Mount House but the exact location is not known. Rugby Park, the home of Kilmarnock Football Club, is then seen to the right where the St Marnock's mineral depot was located. The route then continues to the present Kilmarnock station, passing at the junction with the Barrhead line, Kilmarnock signal box.

St Marnock's mineral depot has now been redeveloped as a housing estate. From north of Rugby Park the original K&TR crossed South Hamilton Street, south of No. 25, and then cut across the town to the corner of what is now Dundonald Road and Portland Road. The line taken by the railway can still be seen with the walls of some gardens being at an unusual angle, clipped by the line of the former railway trackbed.

The original terminus was next to Kilmarnock House and the railway, according to John Wood's Kilmarnock map of 1819, extended more towards Nelson Street but the precise location is unclear. Kilmarnock House has been demolished and the site occupied by the Procurator Fiscal's Office on St Marnock's Street, next to Bank Street, and this is the probable site of the original terminus which was in operation until around 1821. This is in the north-west angle of the crossroads, opposite the Episcopalian Church. Howard Park to the south once formed part of the grounds of Kilmarnock House.

The Holy Trinity Episcopal Church halls (426377) (*) completed by 1896, now occupies the site of the second terminus when the original terminus was moved to this site as the Duke of Portland required the land.

Dalry Junction to Kilmarnock

The section between Kilmarnock and Crosshouse station is covered in Chapter Six as part of the Busby Branch Walk (6.1)

Between Kilmarnock and Dalry, on the 11¼ mile route, were Crosshouse station, originally called Busby station where the Busby branch departed for Irvine, Cunninghamhead station and Montgreenan station and for a short time Dalry Junction station. Local passenger traffic was light with no towns along the route. There were a number of coal pits along the route especially near Montgreenan, where the line passed close to the Doura branch.

Montgreenan station looking towards Kilmarnock in June 1959.
Hamish Stevenson Collection

In recent years the state of the trackbed has deteriorated and the two principal viaducts between Crosshouse station and Dalry Junction, the three-arch viaduct over the Annick Water (364418) and the five-arch viaduct over the Lugton Water (329429), have both been fenced off requiring long detours.

Montgreenan station (340434) (*) located on the minor road north of Benslie opened on 1st February, 1878 and lost its passenger service on 7th March, 1955 and freight services in October of the same year. A siding was in use at the station site for coal traffic three years before the station opened. Access to the platforms was by steps leading down from the road overbridge. The main station building, to the right looking towards Dalry, had red sandstone facing and an awning. The siding was located behind the station building. A goods shed was added later. Local mining communities, at Benslie and Fergushill, and the Montgreenan and Eglinton estates, supported the passenger service until the inhabitants were rehoused in Kilwinning. The remote station even received a visit from King George VI when the Royal train stopped to allow the King to have his lunch. When the army took over the Eglinton Estate in 1942 they used the station. The platforms have been removed but the main station building remains and is now a private residence.

Cunninghamhead station (369414) is found where the B769 crosses over the line by a fine skew-arched bridge. The station opened on 4th April, 1843 as Stewarton but closed on 22nd May, 1848. The station was back in the timetable in November 1850 and was eventually renamed Cunninghamhead on 1st September, 1873 when the Glasgow, Barrhead & Kilmarnock line began operations. The station closed to passengers on 1st January, 1955 and for freight in February 1960.

Apart from serving the small village of Cunninghamhead and the nearby Cunninghamhead Estate there was a lot of business generated by local farms. There were also a goods shed and extensive cattle docks. Nothing remains of the station buildings and there is little to associate the site with the railway. The main station building was similar to that at Stewarton.

Rails leading to the former Andrew Barclay Caledonia works (now Barclay House) with multi-gauge tracks in 2012. *Author*

Andrew Barclay 0-4-0T No. 2086 *Drake* on exhibition at Barclay House. *Author*

Cunninghamhead station looking towards Dalry.
J.F. McEwan/Hamish Stevenson Collection

Dalry Junction station was only in use between November 1850 and December 1859. The station may have been an exchange platform and the base of what looks like a former water tower is visible from passing trains. Dalry Junction was originally known as Kilcush Junction.

Kilmarnock Railway Landmarks

All the sites are close to the present Kilmarnock station (427383).

The former Andrew Barclay Sons & Co. Ltd, Caledonia works, Kilmarnock on West Langlands Street, has been turned into a housing development and Railway Heritage Centre developed by the Klin Group (425382) (*). Rails of several gauges remain embedded in the road leading from WABTEC Rail Scotland, the successor to Barclays in Kilmarnock, across the road, at an angle, to the Heritage Centre.

The exhibition has as its centre piece *Drake*, works No. 2086 built on the site in September 1940 as part of a fleet of six engines. The 0-4-0 saddle engine was commissioned by the Royal Ordnance Factory Woolwich to be used at the Glascoed Arsenal in Wales.

Part of the overhead gantry from the former works remains as a feature in the car park and on the roof of the building is the original metal sign for the works:

Andrew Barclay sign on top of Barclay House, formerly Caledonia Works in Kilmarnock.
Author

Offices
Andrew Barclay and Sons Co Ld

Visible on the end of the building on North Hamilton Street is the double dormer where Andrew Barclay's observatory was located (*).

The supermarket across the road from the former Barclay works occupied the former site of the Britannia engineering works and the Portland Forge. The G&SWR works was located to the west side of the K&TR line.

Along the road is Kilmarnock station (*) and Kilmarnock Water viaduct (*). The Dick Institute features an early painting of the Kilmarnock & Troon Railway with a passenger carriage and coal wagons near Troon harbour. A section of rail and the story of Kilmarnock's industrial history also feature. (*)

Kilmarnock once had a wide variety of different industries, some world leading, but it has suffered a dramatic decline as an industrial town in the post-war era. The railway has survived and the line between Glasgow and Carlisle is a success story. The people of Kilmarnock require more stories like that and are still proud to be thought of as a Railway Town.

Kilmarnock viaduct in 2012. *Author*

North of Kilmarnock

The route that leaves Kilmarnock heading north, part of the original Glasgow Barrhead & Kilmarnock Joint Railway, which opened in 1873 from Kilmarnock to Glasgow, has survived despite Government approval to close it in the 1960s. A vigorous local campaign ensure its continued existence but at a price. The line was singled and with only a passing loop at Lugton the service was restricted to once per hour.

The route passes through attractive rural countryside linking the communities of Kilmaurs, Stewarton and Dunlop, all once noted for textile production. The introduction of power-operated bonnet knitting machines, in the 1860s, created a growing industry in Kilmaurs and Stewarton, indeed Stewarton is still known as the 'Bonnet Toun'. Dunlop cheese was another local product made in several places, not just Dunlop.

Now the rail service has been improved with the completion of a 5.3 mile Dynamic Loop from Lochridge Junction, south of Stewarton to Lugton, which allows two trains to pass without stopping. This will encourage commuters to Glasgow with an improved service. A second platform has been built at Dunlop and at Stewarton enabling a half-hour-service to run. Freight traffic on the route, which provides an alternative to the West Coast main line is also important.

The first station on the railway north of Kilmarnock is Kilmaurs. En route the railway crosses the six-arch Carmel viaduct. The station was closed on 7th November, 1966 but reopened in a slightly different site, nearer the town centre, on 12th May, 1984. The platform has been extended to take longer trains but the present location of the station means that if the route was to be doubled throughout this section then the station would have had to be demolished and moved again, which is unlikely.

On 27th January, 2009, north of Kilmaurs, where the railway crosses the A735 at a bend in the road, a southerly heading diesel locomotive (No. 66067), with 10 tank wagons containing a mixture of gas oil, diesel and kerosene, en route from Grangemouth Refinery to Riccarton fuel depot was partially derailed as the train crossed the rail bridge, due to the collapse of the bridge. The last six wagons derailed south of the bridge and 220,000 litres of fuel spilled contaminating the local river, a tributary of the River Irvine. The last wagon caught fire. Fortunately no one was injured. The cause of the accident was a weakening of the structure due to heavy corrosion which had not been detected during regular inspections. Fortunately the Dynamic Loop was being constructed at the time and the bridge was due for replacement. The replacement deck had already been constructed and this enabled the bridge to be replaced within a month.

South of Stewarton is the 10-arch masonry Lainshaw viaduct constructed of rock-faced ashlar with a moulded string course. The viaduct is built on a curve on the approach to the town (417455) (*) and crosses the valley of the Annick Water. Like other stations on the line Stewarton station closed on 7th November, 1966 but reopened the following year on the 5th June due to a powerful public campaign opposing the closure. In September 2009 a second platform was constructed and the original passenger underpass, which had been infilled, was reinstated.

Dunlop's station also had a brief closure in the 1960s, the dates the same as for Stewarton station, and has since had a second platform reinstated. There was a Dunlop cheese factory near the station but it has closed and a housing estate built on the site. It was reckoned that some of the cheese's flavour was created by using salt from the Saltcoats saltpans. Ironically the railway enabled farmers to get their milk to markets further afield and reduced the supply of milk for cheese making.

Lugton Junction is located south of Lugton station where the Beith branch started, a joint affair operated by the G&SWR and the CR. Lugton station was the next station north on the line and has not been reopened. The station site is in private ownership. Also in Lugton but slightly east was the line built by the Lanarkshire & Ayrshire Railway from Neilston through Lugton to the south of Barrmill where it joined the earlier, opened Barrmill & Kilwinning Railway just north of Giffen. The L&AR also had a station in Lugton, south of Lugton station. These lines are described in Chapter Six.

The Irvine Valley

The railway line along the Irvine Valley branched from the Kilmarnock to Dumfries line at Hurlford. The three valley burghs, as they are known, of Galston, Newmilns and Darvel were an important centre for textiles and each had a station. There were also many coal pits in the area, all closed by the 1930s. The railway, built in stages, branched south of Hurlford station but it was not easy to construct a railway through what in places is a narrow valley. A long 26-arch viaduct and a massive retaining wall at Newmilns were required in addition to rerouting the road.

South-east of Hurlford station, on the line to Dumfries and south of the Darvel line, where the two lines diverged, was the site of the Hurlford locomotive shed. With the Kilmarnock locomotive shed proving not suitable the G&SWR found a new site with room for expansion only two miles from Kilmarnock. Hurlford shed opened in 1876 or 1877, and with the removal of the existing coaling shed on the site, the company had the opportunity to plan the new locomotive shed to meet their needs. The engine sheds had six roads, consisting of two dead-ends each accommodating three roads. The entrances were arched with six arched windows on the gable end above the entrances. Hurlford shed was initially planned to hold 40 engines with room for expansion and far exceeded this with around 100 engines operating from the site around World War I.

To the north of the sheds were the mineral sidings between the engine sheds and the Darvel line, which provided most of the traffic for the shed. The G&SWR designed the site so that the office stores and shops were separate and created a village consisting of two rows of dwellings at the east end of the depot, divided into four. 'The Blocks' were built as a village for staff. A halt was provided at Barleith which was intended for private use when it opened around June 1904 but appeared in public timetables by June 1927. The halt closed on 6th April, 1964 just over two years before the Hurlford shed closed. The site, with rail connected sidings, was taken over by Johnnie Walker, which became part of the Diageo Group and has now ceased operating from the site.

WALK 5.4 HURLFORD TO GALSTON

Distance: 2.75 miles (***).
Start: The walk starts at the cycle track beside the B7073 (456361), at the southern edge of Hurlford and opposite the former Johnnie Walker distribution centre. The trail ends at Barr Tower in Galston.
Terrain: The route is almost completely tarmacked.
Facilities: Cafes, shops in both Hurlford and Galston. No public toilets.

The cycle track follows the route of the former railway. At the start is a road bridge over the railway which is bricked off on the west side. Barleith Halt and the Hurlford shed were on the west side of the bridge. Barleith Halt was immediately to the west of the bridge with the mineral sidings and the residential 'Blocks' to the left of the Halt with the engine sheds lying further west. There is no remnant left of the former railway site which is now occupied by a distribution centre. Opposite the entrance of the distribution centre is an infilled road bridge which took the road over the Gatehead and Hurlford line from Kilmarnock and joined the route to Galston a few hundred yards further on.

Shortly after the start a branch from the cycle path, to the left, follows the start of the Mayfield branch which served the Loudoun Pits to the north of Galston on the north side of the River Irvine. The local coal pits fed coal into the Hurlford mineral sidings.

Looking back towards the Glasgow to Dumfries railway the line can be seen crossing the Cessnock Water by a three-arched viaduct. Ahead is another three-arch viaduct also over the Cessnock Water. The cycle path continues passing Liffnock Yard, a farmstead, passing under another road overbridge and continues until it reaches the outskirts of Galston where there were more pits before the route passes a road depot. The stroll through pleasant countryside is in sharp contrast with the coal mining past of this once busy railway with most signs of the pits removed.

The railway passed under the A719 but the road bridge has been removed. On the far side the trackbed continues as a road and then crosses playing fields. Ahead is Barr Castle and St Sophia's Roman Catholic church, two prominent local landmarks. Keep to the left of a haulage contractor's yard and cross a burn which brings you to Barr Castle. Barr Castle, now a museum, dates from the 15th century and was built to control strategically important crossroads. The tall tower is of red sandstone with the later addition of a hipped roof and porch. In contrast St Sophia's RC church is an arresting red brick Byzantine style church, with a central dome. Both structures would have been familiar to railway travellers.

The site of Galston station (504364) is now a British Telecom exchange on the east side of Station Road. To reach it pass Barr Castle, turn onto Wallace Street and turn right onto Station Road. On the west side of Station Road opposite the former station site the outline of the stone wing arches, to the side of the infilled road bridge, can be found embedded in the embankment. Galston station, 3½ miles from Hurlford station, was a busy station with sidings and was noted for the subsidence caused by coal workings, which meant that the booking office and waiting room were at a rather crazy angle to the platforms.

Cessnock Water viaduct on the Hurlford to Darvel line, a few hundred yards east of Barleith Halt, 2011. *Author*

The bridge east of Newmilns station in 2012. *Author*

Galston enriched by the skills brought over by the Huguenots in the 17th century has long associations with the manufacture of textiles and in the early 20th century lace and muslin. The town lies to the south of the A71, the main road through the valley. To the north of the road lies the shell of Loudoun Castle which burnt down in 1941. The castle grounds were used until recently as an adventure theme park.

From Galston the trackbed continues along a tree-lined stretch of embankment, high above the valley floor, before entering a long deep cutting. Local residents use the first part for dog walking. The Maxwood pit was in this area along with miners' rows.

Newmilns straddles both sides of the River Irvine developed as a centre for textile manufacture and engineering. The main industrial area was to the south of the river around Brown Street. At the west end of Brown Street the former trackbed reaches Newmilns and passes under a road bridge. Beyond the bridge the trackbed is built over, part of the Vesuvius Crucible Co. buildings, which are now closed. Walking along Brown Street you are surrounded by industrial buildings, many listed. Some, like Haddow Aird & Crerar Ltd help keeps the lace making traditions alive in the valley.

At the eastern end of Brown Street, where the road becomes Browns Road, the abutments of a railway bridge can be seen. At the railway bridge take the road to the right which curves uphill crossing the former railway track by a skew-arched bridge (*), with the head of the arch lined with engineering bricks. In the cutting to the west of the bridge was the site of Newmilns station, now built over. Newmilns station was 5¼ miles from Hurlford station. To the east of the road bridge is a massive retaining wall beside the trackbed, whose construction delayed the opening of the railway onward to Darvel. It took three attempts to stabilize the steep hillside and the wall is 34 ft high and some 30 ft thick.

This, however, is not the only railway relic left in Newmilns. Beyond the eastern abutment of the missing railway bridge is the start of the Newmilns viaduct (*) which emerges from a wooded hillside. Squeezed for space the railway company constructed the slightly curved 26-arch viaduct (539373) to take the railway across the River Irvine and through Newmilns. The second arch crosses the River Irvine, while many of the other arches are occupied by small businesses. The viaduct, which is fenced off, can be viewed by walking to Main Street and taking any of the roads to the right.

Darvel, the most easterly of the three valley burghs, was another textile town, often known as the 'Lace Town'. Its lace was once of world renown but the industry declined faced with competition from abroad and lace is no longer manufactured in the town. The railway connection has almost been removed by housing developments. The station site was extensive with the station buildings and its platforms to the north of the site and a goods yard and sidings, along with a turntable to the south. Sadly we are left with 'Station Gate' as the only tenuous link.

Darvel was the terminus of the G&SWR branch but end-on to it was the Caledonian line to Strathaven in Lanarkshire, opened in 1904. Snatches of the former Caley route remain within Darvel and at the eastern end of the town a three-arch viaduct crosses the Glen Water (569379) (*), finished in blue brick, which is visible from East Main Street.

Newmilns station looking towards Darvel on 16th May, 1959. *Hamish Stevenson Collection*

Ex-LMS '2P' class 4-4-0 No. 40644 arrivies at Newmilns station on 16th May, 1959. *Hamish Stevenson Collection*

Darvel station looking west on 21st March, 1964. *Hamish Stevenson Collection*

WALK 5.5 DARVEL TO THE SITE OF LOUDOUNHILL VIADUCT

Distance: 2 miles (***) or 4 miles round trip.
Start: At the eastern edge of Darvel there is a minor road which climbs steeply away from the main road (A71) heading north. A few hundred yards up the hill are the abutments of a railway bridge. Beside the abutments is the start of Irvine Valley Paths Network route to Loudoun Hill which follows the former railway.
Terrain: Conditions underfoot can be muddy. Stout footwear recommended.
Further options: Extend walk and climb the steep Loudoun Hill or at the viaduct walk down to the A71 and return to Darvel by road.
Facilities: Cafes, shops bars in Darvel. No public toilets.

Further up the glen is Lochfield Farm, where Alexander Fleming, whose discovery of penicillin revolutionized the world of medicine, was brought up.

Beside the abutments is the start of Irvine Valley Paths Network route to Loudoun Hill which follows the former railway. This is a superb walk as the railway trackbed cuts across the hillside alternately by cutting or embankment, crossed by overbridges. Ahead is Loudoun Hill a volcanic plug, a prominent landmark visible even from the Island of Arran. The battle of Loudoun Hill was fought between Robert Bruce and an English force on the southern edge of the hill, in 1307, with Bruce's forces being successful.

The walk reaches the remains of Loudounhill viaduct. The viaduct was also known as the Allanton viaduct, after the local farm, or the Priestland viaduct. Only part of the approach to the viaduct now remains with masonry abutments and two piers. The most easterly abutment resides on a small hill. Beyond this was a 13-arch viaduct, constructed of blue engineering bricks, which crossed the valley.

Loudounhill in 2012, with an overbridge over the former railway trackbed and the approach to the viaduct beyond. Loudoun Hill itself is visible in the far distance (*centre*).
Author

Sadly the 13-arch viaduct (602373) was demolished in 1986, condemned as a safety hazard. Demolition, however, was not easy as it was discovered that the viaduct was filled with concrete. The first explosives made little impact. However, the demolition team was eventually successful and a local landmark was removed, which is still sadly missed.

At the eastern edge of the viaduct interchange sidings were built for use by the two railway companies and this is where Loudounhill station was located. The Darvel to Strathaven Railway was closed at the beginning of World War II and the track lifted in 1951.

Loudounhill station, looking towards Strathaven. *Hamish Stevenson Collection*

Chapter Six

Railways of North Ayrshire

It wasn't only Troon that had ambitions as a port. Further north Hugh Montgomerie, a patron of Robert Burns, had become the 12th Earl of Eglinton, in 1796, on the death of his cousin. The 12th Earl had the vision of developing Ardrossan as a harbour, as it was strategically placed for sailing ships to unload their cargoes and avoid having to navigate the upper reaches of the Clyde to reach Glasgow which was difficult for sailing ships. He hoped that a harbour at Ardrossan could be the port for Glasgow.

The next part of the vision was equally bold, build a canal between Ardrossan and Glasgow to take goods from the port to the city. The canal also had the advantage of passing through districts rich in minerals and important towns like Paisley attracting more business. Thomas Telford surveyed the route and on 20th June, 1806 an Act of Parliament was passed to authorize the construction of the Glasgow, Paisley & Ardrossan Canal. However, the canal which started in Glasgow only got as far south as Johnstone before the funds were exhausted. This section opened on 6th November, 1811.

The 12th Earl had already spent a considerable sum on developing Ardrossan harbour, and with funds limited it was not until after his grandson had become the 13th Earl (on the death of his father in 1819) that the harbour project was eventually finished. Additional funds were not available to complete the canal, which was no longer seen as an attractive option with the railway age emerging and with advances in dredging the Clyde allowing ships to sail to the centre of Glasgow, removing one of the principal reasons for developing Ardrossan harbour.

Instead a railway was seen as a more favoured option to complete a link between Ardrossan and Johnstone. On 14th June, 1827 a new Act of Parliament gave assent to the construction of a 22 mile railway, the Ardrossan & Johnstone Railway (A&JR), owned and to be operated by the canal company. The Act decreed that construction, this time, start at the Ardrossan end, due to the failure of the canal to get beyond Johnstone. However, funds again were insufficient and construction stopped this time at Byres, near Kilwinning, a distance of 5½ miles. The railway was built to the Scotch gauge, 4 ft 6 in., and used horse-drawn carriages. Goods traffic was using the line in 1831 with a passenger service starting in 1834. The passenger service was very successful carrying around 30,000 passengers a year by the late 1830s. Goods traffic was less successful and it required a branch from the Ardrossan Railway, at Dubbs Junction, east through Dirrans, to the south of Kilwinning and reaching to Doura to turn around the fortunes of the enterprise. The branch passed through the lands of the Eglinton estate and was partly-funded by local landowners anxious to get their coal from pit to the harbour for export, to generate most of the income for the line.

When the Glasgow Paisley Kilmarnock & Ayr Railway was authorized on 15th July, 1837 it included a connection at Kilwinning with the A&JR and a

ARDROSSAN

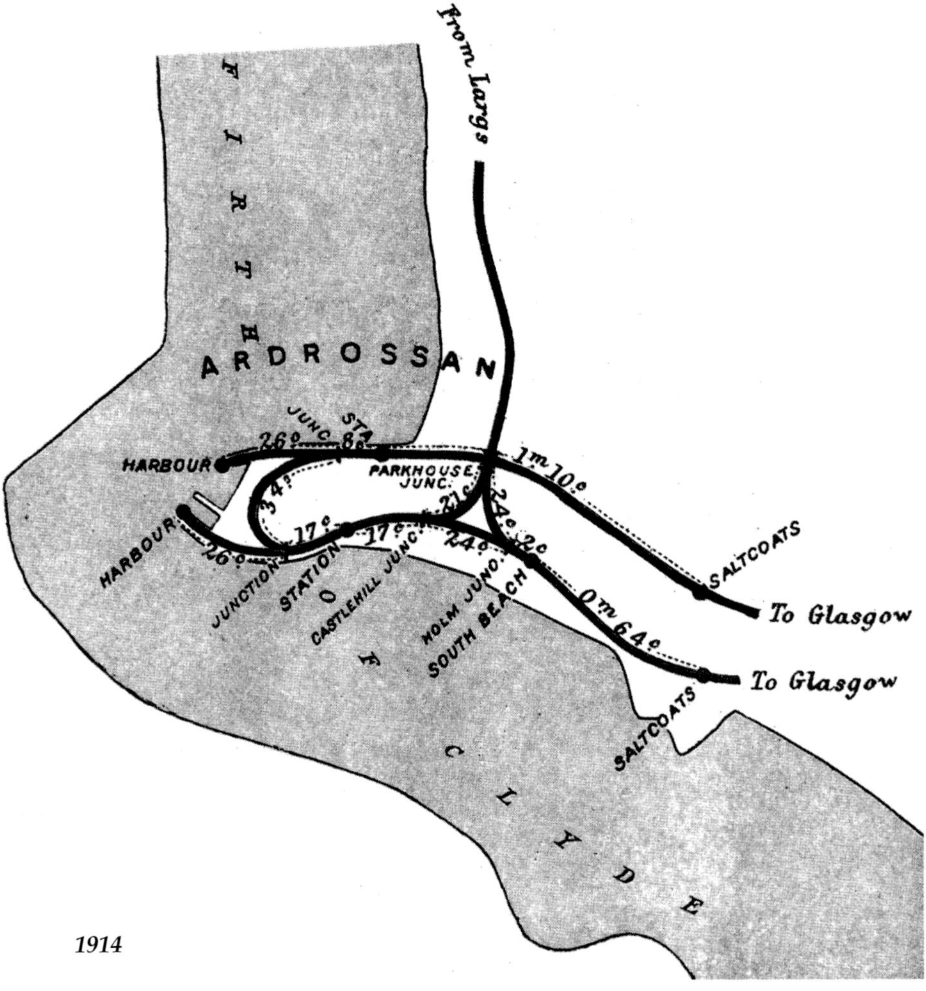

1914

further Act on 23rd July, 1840 separated the A&JR from the canal company. The railway then became known as the Ardrossan Railway and was converted to standard gauge and made suitable for locomotive use. By 1854 the network, including the Doura branch, was absorbed into the G&SWR (*see map page 110*).

When the line to Ardrossan was reopened on 17th August, 1840 there were new stations at Stevenston, Saltcoats and Ardrossan Town and Harbour. The Ardrossan stations were not separately identified for many years in railway timetables. Ardrossan Harbour later became Ardrossan Pier then in 1909 Ardrossan Winton Pier. In the early days the connection with Ardrossan was an important part of the route from Glasgow to London. On arrival at Ardrossan a steamer, the *Fire King* took passengers to Liverpool and then onto London by rail, a journey of 26½ hours. The steamer connection started on 20th August, 1840 and operated on alternate weekdays.

Sir Robert Reid Cunninghame's Iron Road

The Ardrossan & Johnstone Railway was not the first 'railway' in the area. A short waggonway, inspired by the Kilmarnock & Troon Railway, was operating around 1812.

Between Stevenston and Ardrossan coal mining had been established for many centuries on the lands of Sir Robert Reid Cunninghame who managed the Stevenston Coal Co. Cunninghame obtained access to the coal reserves on the Ardeer peninsula and around Stevenston. Some of the coal was exported to Ireland through Saltcoats harbour and the dross used for lime-burning or extracting salt from seawater. Salt production gave its name to Saltcoats, 'cotes' being the cottages of the salt makers which were by the sea.

In 1772 the three mile-long Stevenston to Saltcoats canal, the first commercial canal in Scotland, was opened to ease the flow of coal to the harbour at Saltcoats and the industrialization of the area began. The canal, however, stopped 600 yards short of the harbour and the coal had still to be taken by cart for the final section and this created a problem which would haunt Cunninghame for many years. The final section of canal would have required a series of locks to overcome a protruding stone dyke and was not technically feasible at the time.

The fact that the canal did not reach the harbour was exploited by the 12th Earl of Eglinton, who had become chairman of the North Ayrshire Turnpike Trust and who wanted to entice the coal pit owners away from Saltcoats to his new harbour at Ardrossan. The Turnpike Trustees raised a toll gate at the end of the canal and charged tolls for transporting coal over the final stretch to the harbour. Tolls were subsequently increased and the export of coal from Saltcoats harbour was becoming uneconomical. As a trustee of Saltcoats harbour the 12th Earl also made sure that the harbour dues were higher than those levied at the unfinished Ardrossan harbour.

Sir Robert Reid Cunninghame's solution was to build his own iron road along the shoreline to miss out the toll road. The inspiration came from the waggonway, already in existence at Ayr harbour, but he also visited the Kilmarnock & Troon Railway to learn about the new iron road. Preparation work began in June 1811. He ordered rails from the Muirkirk ironworks and the track was almost completed when the Earl of Eglinton instigated more litigation, which was eventually unsuccessful, but led to the recognition that a rail road was different from a toll road and did not, therefore, fall within the jurisdiction of the Turnpike Act. No tolls could be imposed on a railway.

The short 300 yard waggonway had successfully bypassed the toll roads but was still short of the harbour due to a plot of land owned by the Earl's family, but importantly the coal could reach the harbour by using non-toll roads. Sir Robert Reid Cunninghame, now enthusiastic about the new form of transport, extended his railway to new pits and a mineral line was built which was still operational in 1836.

The Cunninghame's attempts to defend their interests against the Earl of Eglinton were fatally undermined, however, in 1827 when Sir Robert Reid Cunninghame's son reached an agreement with the 13th Earl to extend the railway to the harbour but critically in exchange for allowing a new railway to cross their land. This agreement favoured the 13th Earl of Eglinton who used his new railway, the Ardrossan & Johnstone Railway, to ensure, than when the railway began goods traffic in 1831, coal was sent to Ardrossan harbour and that none passed through Saltcoats harbour. By 1852 he had succeeded and no more coal was being exported through Saltcoats harbour and Cunninghame's short railway was scrapped.

Developments on the Ardeer Peninsula

As the town of Stevenston grew most of the industry was located south of the G&SWR on the Ardeer peninsula. Ironworks, built by Merry & Cunninghame, began production in 1854, and their tall 80 ft furnaces dominated the peninsula. At night the furnaces at Ardeer and those of the Eglinton ironworks, near Kilwinning were visible across the Firth of Clyde on Arran. The folks from Arran must have wondered what was happening in Ayrshire. This was a new venture for Merry & Cunninghame who had already established themselves in Ayrshire by building an ironworks at Glengarnock, in the Garnock Valley. A railway network grew serving the ironworks and coal pits. The Ardeer ironworks closed by the mid-1930s and the mineral railway was lifted shortly after. The local coal pits had largely stopped production around the same time.

In 1873, the industry that was to bring prosperity to the area and transform the Ardeer peninsula began production when Alfred Nobel's Ardeer explosives factory produced its first nitro-glycerine. With restrictive laws on where dynamite could be produced the barren and isolated sand dunes of the Ardeer peninsula were seen as being an ideal location. In time a short railway, jointly operated by the G&SWR and the CR, ran to the explosives factory and was referred to as Nobel's private line but each company also ran separate lines to the explosives factory. The terminus of the private line was Ardeer Platform, built in 1896, and it was one of the busiest stations in the area especially after ICI took over the site in 1926. With expansion of the Ardeer works additional workers' platforms were required in the 1930s and these were provided on the other side of the River Garnock at Snodgrass sidings served by the Ayr to Glasgow line near an access point to the expanding site. Within the factory there were also many miles of 'bogey railways' for transferring explosives around the site and a short branch to Nobel's Wharf on the River Garnock which enabled explosives to be taken away by boat from the site.

After the war explosive production tailed off and the size of the workforce was reduced. Attempts to diversify into new synthetic fibres like Ardil, manufactured from ground nuts, were not successful. A new nylon plant, which necessitated the local golf club moving, was opened in 1965 but its water cooling tower collapsed in a gale, probably due to a building defect, hindering production. The industrial unrest of the late 1970s caused production to stop for some time and in 1981 with the market for nylon fibre in rapid decline the plant was closed. Within 20 years the number employed on this vast site was down to around 500.

Later Developments on the Ardrossan Route

Passenger traffic to the coast was becoming more popular in the later half of the 19th century, with many keen to experience the joys of a day at the seaside, and the G&SWR saw further opportunities to extend its route north of Ardrossan. This it did by stages to to reach Largs eventually. Starting in 1878 the railway north of Ardrossan began with a branch from Ardrossan to West Kilbride and then to Fairlie two years later, with a short extension to Fairlie Pier station (1st July, 1882), and eventually opening to Largs on 1st June, 1885. Fairlie pier was ideally placed for ferries across to the small town of Millport on the island of Cumbrae, and also offered the shortest crossing to Campbeltown on the Kintyre peninsula. Safer access during the gales of the winter months meant that the pier was also used for traffic to the Island of Arran rather than Ardrossan harbour which can be difficult to enter during stormy weather.

When the extension to Largs began operating an additional station known as Ardrossan South Beach was built to allow trains to stop in the town without having to go to Ardrossan Town, then having to reverse.

Kilwinning to Glengarnock – the Ayr to Glasgow line

Between Kilwinning and Glengarnock the branch from Kilmarnock, covered in Chapter Five, joined the line from the south-east at Dalry Junction.

North of Dalry traffic was also increasing and the G&SWR built a relief line, from Brownhill Junction, north of Dalry, to Cart Junction, near Johnstone. The Dalry and North Johnstone loop was opened on 1st June, 1905.

The Glasgow Barrhead & Kilmarnock Joint line (G&SWR and Caledonian Railway) later added a five-mile branch west to Beith from Lugton Junction, just south of Lugton station but this branch did not connect to the Ayr to Glasgow line.

The Lanarkshire & Ayrshire Railway

By the late 1880s about a third of Lanarkshire's coal pits were exporting coal through the harbour at Ardrossan. Despite the monopoly that the Caledonian Railway had over the Lanarkshire pits this meant that at some point the coal had to travel over 'Sou'West' routes and that reduced profits for the Caley. The G&SWR jealously guarded its Ayrshire routes as indeed did the Caledonian railway in Lanarkshire. The Caledonian Railway was frustrated by having to hand over coal to its rival the G&SWR for the final stretch to the ports. There was also local business in Ayrshire from iron furnaces and chemical works which the CR thought it could gain from its rival. The need for its own line to compete with the G&SWR was therefore a priority for the CR and led to the building of the Lanarkshire & Ayrshire Railway.

The two rival railways had reached an agreement to run jointly the Glasgow, Barrhead & Kilmarnock line. A branch from this line to Beith passed through the village of Barrmill. From here the CR built a line for the 6½ miles south to Kilwinning. The Earl of Eglinton was only too pleased to support this intrusion which had the potential to increase business at Ardrossan. With authorization being obtained to complete the route to Ardrossan, the railway was reconstituted as the Lanarkshire & Ayrshire Railway with the Earl of Eglinton as its Chairman.

The 6¼ miles extension from Kilwinning to Ardrossan was opened on 4th September, 1888, followed a few months later with a temporary link to Ardrossan harbour until its own pier was opened on 30th May, 1890 at Montgomerie pier.

The line ran to the east of the G&SWR lines passing through remote countryside until it reached Kilwinning and then travelling north of the G&SWR line through Stevenston, Saltcoats and Ardrossan with the siting of its stations further inland than their G&SWR equivalents and not being as favourably sited as its established rival. However, the route was 3½ miles shorter.

Having finally penetrated Ayrshire the Caley strengthened its grip on G&SWR territory with a branch to the steelworks at Glengarnock, on 1st November, 1889, with the opening of Glengarnock High station and south to Bank Street, Irvine on 2nd June, 1890. The Irvine branch had sidings which served the Eglinton ironworks and local coal pits.

Fierce competition for business, provided by the L&AR, benefited local traders, who welcomed the breaking of a monopoly. The downside was the lack of cooperation between the two companies which resulted in expensive duplication including a track being built to the south of the Beith branch from Lugton as far as Giffen Junction. With the completion of the parallel line the CR could now carry its own coals to Ardrossan.

A further consequence was an equally intense rivalry for the limited steamer traffic to Arran, Ireland and the Isle of Man operated by another Caledonian run company, the Caledonian Steam Packet Co. The G&SWR had worked with privately-owned steamers and their trade was swept away by the Caledonian subsidiary. It took time and investment for the G&SWR to claw back lost business. The company first had to fight an expensive legal battle to enable it to run its own steamers. Then it introduced the *Glen Sannox*, built with little regard for cost and, at that time, the fastest vessel on the Clyde. For the few thousand inhabitants of Arran this competition was great news, with fares being reduced and a wonderful service provided. Apart from peak holiday times the services never ran at full capacity. Eventually the companies came to an agreement on how to share services.

Despite the construction costs, the CR venture was well-supported and indeed encouraged by local interests and initially the L&AR was a success. But with the building of Rothesay Dock at Clydebank in 1907, which was much closer to the Lanarkshire coal pits, much of the coal traffic was diverted from the L&AR. The decline was rapid and by 1932 the line had lost its local passenger services.

Nowadays all that is left of the CR challenge is a track to the Defence Munitions Depot at Giffen from Barrmill and even this is no longer operational. Local passenger traffic had ceased by July 1932, although some excursions used the line for a few years more. Goods traffic had stopped by May 1950. After World War II, however, the building of a short spur between the rival lines at Ardeer allowed the continued use of Montgomerie pier until its final closure in 1968.

Exploring the Railway Heritage

From north of Barassie to Glengarnock

The Ayr to Glasgow line, between Barassie and Irvine is very straight and cuts across sand dunes beside Irvine Bay. During and after the war this was a busy area with Dundonald Camp, an army training camp and later RAF Gailes, a radar station. Before the railway was built, there were, in 1829, experiments with a suspension railway by a local inventor Maxwell Dick in this area. Little is known of this project but Dick, a local publisher and bookseller, also invented a snowplough.

The construction of a golf course, Western Gailes, to enable golfers from Glasgow to enjoy the pollution free atmosphere at the coast, led to the opening of Gailes station (323356) in June 1893 but the golf course was not ready until 1897. The course is often used for prestigious golf competitions. The station brought eager golfers to the coast and closed in January 1967 but by then most golfers probably used their cars. There is a level crossing to enable golfers to reach the clubhouse which is on the seaward side of the railway track. There was a tragic accident in 2007 at the level crossing when the driver of a Ford Transit van was killed by a southbound train.

The approach to Irvine station shows the industrial side of the town, mainly near the harbour. The harbour area is based to the south of the confluence of the Rivers Irvine and Garnock. To the west of the rivers are the sand dunes of the Ardeer peninsula. The town had already unsuccessfully supported a proposal to build a railway from the town to join the Ardrossan Railway near Kilwinning, quite similar to the route eventually built by the Lanarkshire and Ayrshire Railway. The support switched to the line planned by the GPK&AR

Gailes station looking towards Glasgow on 15th July, 1957. *Hamish Stevenson Collection*

and the station was opened in August 1839 and within the year the line had reached Glasgow. Seven years later a branch was added to a newly completed wharf at Irvine harbour.

Initially the town did not benefit from the railway as much as expected. Irvine did not have a wealthy enterprising landowner like Troon and Ardrossan. The Duke of Portland saw that Troon was the preferred destination for the coal extracted from his pits and the opening of the Eglinton ironworks at Kilwinning ensured that a lot of the coal produced in the area was diverted there using the existing Doura branch which delivered coal from the coal pits around Irvine to the ironworks.

A further branch was added to the burgeoning network, a useful cross-country route from Irvine linking to the Dalry line, a few miles west of Kilmarnock at Busby Junction. Partly this was in response to the perceived threat from the Caledonian Railway which at that time was being given encouragement by the Duke of Portland to increase its presence in Ayrshire (*see Chapter Five*). The Busby branch as it was known opened on 22nd May, 1848 and was an important addition linking to the harbour at Irvine which had acquired its own branch a year earlier. It allowed traffic to reach Stevenston, Saltcoats and Ardrossan and later Largs. The route which was double-tracked was another significant revenue generator with numerous coal pits, brickworks and even a pottery at Southhook, whose final glaze was much admired by competitors for its quality. When the Ardeer explosives factory started production, on the peninsula opposite Irvine harbour, a money-spinning but more dangerous traffic resulted. Oil from the refinery, opened at Ardrossan in 1925, was also often sent along this route. The route was always popular for special excursions whether they were Sunday School outings or from local firms like Glenfield & Kennedy in Kilmarnock. The Busby branch joined the Glasgow to Ayr line just to the south of Irvine station, in the area now occupied by a retail park but did not link directly to the harbour.

In 1848 the townsfolk of Irvine had to change the time on the Irvine town clock to synchronise with the times given on railway timetables and so the Irvine town clock was put forward by 17½ minutes. Irvine was catching up with the outside world.

In the mid-1850s the railway network was still not attracting much additional industry to the town, which still relied on the manufacture of cotton. By the late 1870s, however, the area near the harbour was developed with chemical works and forges being established close to the harbour and linked to the railway. In this area the G&SWR had its maintenance department, known as the Vale of Clyde railway works, opened around 1880 on the site of a wagon works. The works, formed around a square, made signal poles, furniture for stations, repaired signalling equipment and made and repaired lamps and employed up to 250 men. For a few years there was even a football club named after the works. The Vale of Clyde railway works closed in 1948 with the work transferred to Barassie carriage and wagon works.

WALK 6.1 BUSBY BRANCH: IRVINE TO KILMARNOCK

Distance: 9 miles - one way (***).
Start: The route of the Busby branch can be followed from Irvine railway station to Kilmarnock railway station with only a few deviations. The route is part of National Cycle Route 73.
Directions from Irvine station to the start of the walk (for those arriving by train): Beyond the Tesco/Sainsbury superstores, in the retail park, there is a roundabout (roundabout 1). Go straight on (A71). The original railway wall, patched with brick is to the left.
Cross the road bridge over the River Irvine and continue straight on (first exit) at the next roundabout (2).
At the third roundabout (3) take the second exit Annick Road (B7081), past a hotel until you reach another roundabout (4) – Newmoor Roundabout.
The New Town Trail joins the former railway trackbed at the roundabout (Newmoor roundabout) close to Greenwood Academy, Dreghorn (340382) to the north of a garage forecourt. There is a regular bus service between Irvine Station and Dreghorn.
Terrain: Surfaced – mainly tarmac.
Facilities: In both Irvine and Kilmarnock there are shops and cafes. Public toilets are at the Rivergate Shopping centre, Irvine and at Burns Mall, Kilmarnock

The land between the bridge and the start of the walk was mostly fields, with the exception of the Warrix Fireclay works and coal pit and Shewalton pit before the development of Irvine New Town started in 1966. Irvine was the only new town in Scotland to be built around an existing community and the only one next to the sea.

Dreghorn, formerly known as Long Dreghorn, was a mining village, which in the late 1960s became part of Irvine New Town. Several housing estates were built in the area, and many families were rehoused from Glasgow. In the 1970s a secondary school was built in Dreghorn, Greenwood Academy, to cope with the burgeoning population, and the present secondary school, built as part of a public private partnership, replaced the first school in 2008.

Not all pupils would be aware that the trail follows a former railway or indeed of the coal mining past of the area, with 16 pits in the area around Dreghorn and Springside, or the very different living conditions in the past.

The area has been transformed and it is difficult to believe that after World War II, only half the houses in Dreghorn had inside toilets. Where the school is situated was the area where miners exercised their greyhounds and fished on the banks of the River Annick. Across the road was the Greenwood Plantation and beside the woods were the infamous Greenwood miners' rows, a few hundred yards from the pit head of the Montgomeryfield pit. The miners' rows are long demolished, but were notorious for flooding in wet weather, causing the contents of the dry closets to seep around the area for people to walk through, often barefoot.

Conditions underground were equally harsh, with miners in winter rarely seeing any daylight, crawling underneath the ground to hack away at coal faces, and setting off explosives in the darkness with a high risk of the coal face collapsing. Accidents were commonplace and there was no National Health Service to treat injuries. Pit ponies, also suffered, being lowered down the shaft at Montgomeryfield pit in a net, their legs bound with rope. After years of toiling underground, in the dark, the ponies were almost blind and when their working lives were over they often ended up being sent to the Eglinton kennels to be processed for food.

Behind the school there is an overbridge, which once led to a farm, but now allows pupils to reach the housing estates to the north, followed by a long stretch of deep cutting, known to the local pupils as 'the Steepies'. At the eastern end was a signal box, which controlled access to the mineral line which led to the Montgomeryfield pit. A path veering to the south-east, at the end of the school playing fields, roughly follows the route of the mineral line which crossed the main street in Dreghorn at a level crossing. Montgomeryfield pit had a brickworks and also screened coal from several local pits.

The trail uses the former railway bridge to cross the River Annick and continues east on a low embankment, in an area prone to flooding. Long lines of coal wagons were stored waiting for repair or dismantling in the later years of the route. There were more coal pits to the north, linked to the railway.

Of Dreghorn station (351385) nothing remains. The level crossing gates which once straddled Station Brae have been removed as have the signal box, platforms and basic station buildings. The outline of the sidings to the west and south of the level crossing can be discerned. Between October 1850 and May 1868 there was no passenger service listed. The station closed on 6th April, 1964. Beside the station were more miners' rows.

To the south is a distinctive octagonal church and the Dunlop Memorial Hall at the top of Brae Head. The hall commemorates John Boyd Dunlop who patented the pneumatic (inflatable) tyre in 1888. His patent was challenged by another Scottish inventor, Robert Thomson but Thomson lost his case. Dunlop set up, initially in Dublin, the first Dunlop factory to manufacture pneumatic tyres but sold out his idea early and made little money from his invention.

Dreghorn station, looking towards Kilmarnock on 7th March, 1964.
Hamish Stevenson Collection

After Dreghorn station the River Annick is crossed again, by a narrower replacement bridge. To the north is a road bridge over the River Annick. A mineral line, the Perceton branch, ran beside the River Annick and linked with the Doura branch further north although trains would not have been able to travel from Perceton to Kilwinning without reversing. Over the years the site of the link appears to have changed.

Ahead is a road bridge over the route, now infilled, and the trail takes a detour linking up with the former trackbed on the other side of the road. Close to the site of the road bridge was the junction of another mineral line this time to the Bourtreehill brickworks with a coal pit at the junction with the Busby branch. The pit known as 'the Brig' or Capringstone No. 8 (Capringstone this time with an 'e' at the end) was of use after it stopped producing coal as it was used to pump water from the shaft into the river and reduce the level of water in nearby mines.

A tree-lined footpath continues the route towards Springside. Springside station opened on 2nd June, 1890 and closed with the rest of the route in 1964. Each platform had a wooden building and there was an additional storage hut on the north platform. A path led down from the road to the halt. The route then passed under the road but the bridge has been infilled. Signs point the direction east and the former mining village is soon left behind.

The land between Springside and the site of Crosshouse station is now rural in nature and makes for a pleasant walk. The trackbed crosses the Garrier Burn three times, firstly by a replacement bridge and secondly using the original bridge.

To the north (left of the trackbed) is Southhook Farm.There is a substantial stone overbridge crossing the line leading to the farm. Located, at this point, were the Southhook Fireclay works, coal pit and sidings. The sidings were shared with the Paddocklaw pit to the north-west.

BR Standard class '3MT' 2-6-0 No. 77016 at Crosshouse station with a Kilmarnock-bound passenger train on 28th March, 1964. *Hamish Stevenson Collection*

Crosshouse station site in 2011. *Author*

Springside station looking towards Irvine with Bourtreehill brickworks in the distance, 27th July, 1957. *Hamish Stevenson Collection*

More fireclay than coal was produced at the pits. The headgear, the winding engine was produced by Andrew Barclay, and chimney and kilns were close to the railway. Miners' rows and a mission hall completed what was a small community. The site was cleared around 1970. The glaze produced at the factory was prized, being free of impurities and very useful in producing large pieces of sanitary ware such as baths and was the envy of competitors. The head offices of the Southhook Pottery Co. were at Bonnyton near Kilmarnock station.

After the Southhook site the trackbed crosses the Garrier Burn for the third time. To the north are the crumbling brick abutments of an old viaduct. Shortly after to the south is an embankment curving towards the south. The embankment led to an ironstone mine, with the ore being smelted on site before being transferred to the Glengarnock steelworks.

Ahead are the first houses in Knockentiber, built over the site of the Plann Fireclay works and coal pits. To the left of the trackbed is a rail bridge, part of the Kilmarnock to Dalry line, which merges with the Busby branch, near the station.

The trackbed then reaches a two-arch road bridge over the two railway routes before they merged at Busby Junction, which was just beyond the bridge. Busby Junction was renamed Crosshouse Junction in 1924, after the regrouping of the railway network, possibly to avoid confusion with another Busby Junction near East Kilbride.

To the west of the bridges was the site of Crosshouse station (399397). A triangular platform filled the vee between the two merging lines with additional platforms on the outside. A footbridge, beside the road bridge, connected all the platforms with the main two-storey station building located next to the road bridge on the north side. On the same platform as the two-storey platform was a single-storey building with a passenger waiting area, behind a glazed screen. There was a goods shed on the north side. In the vee-shaped platform and on the southern platform were further waiting rooms. The station was always well-maintained and had several flower beds. The site is now occupied by a car breaker's yard but one of the buildings, the single-storey building on the north platform, remains although much modified.

The Queen's bridge between Bogside and Irvine sustained damage after a flood in January 1932. Trains had to be diverted via Kilmarnock. *Hamish Stevenson Collection*

Almost since the opening of the line in 1848 there has been a station at this site. The station was originally named Busby, probably named after the local Busbiehead Pit, to the west of the station and was opened in September 1848 but closed on 15th April, 1850. Trains were first shown stopping at Crosshouse, which was on the same site, in April 1873. Crosshouse station closed on 18th April, 1966. The puzzle is why the station was called Crosshouse and not Knockentiber. Both villages were of equal status but Crosshouse station was next to Knockentiber, with the village of Crosshouse being about a mile further to the south.

The trackbed now continues towards Kilmarnock, and crosses the Woodhill Burn by a three-arch viaduct, with brick-lined arches. The trackbed then passes under a road bridge, which has been narrowed and strengthened with concrete. A sculpture made out of railway sleepers lines part of the route, with Kilmarnock clearly visible in the distance. Again there was evidence of more mine workings along the route.

Finally a stub of the former railway is reached with a long double siding, merging to one track at the eastern end. The Kilmarnock Long Lyes, as they are known, have recently been redeveloped to provide a rounding loop for coal trains. The development was to avoid the unproductive mileage from running via Falkland Yard (Ayr) for rounding.

A path runs beside the sidings and finally climbs to street level on Western Road. Beyond the bridge the two tracks merge and become single near the Wabtec works and join the Glasgow line at Kilmarnock station. The single-track branch from Glasgow curves in from the north before reaching Kilmarnock station.

To reach Kilmarnock station from the Long Lyes on foot turn right onto Western Road. The former headquarters of the Southhook Pottery is found beside the railway sidings. The site is now a housing estate but the art deco building on Western Road, part of the pottery, remains as a listed property. The pottery was taken over by Shanks in 1963; its once employed over 500 workers.

Continue south until Bonnyton Road is reached and turn left. Bonnyton Road becomes West Langlands Street and passes the former Andrew Barclay buildings (Caledonia works) to reach Kilmarnock station.

Irvine to Kilwinning

North of Irvine station the railway crosses the River Irvine by the six-span masonry Queen's bridge (313398), named to commemorate Queen Victoria's Coronation. The Irvine town treasurer Thomas Campbell won the contract and locally the bridge is often referred to as Campbell's bridge. The railway then crosses the Bogside Flats to reach Bogside station (310403) which served the Bogside Race Course and golf course. There had been a tradition of horse riding on the town's moor and the 12th Earl of Eglinton laid out a new racecourse at Bogside. The Scottish Grand National was raced here until the 1960s when it switched to Ayr Racecourse. The outline of the course is still clearly visible, but not from the railway, with many of the fence supports remaining but the grandstand has been demolished. Near the centre of the racetrack is Bogside coal bing, one of several pits in the area once linked by a mineral railway to the Doura branch.

Bogside station was located north of the broad bridge over the line and next to what is now the Royal Irvine Golf Course. Many golfers from Glasgow used the station to reach the golf club. Racegoers used the station from 1885 and there was a service on Tuesdays, Thursdays and Saturdays from 1894. The service was restricted during World War I. It was renamed Bogside Racecourse from

Bogside Racecourse station looking south. This photograph was taken on its final day of service, 31st December, 1966. *Hamish Stevenson Collection*

The view from Stevenston bridge in 1996 showing the ICI Organic Division sidings. The Ardeer line is to the right. *Author*

1952 until 1965. When the racecourse closed the name reverted to Bogside until its closure on 2nd January, 1967.

Between the railway and the winding River Garnock was once a heavily industrialized area, initially with several coal pits but later by the expanding Ardeer site which developed on both sides of the river. The ICI Snodgrass siding, visible from the railway was used as a workers' platform, with thousands of employees of the Ardeer works descending on the site. The platform took pressure off Stevenston and Ardeer stations which were extremely busy during shift changes.

North of the Snodgrass siding the line crosses the River Garnock by the four-span Longford bridge and then the modern A78 dual carriageway. Beyond the crossing of the road is Byrehill Junction where a spur connects with the Ardrossan route at Dubbs Junction.

In 1833, before the railway was opened, the surface of the River Garnock was seen to be bubbling, caused by the inrush of the river waters into local pits at Snodgrass, Longford, Bartonholm and Nethermains. Fortunately the miners had time to escape. The next time the tidal waters rose the water level returned to normal but the pits remained flooded. Almost 20 years later the ever resourceful Earl of Eglinton bought the lands, cut a short canal to cut off a loop in the river, drained the water from the loop and pumped out the pit workings. The Earl then leased the coal pits to Bairds of Gartsherrie who had built the Eglinton ironworks just to the north of the river.

Immediately, after Byrehill Junction, to the right was the site of the Eglinton ironworks, now an industrial estate.

The railway then reaches Kilwinning station where the Ardrossan line joins the Glasgow line. The station has two platforms on the Glasgow to Ayr line and two on the Ardrossan line. The station buildings, triangular in plan, occupy the space in the fork of the junction. The station opened on 23rd March, 1840 and with the Ardrossan Railway regauged a timetabled connection with Ardrossan trains was made at Kilwinning by the end of that year.

WALK 6.2 LADYHA' RAILWAY TUNNEL AND A SHORT SECTION OF THE DOURA BRANCH

Distance: 0.75 miles (**).
Start: Eglinton Park Visitor Centre and follow route to Ladyha' coal pit where the tunnel is located. From here a short section of the Doura branch is followed returning through the grounds of Eglinton Country Park.
Terrain: Conditions underfoot can be very muddy.
Facilities: Café and toilets at the Visitor Centre.
Further Options: Explore the grounds of Eglinton Country Park.

Beside the visitor centre there is a short section of railway track believed to date from *circa* 1830 (*). It was found at Millburn near Benslie and is 15 feet in length, the standard length at that time. The rails are flat bottomed which means that they had a greater surface contact with the sleeper and could rest directly on the sleeper. It is likely that the rails were spiked to wooden sleepers. The rails were more typical of the waggonway era as after conversion to standard gauge heavier rails were required to support locomotives. The rails appear to be an early version of a Vignole style rail.

From the centre follow the path which leads over the suspension bridge and then past the walled garden to a tarmac road. Access to Ladyha' coal pit is by a path opposite the walled garden. The first Ladyha' pit was sunk in 1843 and linked by rail the short distance to the Eglinton ironworks. Due to increasing demand for coal at the ironworks a further pit was sunk in 1885.

The buildings associated with the coal pit have been demolished but the 231 yards-long brick-lined railway tunnel (314425) (*) remains which covered the final approach to the coal pit. The construction of a tunnel would have added cost and does not seem necessary, a cutting would have sufficed. The suggestion was that the tunnel was constructed so that the railway could not be seen from the castle but this is unlikely given that the furnaces of the Eglinton ironworks dwarfed even the castle. Would a railway have made any difference to the view? Anyway the pit buildings would have been more prominent than the railway to residents of the castle. The answer may lie a short distance away in what is now a field to the south where, at the time of the coal workings, there were extensive glasshouses for growing vegetables. It is believed that soot from the steam engines would have blackened the glass, something that the Earl did not want. Given the height of the blast furnaces and the direction of the prevailing wind, pollution from the ironworks may not have been significant. The coal pit at Ladyha' struggled after the closure of the ironworks in 1924 and finally closed in 1934.

The tunnel is waterlogged and metal grilles prevent entry. During the war it was used as a bomb shelter and for storage. A footpath leads to the other end of the tunnel and the trackbed can be followed to Irvine Road (A737), close to the junction with Bannoch Road.

Across the road, and on the far side of the River Garnock, were the Eglinton ironworks. The site has been cleared and the slag heap removed and was used in the construction of Hunterston deep water terminal, further up the coast. The former railway bridge over the River Garnock is still in use, part of a path from the Irvine Road, which carried the Doura branch from Dubbs Junction over the

Vignole-style rails on display at Eglinton Country Park. *Author*

Ladyha' Colliery tunnel, now within Eglinton Country Park, 2009. *Author*

river. The ironworks were situated between the B779 and the Ayr to Glasgow railway bounded by the Doura branch to the south. They were served by multiple sidings, mainly from the G&SWR but latterly there were a few sidings provided by the Lanarkshire & Ayrshire Railway which passed to the east of the site.

To the south of the junction of the Irvine Road and Bannock Road were sidings with the Doura branch. In this area was the likely terminus of the passenger service, which began in 1834, between Dirrans and Ardrossan. It was at the intersection of Irvine Road with the Doura branch but no evidence of the terminus, which was never listed as a railway station, exists.

On the Irvine Road side of Bannock Road is a footpath which follows the line of the Doura branch. Demand for coal to be removed from coal pits along this line, chiefly to Ardrossan, was strong and 80,000 tons a year were being transported by 1840 before the route was converted to standard gauge to allow for steam haulage.

The footpath is followed until a T-junction is reached where the road is crossed and the country park is entered. At the gate turn left (do not follow the track in front of you) and there is a cutting, lined with some of the original rail fence posts. Continue until a fence blocks the route. Ahead is the coal bing for the Moncur pit which lay beside the Doura branch. Beyond this point the route is very fragmented and you should turn right and follow the route back towards the visitor centre. On the way it is worth exploring Tournament bridge and the remains of Eglinton Castle.

Archibald the 13th Earl of Eglinton is forever known as the 'Tournament Earl' for a wild extravaganza held beside the castle in 1839. Around 100,000 people were attracted to witness the enactment of a three-day jousting tournament complete with a procession of knights in full armour and their retinues in period dress. The grounds were transformed with a banqueting hall, a pavilion and a grandstand capable of holding 2,000 people and the newly opened Ayr to Irvine line played a part. The locomotive, the *Marmion*, conveyed almost 3,000 people to the tournament. It is not known if passengers were charged extra for taking lances and suits of armour on the trains! Unfortunately, the weather was awful for the first two days, turning the jousting field into a sea of mud and contributing to the banqueting hall collapsing. By the third day the weather had improved and a truncated event was held. The event was won by the Earl himself and the silver Eglinton Trophy presented to him is on display at the headquarters of North Ayrshire Council in Irvine. The event was seen as hopelessly 'over-the-top' and did little for the Earl's reputation.

By the time of Archibald Seton Montgomerie, the 16th Earl and his family were forced to leave the estate, due to financial problems, in 1925, creating more unemployment in an area which had just suffered the closure of the Eglinton ironworks. The estate suffered during World War II, when the army took over, with some of the turrets of the castle being used for explosives practice and the grounds were left in a poor state. In 1958 the Wilson family opened a pet food factory, which closed in the 1980s, and some of the buildings, now largely ruins, remain.

The Country Park is run today by North Ayrshire Council, which took over the running from the Irvine Development Corporation. The visitor centre can provide more information about the country park and its history. Check for opening times.

There are two further features linked to the railway worth visiting. There is a fine example of an early waggonway bridge, near South Fergushill Farm,

Waggonway bridge beside the B785 near South Fergushill Farm. *Author*

(326432) (*) beside the B785 where it crosses the Lugton Water. Due to bends in the road parking close to it is not advised.

Further south on the same road, opposite the old South Millburn Farm, is a ruined cottage (337426) (*) which it is thought may have been a waggonway crossing keeper's cottage, controlling waggonway traffic entering the Eglinton estate. Elongated rectangular windows in both gables would have enabled checking of passing waggonway traffic. A waggonway branch left the Doura branch at this point. It was here that the waggonway rails, now at the visitor centre in Eglinton Park, were found.

The Doura branch continued south, passing under the A736, west of Sourlie roundabout and Lawthorn and Girdle Toll areas of Irvine. South of the B769, near Perceton, little remains.

Kilwinning to Ardrossan

The railway that the G&SWR took over passes through the south-east part of Kilwinning, passed Dubbs Junction and then under the A78 before reaching Stevenston station. In a journey of just over two miles it skirts the northern edge of the Ardeer peninsula. Many remnants of the former ICI works remain along with overgrown sidings no longer in use. Buildings set apart from each other, part buried in sand dunes so that an explosion in one would not set off a contagion, remain in mute testimony to a once vibrant site.

Over 14,000 people were once employed. The railway played a vital role for almost 70 years as the 'Dynamite Train' brought workers to the site. Travelling from Largs, the train picked up workers from all points south and took them through to the long platform terminus at Ardeer, which was privately owned by the factory. The early wooden platform was replaced by a brick and concrete platform and a long shelter was later added. The platform had to be long enough to accommodate two trains at one time, when the workers' trains arrived at changes of shift. One perk for the railway workers at the station and signal box was that they got the same pay rises as that given by the company to their workers, making the assignment an attractive posting.

Other trains converged from Kilmarnock and Ayr, some depositing workers at Stevenston station to cross the footbridge for the next stage of their journey. There was even a train for those working the night-shift. Those travelling home by train had a bad habit of jumping from the train, particularly at Stevenston and Saltcoats stations, before the train had stopped at the platform anxious to avoid the long queue to hand their tickets over. Eventually the police were called and warnings issued to the miscreants. After the Coronation of King Edward VII in 1902 the Nobel site was visited by dignitaries from the British Commonwealth and their guests who were touring sites, around the country, by a special train.

A decline in the work force, competition from buses and the rise of the private car combined to bring about the closure of Ardeer Platform on 3rd October, 1966. The platform, now overgrown, still remains at Ardeer (281404) (*), close to Nobel House inside what still remains a vast industrial site. Also inside the site is Africa House originally built as the South Africa Pavilion for the 1938 Glasgow Exhibition. After the exhibition it was dismantled and reconstructed on the Ardeer site by ICI. The architect was George Miller, the only son of the famous railway architect James Miller.

The level crossing at Stevenston station still causes hold-ups for road traffic but with fewer people travelling to the Ardeer peninsula the congestion is not as severe. The station buildings have been replaced by basic but functional shelters.

Saltcoats station retains the two-storey red sandstone building. Originally the building housed the offices and station house but is now a café. On the Glasgow platform is a long single-storey sandstone building, containing the booking office, with a glazed canopy. It was a station designed to impress the tourists flocking to the coast for their day at the beach.

Other stations en route to the terminus at Ardrossan Harbour station, Ardrossan South Beach and Ardrossan Town have received the Stevenston treatment with the Town station buildings, once with an impressive sandstone frontage onto Princes Street, having been demolished. The Town and Harbour stations, only a short distance apart, were not separately identified in early timetables until around 1850. Ardrossan Harbour was known as Ardrossan Pier and then Ardrossan Winton Pier and then Ardrossan Harbour again in 1967. In some early timetables the present Ardrossan Town was known as Ardrossan Princes Street and the addition of the 'Town' suffix was only made in 1953.

Stevenston No. 1 signal box on 17th June, 1978. In the background is Stevenston station. Also shown is the abutment and intermediate pier of the Lanarkshire & Ayrshire Railway.
Stuart Rankin

The tablet from the Ardeer branch is exchanged at Stevenston No. 1 signal box on 27th March, 1964.
Hamish Stevenson Collection

Ardeer Platform, viewed from the end buffer stops on 27th March, 1964.
Hamish Stevenson Collection

Ardeer Platform viewed from the other end. On 27th March, 1964, ex-LMS Stanier 'Black Five' 4-6-0 No. 44723 waits to leave with its passenger train. Nobel House can be seen beyond the train.
Hamish Stevenson Collection

BR Standard class '3MT' 2-6-0 No. 77017 with an Ardrossan-Darvel passenger train is seen at Holm Junction on 27th May, 1961. The Largs branch is to the right and the line to Ardrossan Town to left. Ardrossan engine shed is in the background. *Hamish Stevenson Collection*

Holm Junction on 19th November, 1986. Ardrossan engine shed has been demolished by this time. *Hamish Stevenson Collection*

LMS '2P' class 2-4-0 No.626 stands at Winton Pier station, Ardrossan on 9th April, 1949. Another train lurks beneath the train shed roof. *Hamish Stevenson Collection*

The almost mile-long line to Ardrossan Harbour branches from the Largs line at Holm Junction, a very short distance beyond Ardrossan South Beach station and crosses Princes Street by a level crossing on the final approach to the harbour. Within the triangle of land created by the branching of the two lines was Ardrossan shed, over looked by the ruined Ardrossan Castle perched on a hill. Cromwell took many of the stones from the castle to build his fort at Ayr.

Ardrossan shed replaced the original shed which was located between Ardrossan Town and Ardrossan Pier station as it was then known. A spur was built from Castlehill Junction, just short of Ardrossan Town to Parkhouse Junction on the Largs branch. The later shed had two 2-road brick sheds and may have replaced an earlier wooden shed on the triangular site. Ardrossan shed was also responsible for most of the passenger traffic between Glasgow and Largs and was particularly busy at peak holiday times. Ardrossan shed was responsible for harbour workings at Ardrossan, the ICI traffic, including the Snodgrass sidings and some traffic to Irvine and along the Busby branch. With the end of steam workings the Ardrossan shed closed in 1965 but remained in use for signing on until 1969. The track was lifted in 1971 and the sheds demolished in 1975. The spur between Castlehill and Parkhouse Junction closed in 1969 and was lifted by 1977. There is still an electrified siding from Holm Junction into the former Ardrossan shed area.

The Largs Branch

The Largs branch remains open and while holiday traffic has declined, commuter traffic to Glasgow continues. With the building of the Hunterston Ore Terminal the branch has seen long freight trains carrying coal to power stations in England as well as to Longannet in Fife. While the route north of Saltcoats remains double-track only the northbound line was electrified. The southbound line is used for freight traffic from Hunterston. Beyond Hunterston the second

Hunterston ore bunkers under construction in June 1976. *Hamish Stevenson Collection*

track has been removed. This resulted in the removal of the southbound platforms at West Kilbride and Fairlie and two of the four platforms at Largs.

Beyond Ardrossan the railway continues high above the shore line, on a raised beach and is several hundred yards from the coastline until Fairlie. Just after the rail bridge over the Ardrossan bypass, the Montfode sidings were located (224442), to the west of the line. Camouflaged oil tanks were built here during the war as an alternative storage facility if the refinery at Ardrossan had been targeted.

West Kilbride station (208484) (*) has been enhanced by the art deco style architecture of James Miller, the renowned railway architect. His work replaced some of the original station which was burnt down in a fire. Since electrification the station building is no longer used by the railway and has been used for a variety of retail and food outlets. Less glamorously the station sidings, now closed, saw an increase in business with the delivery of cement for the construction of the nearby Hunterston power station in the 1960s.

Beyond West Kilbride, the railway passes inland of the Portencross peninsula, where the Hunterston power station is located and just south of Fairlie is the Hunterston terminal. The terminal is a coal handling port and ships of any size can use the mile-long jetty. Originally intended for importing iron ore for the now closed Ravenscraig steelworks, the terminal now transfers coal to a railhead for onward transportation to power stations at Longannet in Fife and Drax in Yorkshire.

Continuing north, just before Fairlie station were the Scottish Nuclear Sidings which allowed lead-lined steel flasks, containing radioactive material, to be loaded onto special wagons for transport to Sellafield. The sidings are now disconnected from the railway.

Fairlie station remains in use. Now known just as Fairlie, the station became known as Fairlie Town, in 1952, until locals pointed out that Fairlie was really a village and the name was changed to Fairlie High until the 'High' was dropped years later. There was also a signal box at Fairlie called Fairlie High, presumably not the tallest signal box!

North of the station the railway enters the 990 yards-long Fairlie tunnel. In 1940, during a severe winter, the tunnel was blocked by a snowfall and while explosives were being used to clear the tunnel, engine driver Alf Burden was killed when he fell from his cab.

After the tunnel was the short 400 yard branch to Fairlie Pier. The pier at Fairlie was wooden and extended a hundred yards from the shore. It was a busy pier, with boat trains arriving from Glasgow and Kilmarnock to connect with the steamer to Millport, just across the water on the island of Cumbrae, and sailings to Arran. The pier even justified its own locomotive shed. Due to objections from Lord Glasgow, the local landowner, an extension north to Largs was delayed and since a shed was required immediately to service the traffic it was built at Fairlie. Even after the original shed burnt down in 1917 a new shed, this time a more substantial one of brick, was opened the following year still at Fairlie Pier. The shed was closed in 1930 and the work transferred to Ardrossan.

In latter days some of the steel for construction of the Hunterston power station was unloaded at the pier. The pier closed in 1971, the days of cars being run onto the *Glen Sannox* over two planks of wood long gone. The shed was used by a local boat builder until its eventual demolition in 1987. The area has been redeveloped and the polytunnels of the Fairlie Organic Gardens were erected on top of the foundations of the locomotive shed.

Beyond the site of Fairlie Pier was Admiralty siding which is no longer connected to the Largs branch. The siding was the base for the NATO Boom Defence, equipped to stop the underwater infiltration of boats in the Clyde in the event of war. The site is now used as a boat storage and repair yard with most of the track remaining embedded in tarmac.

North of Fairlie the railway hugs the coast line, some of which was reclaimed from the Firth of Clyde.

Fairlie High looking towards Largs with two camping coaches in the siding on 27th July, 1957. *Hamish Stevenson Collection*

A busy scene at Largs station with visitors arriving for a day 'doon the watter' in 1910.
Hamish Stevenson Collection

The train information board at Largs station in 1975. *Hamish Stevenson Collection*

Fairlie Pier looking to the terminal end, 27th July, 1957. *Hamish Stevenson Collection*

Largs

Exactly five years after the railway reached Fairlie the extension to Largs was open, a route agreed with Lord Glasgow, the local landowner, for the public. The Directors of the G&SWR had already visited the wooden station and the local company of the Rifle Volunteers had been taken to Fairlie by special arrangement.

The original wooden station buildings did not survive the 1930s and were replaced with a new Victorian-style building, platforms and roof. Electrification meant that only two of Largs original four platforms now remain in use.

Tuesday 11th July, 1995 brought the bleakest day in the history of Largs station when the 6.15 am ScotRail train from Glasgow ploughed through the buffers, due to brake failure, and came to a juddering halt in the Main Street having demolished two shops en route. Fortunately no one was killed but five people were injured. On a personal note, I was alarmed whilst watching breakfast news that morning as my uncle and family, at that time, lived in Crawford Street directly opposite the station and it was not immediately clear that they were not affected. Fortunately, they were unharmed and their building not touched.

The station is again open after a long battle with developers who wanted hotels and flats on the site. Largs is an attractive seaside town, still busy with those wishing to spend some time at the seaside, enjoying an ice cream at the famous Nardini's Cafe or wanting to cross to the island of Cumbrae using the regular ferry service.

Kilwinning to Glengarnock

North from Kilwinning the railway passes through the expanding northern edge of Kilwinning, crossing the River Garnock and keeps the river company on the approach to Dalry. South of Dalry, at Dalry Junction, the disused branch from Kilmarnock, which is covered in Chapter Five, joins the line from the south-east.

Dalry

The small town of Dalry was once a thriving industrial centre based on textiles, ironworks, coal mining and brick making. Originally industry was based more on textiles but with the development of the Blair ironworks in 1845, the area became more heavily industrialized. The ironworks, taken over by Bairds in 1852, required coal and many pits were sunk in the area. Bairds had several sidings to the south of the town although the ironworks were located on the east bank of the River Garnock to the north of Dalry station.

On the approach to Dalry from the south the railway passed the Douglas brickworks and Monkcastle Fireclay mine to the west with its own internal railway system which closed in 1945. The site is now occupied by a car auction company.

The railway station opened on 21st July, 1840 and when the North Johnstone Loop opened in 1905 the station was enlarged to four platforms. With the decline of local industry the station was not so busy and after electrification the station reverted to two platforms and in keeping with many stations is now unmanned. A housing development now occupies the former sidings.

North of Dalry there are exchange sidings serving the DSM Nutritional Holdings, a Dutch company, who took over the site from Roche and continue vitamin C production along with other products. The Swinlees sidings which served coal pits in the area to the west of the railway were slightly to the north but the exchange sidings, if the sidings had been operating at the same time, would have overlapped.

Such was the high volume of traffic on this stretch of railway that the G&SWR built a loop line from Brownhill Junction, north of the Swinlees branch, through Kilbirnie to Cart Junction near Elderslie. Between Brownhill Junction and Dalry the problem was solved by laying four tracks. The junction site is signposted and obvious to travellers by train. At the junction, the southbound Lochwinnoch Loop crossed above the main line and joined from the east side, the line south onwards then becoming four tracks. There were two separate single-track Loop line bridges over the River Garnock north of the junction and sidings between the northbound Loop line and the main line at the junction. The first part of the 'Loop line' can be followed from the train as the line approaches Glengarnock station.

Glengarnock

Glengarnock station was originally named as Kilbirnie and opened on 14th June, 1840. The ironworks were located south of Kilbirnie Loch and eventually as the community around the ironworks grew, with an influx of workers for the ironworks, the inhabitants adopted the name Glengarnock. By 1888 the station was renamed as Glengarnock and Kilbirnie and with the opening of the northbound Loop line, which passed through Kilbirnie adding a new station in the town, the station was again renamed this time as Glengarnock.

The station was located beside the ironworks which were started by Merry & Cunninghame, who also operated the Ardeer ironworks, but their interest ended in the late 1800s. Steelmaking began in 1884. After a period of economic depression David Colville & Son then took over the site in 1916 to support the war effort and its increased demand for munitions. The plant was nationalized and survived until 1985. The steelworks have been demolished and replaced with an industrial estate. Much of the slag from the steelworks was dumped in Kilbirnie Loch. While the steelworks largely employed men the other major employer in the area, the W. & J. Knox Threadmills, had a predominately female workforce. The thread mills specialized in producing fishing nets and nets for the British Army. After a management buyout they are still operating.

The industry in the area attracted the interest of the Caledonian Railway with a branch from the Lanarkshire & Ayrshire Railway being built. This line, as well as competing for business from the steelworks, created two new stations, in 1899, Glengarnock and Kilbirnie which became Glengarnock High and Kilbirnie South respectively on 2nd June, 1924 as part of an exercise by the LMS to avoid confusion. The stations closed in 1930 having been operational for only 40 years. Kilbirnie South lost its freight service the same day while freight services at Glengarnock High survived until 1945. There are no remains of either station. Passenger services consisted of nine return journeys between the station and Giffen Junction where passengers could travel north to Glasgow or south to Ardrossan.

North of Glengarnock, the Ayr to Glasgow line passes Kilbirnie Loch, to the left, with bonded warehouses owned by Chivas Regal to the right. Near this site was a siding at Bark Mill by the Main Burn, later known as Muirs sidings. A furniture factory was set up here, by Matthew Pollock one of the founding fathers of furniture making in nearby Beith. The railway siding saved time, in transporting the furniture to other markets, and helped establish Beith as a furniture-making town. Eventually the business moved to Beith and the siding closed.

At the northern end of the loch, north of the road bridge over the line, was Beith station, the last in Ayrshire before Renfrewshire is reached. The station closed on 4th June, 1951. From 2nd June, 1924 it was renamed Beith North.

Walk 6.3 Glengarnock to Lochwinnoch - part of the Lochwinnoch Loop

Distance: 4 miles (***).
Start: Glengarnock station and ends at Lochwinnoch station - both stations on the Ayr to Glasgow line and follows a section of the Dalry and North Johnstone Loop. The trackbed is part of the National Cycle Route 7.
Terrain: Route is tarmacked throughout.
Facilities: Cafes in both Glengarnock and Lochwinnoch. Public toilets at Main Street, Glengarnock.
Further options: Continue on cycle route.

From Glengarnock station head along Main Street and turn right at Garnock View. The road passes under an old Caledonian Railway bridge, part of a loop line, and reaches Caledonian Road where you turn left. The Glengarnock

Kilbirnie South station in 1949. The station was closed at the time and had become overgrown. A (simplified) track layout remained until the 1950s. *Hamish Stevenson Collection*

The station site at Kilbirnie South in 2012. The site is now occupied by Anam Cara care home. *Author*

steelworks were located in the area between Caledonian Road and Kilbirnie Loch. Much of the former steelworks site is now an industrial estate.

The cycle route is joined a short distance along Caledonian Road. The route initially follows the former Caledonian route and passes the site of Glengarnock High of which there are no remains. The Caley had a further station in Kilbirnie, later known as Kilbirnie South. This was located in the Dean Road area of the town and no remnants of the station remain.

To the left are playing fields and the ground of Kilbirnie Ladeside, the local football team. Beyond the playing fields the embankment of the loop line can be seen. The remains of the island platform of Kilbirnie station (320546) are found a short distance along the track. The station closed along with the other stations on the loop on 27th June, 1966.

After the station the route continues under bridge 51, which carries the A760, at an angle, across the trackbed. The A760 remains close to the former trackbed until Lochwinnoch. A feature of this walk is the number of bridges across the line which for the next few miles is largely through a cutting. Some of the bridges are wooden water conduits to take the water across the trackbed which has drained from the high moorland to the left. This section of the route required a lot of engineering to keep the trackbed dry. Between bridges Nos. 51 and 50 there is a sculpture made out of old railway sleepers patterned with nails in the shape of cyclists which reinforces the change of use on the route.

Bridge No. 50 is a fine three-arched skewed bridge with engineering bricks at the head of each arch. The next bridge is a very tall single-skewed arch made from concrete. There is quite a variety of bridge styles in a short distance including plate girder bridges. The trackbed is guided away from a flooded section and at last there are views across the northern edge of Kilbirnie Loch to Beith with the prominent steeple of the Beith Parish Church.

North of Kilbirnie Loch the route leaves Ayrshire and enters Renfrewshire. From bridge 38 the section of cutting ends and the trackbed is carried on a long section of embankment with streams now being bridged by the railway.

The railway crosses over the A760 and just after to the left of the track are the ruins of the 16th century Barr Castle, the remains of a four-storey building which has passed through many owners. The gable ends have collapsed leaving exposed the chimney stack.

Local landowners began to drain the Barr Loch, which the castle overlooks, from the 17th century, to provide agricultural land. The process of draining was aided by the silt brought down by the River Calder which began to separate Barr Loch and Castle Semple Loch, which lies further north beside Lochwinnoch, into two separate lochs. In maps from the early part of last century the Barr Loch is shown as a drained area and it was only flooded again in 1946.

The trackbed enters the village, now a dormitory village for nearby towns like Paisley and Glasgow, by crossing the A760 road and the River Calder. The railway once passed through the centre of Lochwinnoch on an embankment. The station site on the closed loop line has now been redeveloped. The village grew around its mills but like Beith it developed a furniture making industry. Furniture for many of the great Clyde-built liners and the *Titanic* was crafted here.

Beith (Town) with the engine shed and furniture works to the left on 27th April, 1957.
Hamish Stevenson Collection

Beith (Town) branch engine, ex-Caledonian Railway '439' class 0-4-4T No. 55203, being watered on 27th April, 1957.
Hamish Stevenson Collection

Follow the signs and continue beside the A760 between the Barr and Castle Semple lochs to reach Lochwinnoch station. Castle Semple is used extensively for water sports and on its southern bank is a RSPB hide not far from the present station on the Ayr to Glasgow line. The cycle route continues north towards Paisley.

The current Lochwinnoch station lost its name when the loop line opened and became known appropriately as Lochside. Lochside closed between 1955 and 1966 and was renamed Lochwinnoch on 13th May, 1985.

Branches from the Glasgow to Kilmarnock line

Lugton South Junction to Beith (Town)

While the track remains from Lugton Junction to Barrmill and then south through Giffen to the Defence Munitions Beith, the route is closed and has not seen traffic since 1996. The Ministry of Defence have declared the route surplus to requirements and the line is severed at Lugton Junction. The station in Barrmill (368516) was closed on 5th November, 1962 with a freight service lasting until 1964. A housing development now occupies the site.

The main sources of employment in the village were the Crawford Thread Mills which closed in 1951 and the nearby limestone quarry at Dockra to the north-west of the village, linked to the railway, which closed in 1972. The local MOD munitions factory employs some locals but there are also a number of small-scale employers and many commute from Barrmill to Paisley or Glasgow. There are whisky bonds (Chivas Regal) to the north of the village.

The railway continued almost two miles to the west to reach the terminus at Beith. The trackbed passes close to the northern edge of the munitions work which may explain why it has not been developed as a cycle path.

Barrmill station looking towards Lugton on 27th April, 1957, The branch to Giffen is behind the station with Giffenmill viaduct (on Lanarkshire & Ayrshire line) visible in the distance. *Hamish Stevenson Collection*

Beith had acquired a reputation for making furniture and leather manufacture. With the arrival of the railway from the east the manufacturing of furniture thrived in the town and the tag 'Beith Made' was the benchmark for quality. Furniture and fitting made in Beith graced many of the great ocean liners like the *Queen Mary* and the *Queen Elizabeth*. By 1983 furniture manufacture had ceased in Beith, destroyed by foreign competition and self-assembly furniture. The manufacture of ropes was another local industry, which had died out by the 1920s, also unable to compete with cheap imports.

The station (345535) (*), which was renamed Beith Town on 28th February, 1953 had a curved single platform overlooked by the West of Scotland Furniture Company's sidings. In addition there was a goods shed and an engine shed. The engine shed was a single-track stone structure with an arched entrance. Only the station master's cottage and the road bridge (A737) over the trackbed remain. The station site is now a housing estate and the buildings associated with the furniture factory and sidings have been demolished.

Lanarkshire & Ayrshire

The former L&AR route left the site of Lugton High (414527), passed over the A735 and after a short distance passed under the joint line to Kilmarnock, in sight of the joint line to Beith, an over-abundance of railway tracks for such a remote area. Only the concrete abutments of the rail bridge, over the A735, remain and little of the station. The two platforms have gone with only the station master's house and part of the wooden steps leading up to the platform remaining.

Lugton (High) station looking north-east. The photograph probably dates from around 1950 since the rails, near to the building, are still shiny and the Giffen Junction via Gree route was taken out of use on 17th December, 1950. *Hamish Stevenson Collection*

Their loss is not felt as deeply as the removal of the 11-arch Gree viaduct (404523). The 'S-shaped' viaduct which crossed the Lugton Water lasted for 105 years before it was demolished in 2008. An early example of a concrete viaduct it was built without steel rod reinforcement and was showing signs of age. A local landmark and 80 feet high at its highest point near its eastern end, it also marked the boundary between East and North Ayrshire with seven of its arches residing in North Ayrshire. Irish navvies were employed in constructing this section and it is rumoured that two were killed during the viaduct's construction.

Immediately to the west of the viaduct was Gree Goods which dealt mainly with cattle and livestock. Beyond the A736 the infilling of cuttings has made this section difficult to follow. Just before the trackbed passed under the road to Barrmill there were more sidings but this area is now a landfill site. The railway then crossed the Dusk Water by a seven-arch viaduct, known as Giffenmill viaduct (368512) which was demolished in 2006, its loss felt by villagers who saw it as an iconic landmark in Barrmill. Beside the viaduct was the site of the Crawford Thread Mills. The route then linked with the branch to Giffen station, at Giffen North Junction on the original Barrmill and Kilwinning route. During 1930 the track between Barrmill Junction and Giffen North Junction was lifted but was re-laid by the end of 1950. Whilst the track is still down the locals are not deterred to use the trackbed to walk their dogs safe in the knowledge that no train will travel on the route.

Consignments of munitions using the railway were considered too obvious a target for terrorists and so the route to Giffen station will never see another train and the trackbed is now surplus to requirements. The platforms remain at the Giffen station (359506) site. When the station opened on 4th September, 1888, it was known for just over a year as Kilbirnie Junction and even more briefly as Giffen Junction. The station was five miles from Lugton East Junction. South of the station the exchange sidings, for the MOD site, also remain with the tracks still in place. The MOD site has expanded in size with the MOD buying a number of local farms. The original MOD site was closer to the station. The MOD facility at Beith is a high security operation and walkers in the area can be stopped for security checks.

Giffen Junction, formerly Kilbirnie Junction is south of the station. From here the Kilbirnie branch headed towards Glengarnock (High) and Kilbirnie (South) stations. En route was Brackenhills station (337520). This station once served the sizeable community at Barkip, a mining and quarrying community of which little remains. Barkip was connected to the ironworks at Glengarnock by the Barkip Railway. The Barkip Railway, opened *circa* 1856, used a cable-worked incline on the section closest to the ironworks, such was the gradient, and supplied coal, limestone and ironstone to the ironworks from various local pits and quarries.

The Lanarkshire & Ayrshire Railway was built using part of the route of the Barkip Railway near Brackenhills. Brackenhills station, closed in 1930, was open for only 24 years. The platform just to the east of the A737 remains as does the loading bank and station master's house. North of the road the railway entered a cutting, which the L&AR had to deepen, known locally as 'The Gurdie', to remove the need for the incline, which has now been largely filled in. From here the L&AR deviated from the Barkip Railway to reach the former ironworks, now steelworks, further to the south.

Giffenmill viaduct (Lanarkshire & Ayrshire Railway) taken from train on the Barrmill to Giffen section on 9th June, 1962. This structure was subsequently demolished.

Hamish Stevenson Collection

Giffen station looking towards Barrmill. *Hamish Stevenson Collection*

Giffen looking northwards. Ex-Caledonian Railway McIntosh '812' class 0-6-0 No. 57581 has arrived with a railtour on 9th June, 1962. *Hamish Stevenson Collection*

The site of Giffen station in 2012. *Author*

Giffen North Junction with the trackbed of the L&AR line towards Lugton (High) to the right and Giffenmill viaduct in the distance. The view along the track is towards Barrmill, 24th May, 1960. *G.H. Robin/Hamish Stevenson Collection*

The platform at Brackenhills, view looking towards Giffen on branch line to Kilbirnie South, 6th October, 1949. *Hamish Stevenson Collection*

East of the station site, a tramway from Hillhead quarry, to the north, fed limestone down to the Kilbirnie branch. The limestone was dropped from a gantry above the railway, into railway wagons, to be taken to the now steelworks at Glengarnock.

Between Giffen station and Kilwinning the trackbed has deteriorated and is difficult to walk. In this section was Auchenmade station (343484) (*), south-west of the B707 and 6.75 miles from Lugton East Junction. The two platforms remain and the area was once occupied by four sidings. One of the sidings was privately operated by the Auchenmade quarry and brickworks until around 1909. Auchenmade also supervised the Lissens Goods station to the south (328470) (*), which closed on 30th March, 1953, and the sidings operated by the Lylestone quarry.

North of Kilwinning where the L&AR passed over the Kilmarnock to Dalry branch is not accessible. Shortly after the L&AR crossed the River Garnock, north of Kilwinning by a seven-arch viaduct (304444) (*). Thereafter housing developments have obliterated the trackbed between the viaduct and the station.

In Kilwinning the Caledonian station site is occupied by Caley House (300434) and the goods yard is now occupied by James Watt College. The station became known as Kilwinning East on 2nd June, 1924 and closed on 4th July, 1932.

Kilwinning to Irvine (Lanarkshire and Ayrshire Branch)

This short 3¼ mile branch has passed into oblivion. From Kilwinning East the railway passed under the road and immediately branched south, passing to the east of the Eglinton ironworks, crossed the River Garnock near Nethermains bridge and crossed what is now Ravenspark Golf Course. A metal-sided bridge, which once crossed the line, remain in the grounds of the golf course, 100 yards east of the club house, and further south traces of an embankment, on the golf course, can be seen near Sandy Road. The route passed under Sandy Road to reach Bogside Halt (315404), 2¾ miles from Kilwinning East, which is now lost

Kilwinning East. The station nameboard reads 'Kilwinning East change for Irvine'.
G.E. Langmur/Hamish Stevenson Collection

The derelict Bogside (Moor) station on the Lanarkshire & Ayrshire Railway's Irvine branch. This view is looking towards Irvine in 1930. *Hamish Stevenson Collection*

to the sports field of Irvine Royal Academy. The halt was in use by 1900 and was noted as a golfers' station and for some of the time it was open the station master at either Irvine or Kilwinning had to be informed if you wanted to get off at the halt. On 2nd June, 1924 it became known as Bogside Moor and according to some sources Bogside Moor Halt. It closed on 28th July, 1930.

The route then passed under the nearby A737, just south of Fleming Terrace and then ran parallel to Old Caley Road before widening out into the goods yard and the terminus at Bank Street close to the junction of East Street (323392). What was once a journey through open fields has now been built over, mainly by council housing.

Irvine Bank Street station (L&AR). *Professor C.J. Fordyce/Hamish Stevenson Collection*

The station, which became known as Irvine Bank Street on 2nd June, 1924, only survived until 28th July, 1930. The line was used for freight until 1939 and in 1936 a special train carried football fans to a match in Clydebank. The local passenger service to Kilwinning, known as the 'Riviera Express', maybe with a touch of irony, consisted of only an engine and one carriage. The station had two platforms, although one was very short. The main platform and station concourse was covered by a large canopy which was at an angle to the street. One of the waiting rooms at the station was used as an overspill classroom, for the local primary school, after the station was closed. Part of the station buildings on Bank Street was subsequently used by the *Irvine Times* newspaper.

Kilwinning to Ardrossan Montgomerie Pier

From the junction with the Irvine branch until Stevenston station the former L&AR is not easy to explore due to the ground conditions. In June 1947 a spur was built linking the former G&SWR with the L&AR just to the east of Stevenston, which lasted until 1968.

WALK 6.4 STEVENSTON MOORPARK STATION TO SALTCOATS NORTH
THE OLD CALEY RAILWAY LINE WALK

Distance: 1.5 miles (***).
Start: Head north from Stevenston station along Station Road to Moorpark Road West where Stevenston Moor Park station (267415) (the 'Moor Park' was added on 2nd June, 1924) was located. The Thistle Day Centre now occupies the former station site. From the car park of the Day Centre the trackbed can be found behind the tenements on Moorpark Road West.
Terrain: Mostly tarmac.
Facilities: Cafes, shops and public toilets at Saltcoats, Stevenston and Ardrossan.

Part of the embankment, in the section from the former station site, was built over the three mile-long Stevenston to Saltcoats Canal. With the arrival of the Ardrossan & Johnstone Railway the canal had fallen into disuse.

With a caravan park to the left the trackbed crosses Auchenharvie Golf Course. The Old Caley Railway Line Walk officially starts at the club house. Beside the putting green is a memorial cairn commemorating a pit accident when water flooded into the workings, from the sea, killing nine men. The last of the pits in the area closed in 1930s. The small lochs, a feature of the golf course, were formed by the flooding of former pit workings. On the golf course are the remains of the Auchenharvie Engine House (257414), dating from the early part of the 18th century, which contained a very early example of a beam engine used to extract water from the coal pits. The local leisure centre, seen to the right, is built on the site of Sir Robert Reid Cunninghame's residence, Seabank House. The trackbed then crosses over Canal Street by a replacement bridge.

Stevenston (Moorpark) station on the Lanarkshire & Ayrshire line, looking east.
Hamish Stevenson Collection

On the bridge, on 5th August, 1939 the 12.30 express train from Glasgow Central to Ardrossan Montgomerie Pier hit an obstacle on the track. The engine and tender were derailed and ended up down the embankment with the first three of the seven carriages also derailed. The driver and fireman and two others were killed and 59 injured. Speed was not an issue and it is thought that someone had laid a stone or stones on the line.

The Caley route was often used in the summer for express trains to the coast and for a time the stations on this part of the route were re-opened, so popular did a special cheap promotion known as the 'Evening Breathers' prove.

The Old Caley Railway Line Walk continues until Jack's Road passing through a wide cutting. The bottom of the cutting has been raised, thereby

The 'Old Caley Railway Line Walk' (L&A) at Saltcoats. Notice the reduced headway.
Hamish Stevenson Collection

reducing the headroom at some of the overbridges. Beyond the bridge over the trackbed at Jack's Road was the site of Saltcoats North station (244419) similar in style to Stevenston Moorpark. The next stretch has been built over until close to Ardrossan Academy where the line enters a deep and impassable cutting. The cutting is crossed by an aqueduct which takes the Stanley Burn over the trackbed and which was used to supply water to the Ardrossan shed.

Close to Glasgow Street, in Ardrossan, the trains travelling on the Largs branch pass over the former L&AR. The disused trackbed, however, now stops at Glasgow Street. On the seaward side, housing built on the site of a goods yard, has removed all traces of the railway until Montgomerie Road where the platforms, somewhat overgrown, remain for Ardrossan North station (228425) (*), originally known as Ardrossan Town until 1924. This was the terminus for the line until Ardrossan Pier was opened two years later. The LMS removed the steel framed awnings from Ardrossan North station and re-erected the awning to provide a new concourse for Buchanan Street station in Glasgow. There were sidings at the station which served the Shell refinery and bitumen works and a connection with the Ardrossan Harbour branch west of Ardrossan (G&SWR) which closed in 1969.

There was one more station, Ardrossan Pier (225423), renamed Montgomerie Pier in 1924. The station was a two-platform terminal which had an iron-framed wooden-clad building which originally had a glazed roof supported on lattice girders. Sadly, like so much on this route, the station has gone, replaced by private flats which overlook the Ardrossan Marina. Rail services to Montgomerie Pier and the Shell Mex plant continued until 1968 with the refinery closing in the 1980s.

Saltcoats North station on 3rd September, 1960. Caledonian Railway 4-2-2 No. 123 stands at the platform on an enthusiasts' railtour. *Hamish Stevenson Collection*

Ardrossan North station with the oil refinery in the distance, 3rd September, 1960.
Hamish Stevenson Collection

BR Standard class '4MT' 4-6-0 No. 76114 waits with a passenger train at Ardrossan Montgomerie Pier station on 14th August, 1964. *Hamish Stevenson Collection*

Ardrossan North station and the refinery sidings in June 1976. An Andrew Barclay-built fireless locomotive, Works No. 1952 of 1928, can be seen in the distance on the right.
Hamish Stevenson Collection

Ardrossan North and the location of the refinery sidings as seen in 1996 with the Arran ferry in distance. *Author*

Acknowledgements & Sources

My thanks are due to my son Scott for producing the maps and for his companionship on the journeys and for Christine for her continued support and for editing the text.

Thanks are also due to Malcolm Ferguson for his support and to Tony Jervis, who could always find an answer to my many questions, to Fergus Gibson, Neil Rowan, Richard Scott, Bob Smillie and John Hume for their knowledge and advice, to Roger Griffith (user: rosser1954) for historical information, to Sheena Andrew and Frank Beattie, and to Tom Barclay and staff at Carnegie Library, Ayr. My thanks also to my publisher, the Oakwood Press and in particular to Ian Kennedy for designing the layout.

I would particularly like to thank Hamish Stevenson for permission to use photographs from his collection and for his continued help and friendship. Other than myself, Andrew J. Arnot, Stuart Rankin and David Rutherglen all other photographs are from his collection.

The author can be contacted by email at alasdairwham@googlemail.com

Royalties from this book are being donated to Room 60, part of the outreach of Newton Wallacetown Church of Scotland.

Thanks to Carnegie Library for access to newspapers and research support.

The following books were of use to the author in preparing this book and are recommended if you are looking for extra information:

Among Thy Green Braes, edited by John Moore, 1977, Cumnock & Doon Valley Council
Ayrshire Coastal Path, James A. Begg, 2008, Rotary Club of Ayr
Ayrshire's Lost History, Mining, Guthrie Hutton, 1996, Richard Stenlake Publishing
Ayrshire: The Story of a County, John Strawhorn, 1975, Ayrshire Archaeological & Natural History Society
Beith, Barrmill and Gateside, Donald L. Reid 2011, Donald L. Reid and Barrmill Jolly Beggars Burns Club
Civil Engineering Heritage, Scotland Lowlands and Borders, Roland Paxton and Jim Shipway, 2007, Royal Commission on the Ancient and Historical Monuments of Scotland
Discovering Ayrshire, John Strawhorn and Ken Andrew, 1988, John Donald Publishers Ltd
Dalmellington Iron Company, David L. Smith, 1967, David & Charles
Glasgow and South-Western Railway, Campbell Highet, 1965, Oakwood Press
Glasgow and South-Western Railway, Stephenson Locomotive Society, 1950
G&SWR Ayr and Cumnock Branches, Stuart Rankin, 2000, G&SWR Association
Girvan and Portpatrick Railway, C.E.J. Fryer, 1994, Oakwood Press
Historic Alloway, 2000, Ayrshire Archaeological & Natural History Society
History of Ayr, John Strawhorn, 1989, John Donald Publishers
History of Irvine, John Strawhorn, 1985, John Donald Publishers
Industrial Archaeology of Scotland, Lowlands and Borders, John R. Hume, 1976, Batsford Publishers
In the Shadow of the Dynamite, John Miller, 1999
James Miller and the Golden Age of Steam, Scott Wham, BSc. Dissertation, Strathclyde University, unpublished
LMS Engine Sheds, Volume Seven, The Glasgow and South-Western Railway, 1990, Irwell Press
Lost Ayrshire, Dane Love, 2005, Birlinn Limited
Post-War Kilmarnock, Frank Beattie, 2008, The History Press Ltd
Private and Untimetabled Railway Stations, Godfrey Croughton, R.W. Kidner, Alan Young, 1982, Oakwood Press
Proud Kilmarnock, Frank Beattie, 2002, Fort Publishing Ltd
Rails to Ayr, Harry Broad, 1968, Ayrshire Archaeological & Natural History Society
Rails to Turnberry and Heads of Ayr, David McConnell and Stuart Rankin, 2010, Oakwood Press
Railway Heritage of Britain, Gordon Biddle and O.S. Nock, 1983, Sheldrake Press Ltd
Railway Passenger Stations in Great Britain, Michael Quick, 2009, Railway & Canal Historical Society
Regional History of the Railways in Great Britain, Volume 6 Scotland (second edition), John Thomas, 1984, David St John Thomas
River Ayr Walk (second edition), Dane Love, 2006, Carn Publishing
Robert Reid Cunninghame of Seabank House, 1997, Ayrshire Archaeological & Natural History Society
Scottish Collieries, Miles K. Oglethorpe, 2006, RCAHMS, Scottish Mining Museum
Scotland (Part III) Thorough Guides, M.J.B. Baddeley, 1903, Dulau and Company
Tolls and Tacksmen, David McClure, 1994, Ayrshire Archaeological and Natural History Society

Index